The Citrix® CCA MetaFrame™ 1.8 for Windows® Cram Sheet

This Cram Sheet contains the distilled, key facts about the Citrix MetaFrame 1.8 CCA exam. Review this information last thing before entering the test room, paying special attention to those areas where you feel you need the most review.

CITRIX METAFRAME 1.8 AND OPTIONAL PRODUCTS

1. Citrix offers optional products that enhance MetaFrame manageability, scalability, and Web publishing capabilities. These products are Load Balancing, Installation Management Services (IMS), SecureICA, and Resource Management Services (RMS).

2. Load Balancing is a system service that routes Independent Computing Architecture (ICA) clients to the least busy serve. It allows you to load balance multiple WinFrame and MetaFrame servers into a single server farm. It provides high availability but not fault tolerance.

3. IMS allows an application to be simultaneously installed onto multiple servers in a load-balanced server farm. It's composed of three elements:
   - *IMS Packager*—Readies the application files for installation
   - *Application Publishing Enhancements*— Loads the prepared files onto the servers
   - *Installer*—Executes the installed files; is the only licensed component

4. SecureICA provides security for traffic between servers and clients. You must install and license it on the MetaFrame server, and you must install any unlicensed component on the client. The North American version provides 40-, 56-, and 128-bit RC-5 encryption; the international version offers only 40-bit encryption. Clients must have an encryption level equal to or greater than that on the server connection.

5. RMS provides application and system management for WinFrame, MetaFrame, and Terminal Server Edition (TSE) on Windows NT networks. It's composed of three components:
   - *Data Collection*—Is installed on MetaFrame servers to collect information on user access and application usage (Excel and text files are not compatible with RMS). This is the only licensed component of RMS.
   - *Data Source*—Is any open database connectivity (ODBC)-compliant database.
   - *Analysis Tools*—Offer detailed monitoring of applications, users, and billing fees.

TERMINAL SERVER/METAFRAME INSTALLATION

6. Microsoft's minimum hardware requirements for a TSE server are as follows:
   - 32-bit x86 microprocessor (such as Intel Pentium or higher).
   - Memory: 32MB of RAM, plus 4MB to 12MB for each connected user.
   - A monitor with VGA or higher resolution with a maximum of 256 colors.
   - 3.5-inch floppy drive.
   - CD-ROM drive.
   - NT-compatible Network Interface Card (NIC).
   - A network protocol, preferably Transmission Control Protocol/Internet Protocol (TCP/IP).

34. WinFrame and MetaFrame servers can be load balanced across a local area network (LAN) or a wide area network (WAN).

35. Load Balancing is not the same as a server farm.

36. Citrix's Load Balancing Services is sold separately and the license must be installed on each load balanced Citrix server.

37. With Load Balancing, users are redirected to the least busy server.

38. The application that will be load balanced must be installed on each server.

39. Using the default settings means that the user load is the only relevant factor utilized when you are routing an ICA connection to the least busy server.

40. The Advanced Load Balancing tab has six settings: Pagefile Usage, Swap Activity, Processor Usage, Memory Load, Sessions, and the Overall adjustment parameters.

WEB CONNECTIVITY

41. Citrix's Application Launching and Embedding (ALE) technology executes applications in two ways: as either launched or embedded applications. ALE allows you to launch Windows- and Java-based applications from, or embedded within, an HTML Web page. You can access the applications with a Web browser via an ICA Web client.

42. Here are some details on launched applications:

- When a user clicks on a hyperlink that is associated with a launched application, it runs in a separate window on the client's local desktop.
- Launched applications can be maximized, minimized, and resized just like an application running on the local desktop.
- When the Web browser is closed, the launched application continues to run.
- With launched applications, a user can have multiple published applications running and still browse the Internet.
- To use application launching, the full client (wfica32.exe) must be installed on the client's workstation.

CORIOLIS™
Certification Insider Press

43. Here are some details on embedded applications:

- Embedded applications run within a Web page.
- Closing the Web browser also closes the application.
- If the browser window is scrolled or resized, so is the application.

44. Citrix ICA Web clients support application launching with any Web browsers that support configurable Multipurpose Internet Mail Extensions (MIME) types, like Internet Explorer and Netscape Navigator.

45. Citrix has developed three ICA Web clients: an ActiveX control, a Netscape plug-in, and a Java applet. Both Microsoft's Internet Explorer and Netscape's Communicator and Navigator browsers support each of the ICA clients.

46. The Web clients do not support seamless windows or client LPT-port and COM-port mapping.

47. The Internet Explorer ActiveX control Web client can be automatically downloaded from a Web page on the Internet or an intranet.

48. The Netscape plug-in must be manually downloaded and installed.

49. Two Java clients run in completely different modes, Application Mode and Applet Mode:

- When running in Application Mode, the Java Virtual Machine (JVM) resides on the client instead of on the server. Applications run in a separate window on the user's desktop.
- When running in Applet Mode, the client along with the application executes completely on the server. The Java Applet Mode client is downloaded from the Web server each time an ALE object is accessed.

50. Two types of files are required to establish an ICA session:

- *ICA files*—Are plain-text files that can be created with the ALE Wizard in PAM. They contain connection files containing a series of command tags needed to establish an ICA connection. The ICA files are downloaded from the Web server to the client's browser.
- *HTML files*—Are plain-text files that point to ICA files that define the ICA connection parameters. You create them in PAM. ICA and HTML files must be located together on the Web server.

16. ICA PassThrough enables non-Win32 clients to take advantage of the Program Neighborhood (PN) features.

17. An asynchronous ICA connection is a remote access solution and does not use Remote Access Service (RAS).

18. PN can be broken down into three main components:
    • *Application sets*—You can have only one set per server farm.
    • *Custom ICA connections*—You must specify a description, connection type, and network protocol. This feature is virtually identical to the older RAM utility.
    • *Common settings*.

19. PN supports only Win32 ICA clients; all other clients must use the Remote Application Manager (RAM) tool, ICA PassThrough, or a Web page. You use PN to configure the client bitmap cache settings (i.e., a directory for the images, the minimum size of the bitmap to be cached, and the maximum size of hard drive space that can be used for the cache).

METAFRAME ADMINISTRATION UTILITIES

20. You use the Citrix Connection Configuration (CCC) utility to create or modify ICA connections, including connection permissions. User Manager for Domains settings take precedence over CCC settings when the Inherit User Config box is checked.

21. You use Citrix Licensing to activate all Citrix licenses after you obtain the activation code from Citrix.

22. You use Citrix Server Administration to manage sessions, connections, domains, and servers (but you initially create ICA connections in the CCC utility). You also use it to configure ICA browsers and gateways. You must configure ICA gateways on Citrix servers on both networks to be connected. A network that accesses another network across a gateway must enter the Internet Protocol (IP) address of the network it wishes to access.

23. You use ICA Client Creator to create ICA client installation diskettes.

24. Clients use ICA Client Printer Configuration to create and connect to ICA client printers.

25. You use ICA Client Update Configuration to add the latest versions of the various ICA clients to the client update database.

26. You use Load Balancing Administration to configure the Load Balancing settings on Citrix servers.

27. You use the Published Application Manager (PAM) to publish and manage applications on MetaFrame servers (a user must be a member of the local or global administration group to publish applications). You also use PAM to manage server farms, including migrating a Citrix server from one server farm to another.

28. You use the Shadow taskbar to shadow one or several user sessions. You can use the Shadow button to shadow only one user at a time.

29. Restrictions/limitations of session shadowing are:
    • Shadowing must take place within an ICA session rather than from a console session. A MetaFrame/WinFrame console can neither shadow nor be shadowed.
    • You initially configure session shadowing in the CCC utility, but you do the actual shadowing from the Server Administration utility.
    • The window size and number of colors of the client session must be equal to or less than those of the session doing the shadowing.
    • Only an administrator (or a user who has been assigned Special Access permission in the CCC utility) can initiate or end a shadowing session.
    • Audio is not available when you are shadowing.
    • Administrators can shadow users only within the domain they are logged onto.
    • RDP sessions cannot be shadowed.

CITRIX LOAD BALANCING

30. Applications can be published across multiple servers in a server farm, using PAM.

31. A server in a load-balanced farm can be taken down for regular maintenance and the published applications will still be available from a different load-balanced server.

32. Load Balancing allows you to centrally manage load-balanced servers from one console.

33. Load Balancing offers high availability of network resources but not fault tolerance.

- One or more hard disks, with 128MB minimum of free hard disk space (300MB is recommended). MetaFrame requires an additional 30MB of hard disk capacity for a complete installation.

- If a server has multiple hard drives that use a stripe set configuration (e.g., Redundant Array of Independent Disks—RAID—0 or RAID 5), the Performance Monitor might show a high reading for the Disk Queue Length counter. This counter should read no greater than 1.5 to 2 times the number of spindles on the physical disk(s).

- Drive remapping allows clients to use the traditional C: and D: drive letters to access their local drives. If you choose not to remap the servers' drives from C: and D:, the clients' local drives show up as V: and U: rather than C: and D:

- You can install Citrix MetaFrame on a TSE operating system only. You cannot install it directly over Windows NT 3.51 or NT 4, or WinFrame versions 1.6, 1.7, and 1.8.

NT DOMAINS: USER PROFILES AND POLICIES

7. After a domain controller authenticates a user, Windows NT first loads the user profile and then loads the system policy. The complete logon process is as follows: User Profile|User Policy|Group Policy|Computer/System Policy.

8. When an administrator makes a change to a user profile or system policy, the changes do not go into effect until after the user logs off and then back on to the network.

9. In the NT environment, policies take precedence over profiles. Individual policies take precedence over group policies. Machine policies take precedence over all policies.

10. A MetaFrame server is generally configured as a member server—not as a Primary Domain Controller (PDC) or Backup Domain Controller (BDC)—so anonymous users are local users, not domain or global users.

ICA CLIENTS

11. Here is a list of ICA clients and the protocols they support:

- 16-bit Windows (Windows 3.x) clients support NetBIOS, Internetwork Packet Exchange/Sequence Packet Exchange (IPX/SPX), and TCP/IP.

- Win32 (Windows 9.x, NT, and 2000) clients support NetBIOS, IPX/SPX, and TCP/IP.

- Windows CE clients support TCP/IP only

- Web clients (Netscape Navigator plug-in/Microsoft Internet Explorer with an ActiveX control) use only TCP/IP.

- DOS 16 and 32 clients can use NetBIOS, IPX/SPX, or TCP/IP.

- Unix clients support TCP/IP only.

- Macintosh clients support TCP/IP only.

- Java clients support TCP/IP only.

12. The available ICA clients that Citrix MetaFrame supports are located on the Citrix MetaFrame CD-ROM or in the %SystemRoot%\System32\Clients\ICA directory.

13. The ICA packet components are:

- *Frame Head*—This is an optional preamble that is used with the reliable protocol to support error-free streaming communications such as asynchronous and TCP/IP.

- *Reliable*—This is an optional preamble used with IPX and asynchronous sessions for error detection and correction.

- *Encryption*—This is an optional encryption preamble for use with the basic encrypted ICA packet.

- *Compression*—This is an optional preamble used to manage compressed data traffic.

- *Command*—This is a required ICA command byte that must precede any Command Data. Command is the *only* required ICA packet component.

- *Command Data*—This is optional data tied to the specified command.

- *Frame Trailer*—This is an optional trailer used with TCP/IP and asynchronous connections.

14. The ICA protocol uses TCP port 1494 for ICA connections.

15. Remote Desktop Protocol (RDP) is Microsoft's thin-client protocol. Compared to ICA, RDP uses more bandwidth, does not support non-Windows clients, and uses only the TCP/IP protocol. MetaFrame uses SpeedScreen 2 to reduce network congestion and to speed up network traffic by up to four times over slow connections.

Citrix® CCA MetaFrame™ 1.8

for Windows®

Roddy Rodstein
Phil Duffield

Citrix® CCA MetaFrame™ 1.8 for Windows® Exam Cram

Limits of Liability and Disclaimer of Warranty

The author and publisher of this book have used their best efforts in preparing the book and the programs contained in it. These efforts include the development, research, and testing of the theories and programs to determine their effectiveness. The author and publisher make no warranty of any kind, expressed or implied, with regard to these programs or the documentation contained in this book.

The author and publisher shall not be liable in the event of incidental or consequential damages in connection with, or arising out of, the furnishing, performance, or use of the programs, associated instructions, and/or claims of productivity gains.

Trademarks

Trademarked names appear throughout this book. Rather than list the names and entities that own the trademarks or insert a trademark symbol with each mention of the trademarked name, the publisher states that it is using the names for editorial purposes only and to the benefit of the trademark owner, with no intention of infringing upon that trademark.

The Coriolis Group, LLC
14455 N. Hayden Road
Suite 220
Scottsdale, Arizona 85260

(480)483-0192
FAX (480)483-0193
www.coriolis.com

Library of Congress Cataloging-in-Publication Data
Rodstein, Roddy.
    Citrix CCA metaframe 1.8 for Windows / Roddy Rodstein and Phil Duffield.
        p.   cm. -- (Exam cram)
    Includes index.
    ISBN 1-57610-945-3
    1. Client/server computing.   2. Microsoft software--Examinations--Study guides.   3. Citrix MetaFrame.   I. Duffield, Phil.   II. Title.   III. Series.
QA76.9.C55   R65   2001
005.4'4769--dc21   2001028381
                                                      CIP

Printed in the United States of America
10 9 8 7 6 5 4 3 2 1

President and CEO
Keith Weiskamp

Publisher
Steve Sayre

Acquisitions Editor
Lee Anderson

Development Editor
Deborah A. Doorley

Product Marketing Manager
Brett Woolley

Project Editor
Stephanie Palenque

Technical Reviewer
Leonard Rasch

Production Coordinator
Todd Halvorsen

Cover Designer
Laura Wellander

Layout Designer
April Nielsen

Ó CORIOLIS™

The Coriolis Group, LLC • 14455 North Hayden Road, Suite 220 • Scottsdale, Arizona 85260

ExamCram.com *Connects You to the Ultimate Study Center!*

Our goal has always been to provide you with the best study tools on the planet to help you achieve your certification in record time. Time is so valuable these days that none of us can afford to waste a second of it, especially when it comes to exam preparation.

Over the past few years, we've created an extensive line of *Exam Cram* and *Exam Prep* study guides, practice exams, and interactive training. To help you study even better, we have now created an e-learning and certification destination called **ExamCram.com**. (You can access the site at **www.examcram.com**.) Now, with every study product you purchase from us, you'll be connected to a large community of people like yourself who are actively studying for their certifications, developing their careers, seeking advice, and sharing their insights and stories.

I believe that the future is all about collaborative learning. Our **ExamCram.com** destination is our approach to creating a highly interactive, easily accessible collaborative environment, where you can take practice exams and discuss your experiences with others, sign up for features like "Questions of the Day," plan your certifications using our interactive planners, create your own personal study pages, and keep up with all of the latest study tips and techniques.

I hope that whatever study products you purchase from us—*Exam Cram* or *Exam Prep* study guides, *Personal Trainers*, *Personal Test Centers*, or one of our interactive Web courses—will make your studying fun and productive. Our commitment is to build the kind of learning tools that will allow you to study the way you want to, whenever you want to.

Visit ExamCram.com now to enhance your study program.

Help us continue to provide the very best certification study materials possible. Write us or email us at **learn@examcram.com** and let us know how our study products have helped you study. Tell us about new features that you'd like us to add. Send us a story about how we've helped you. We're listening!

Good luck with your certification exam and your career. Thank you for allowing us to help you achieve your goals.

Keith Weiskamp
President and CEO

Look for these other products from The Coriolis Group:

Citrix CCEA MetaFrame 1.8 for Windows Exam Cram
by Anoop Jalan

MCSE Migrating from NT 4 to Windows 2000 Exam Cram
by Kurt Hudson, Doug Bassett, Deborah Haralson, and Derek Melber

MCSE ISA Server 2000 Exam Cram
by Will Willis and David Watts

MCSE Exchange 2000 Administration Exam Cram
by David Watts and Will Willis

MCSE Exchange 2000 Design Exam Cram
by William Baldwin

MCSE SQL 2000 Administration Exam Cram
by Kirk Hausman

MCSE SQL 2000 Database Design Exam Cram
by Richard McMahon

MCSE Clustering Using Advanced Server 2000 Exam Cram
by Jarret W. Buse and Diana Bartley

This book is dedicated to the memory of my parents, Sam and Hazel Duffield,
who taught me that reading and education were the keys
to both material success and personal growth.
Their encouragement and support helped me to make it through college
and to become a lifelong reader and student.
—Phil Duffield

About the Authors

Roddy Rodstein is a Citrix Silver Solutions Provider, CCEA, CCA, MCSE, MCP+I, and CCNA. In 1997 he established Rnetworkx, a network consulting company providing Microsoft Windows 2000/Citrix MetaFrame Corporate ASP services in Southern California. Since 1999 Roddy has focused on ASP projects in California and most recently in central Europe. He is currently involved with an ASP project in Central Europe and is assisting in the deployment of hosted applications in English, German, and Dutch. His personal interests include traveling (Central and North America, Europe, and Asia) snowboarding, foreign languages (German and Spanish) and foreign foods, particularly Mexican, Japanese, and Indian. Roddy can be reached via email at **roddys@rnetworkx.com** or from his home page at **http://rnetworkx.com**.

Phil Duffield, CCA, i-Net+, has worked on computers and computer networks since 1987. Starting on Novell NetWare networks, Phil spent the 1990s working on Windows NT integration, documentation, and sales. Since 1997, Phil has worked for a Los Angeles area LAN/WAN networking company on numerous Windows NT/Citrix MetaFrame projects. Phil's personal interests include American literature, wilderness hikes, and high- tech gadgets. Phil can be reached at **philduffield@hotmail.com**.

Acknowledgments

I owe a special level of gratitude to Phil Duffield, for sharing his insight and friendship over the years. Many thanks to the Coriolis team for their talent and professionalism, especially Acquisitions Editor, Lee Anderson; Development Editor, Deborah Doorley; Project Editor, Stephanie Palenque; and Technical Reviewer, Leonard Rasch for offering us this fantastic opportunity. Thanks also to the rest of the Coriolis team who worked on this book: Todd Halvorsen, Laura Wellander, April Nielsen, and Brett Woolley. I would also like to thank Chris Henchy at Hench.net, who let me test hardware and software in his network lab. Many thanks to my family, especially my mother Marcia Haenle, for her guidance and support.

Finally, thank you to Catherine, you have given so much encouragement and support during the long nights and weekends I was writing this book. A mere "thank you" does not suffice.
—*Roddy Rodstein*

This book could not have been written without the help of many friends and associates.

First, I want to thank my co-author and friend, Roddy Rodstein, whose unflagging energy and enthusiasm were crucial to the completion of our project.

Many thanks are also due Deborah Doorley, Stephanie Palenque, and Bonnie Trenga of Coriolis for their kind and patient editorial assistance. Thanks also to the rest of the Coriolis team who worked on this book: Todd Halvorsen, Laura Wellander, April Nielsen, and Brett Woolley. Kudos are also due to Leonard Rasch for all of his excellent Citrix/Windows technical advice and feedback.

Finally, I wish to thank Butch Barkstelle of SIA Networks for helping me to understand and appreciate the role of MetaFrame in real-world networks. His combination of engineering expertise and business acumen has served as an inspiration to his friends and co-workers since 1987.
—*Phil Duffield*

Contents at a Glance

Chapter 1   Citrix Certification Exams   1

Chapter 2   Introduction to Citrix MetaFrame   9

Chapter 3   Network Models   25

Chapter 4   Installing Microsoft NT 4 Terminal Server
Edition (TSE) and Citrix MetaFrame 1.8   43

Chapter 5   Windows NT Domains, User Logons,
and Policies   65

Chapter 6   Independent Computing Architecture (ICA)
Features and Client Configurations   83

Chapter 7   MetaFrame Administration   113

Chapter 8   Citrix Load Balancing   145

Chapter 9   Configuring Web Connectivity   169

Chapter 10   Sample Test   195

Chapter 11   Answer Key   231

Table of Contents

Introduction xvii

Self-Assessment xxv

Chapter 1
Citrix Certification Exams 1
   Assessing Exam-Readiness   2
   The Exam Situation   3
      Multiple-Choice Question Format   4
   Exam-Taking Basics   5
   Question-Handling Strategies   6
   Mastering the Inner Game   7
   Additional Resources   8

Chapter 2
Introduction to Citrix MetaFrame 9
   MetaFrame 1.8 and Thin-Client Computing   11
      Core Features of Citrix MetaFrame   12
      Key Features of Citrix's Server-Based, Thin-Client Networks   12
      Additional Citrix Products   14
   Practice Questions   19
   Need to Know More?   24

Chapter 3
Network Models 25
   Peer-to-Peer Network Model   27
      Pros and Cons Comparison   28
   Traditional Network Model   29
      Pros and Cons Comparison   30

Client/Server Computing Model   30
    Pros and Cons Comparison   31
Network Computing Model   32
    Pros and Cons Comparison   32
Server-Based Computing Model   33
    Pros and Cons Comparison   34
ASP Model   35
    Pros and Cons Comparison   36
Practice Questions   37
Need to Know More?   42

Chapter 4
Installing Microsoft NT 4 Terminal Server Edition (TSE) and Citrix MetaFrame 1.8 43

Introduction to Microsoft Server NT 4 TSE   44
    Scalability and Sizing   45
    Terminal Server Hardware Requirements and
        Preinstallation Issues   47
Microsoft NT 4 TSE Installation Procedure   49
Citrix MetaFrame Preinstallation Issues   53
    Remapping   53
    Citrix License Activation   54
Citrix MetaFrame Installation   55
    Anonymous User Accounts   56
    Uninstalling MetaFrame   57
Optimizing Terminal Server   57
Practice Questions   59
Need to Know More?   63

Chapter 5
Windows NT Domains, User Logons, and Policies 65

Domain Models Introduction   66
    Windows NT Trust Relationships   67
    The SAM and Domain Controllers   67
    The Four Windows NT Domain Models   68

User Authentication and the Logon Process   72
  Logon Process   72
  User Profiles and System Policies   73
Practice Questions   75
Need To Know More?   82

Chapter 6
Independent Computing Architecture (ICA) Features and
Client Configurations 83
A Tale of Two Clients: Citrix ICA vs. Microsoft RDP   84
Citrix ICA Protocol and Client Overview   85
  ICA Clients and Network Protocols   86
  ICA Connection Types   86
  ICA Packet Architecture   89
  CCC Utility   89
  ICA Client Installation   93
  Installing Win32 Clients   95
  Program Neighborhood (PN)   95
  RAM   97
  ICA PassThrough Technology   98
Additional ICA Client Features   98
  Client Caching   98
  SecureICA   99
  Seamless Window   101
  Client Printing in a Seamless Desktop Environment   102
  Mapping Client COM Ports, Clipboard, and Audio   103
Practice Questions   105
Need to Know More?   111

Chapter 7
MetaFrame Administration 113
MetaFrame Administrative Tools Overview   114
  Server Farms   115
  ICA Administrator Toolbar   118
  Citrix Server Administration Utility   120
  Load Balancing Administration Tool   122

PAM   125

CCC Utility   129

Session Shadowing   132

Citrix Licensing Tool and Licensing Procedures   135

ICA Client Update Configuration Tool   136

ICA Client Creator Tool   138

ICA Client Printer Configuration Tool   138

Practice Questions   139

Need to Know More?   144

Chapter 8
Citrix Load Balancing 145

Load Balancing Overview   146

The Load Balancing Process   147

Basic and Advanced Load Balancing Configurations   148

ICA Browser Service   151

The **qserver** Command   152

ICA Browser Tab   153

ICA Member Browsers   154

Dedicated ICA Browsers   155

ICA Gateways   156

Creating an ICA Gateway   157

Accessing Citrix Servers behind a Firewall   158

NAT Explained   159

Configuring Alternate IP Addresses on Citrix Servers   160

Practice Questions   161

Need to Know More?   168

Chapter 9
Configuring Web Connectivity 169

ALE   170

Launched vs. Embedded Applications   171

Intranets and Extranets   172

Citrix Web Computing Components   173

MIME Types Explained   173

Web Servers   174

Citrix Servers   174
ICA and HTML Files   175
Web Clients   182
Practice Questions   185
Need to Know More?   193

Chapter 10
Sample Test 195

Chapter 11
Answer Key 231

Glossary 255

Index 275

Introduction

Welcome to *Citrix CCA MetaFrame 1.8 for Windows Exam Cram*! Whether this is your first or your fifteenth *Exam Cram* book, you'll find information here and in Chapter 1 that will help ensure your success as you pursue knowledge, experience, and certification. This book aims to help you get ready to take—and pass—the Citrix certification Exam 218, titled "Citrix Certified Administrator for MetaFrame 1.8."

Exam Cram books help you understand and appreciate the subjects and materials you need to pass Citrix certification exams. *Exam Cram* books are aimed strictly at test preparation and review. They do not teach you everything you need to know about a topic. Instead, we (the authors) present and dissect the questions and problems we've found that you're likely to encounter on a test. We've worked to bring together as much information as possible about Citrix certification exams.

Nevertheless, to completely prepare yourself for any Citrix test, we recommend that you begin by taking the Self-Assessment included in this book immediately following this Introduction. This tool will help you evaluate your knowledge base against the requirements for a CCA under both ideal and real circumstances.

We also strongly recommend that you install, configure, and fool around with the software that you'll be tested on, because nothing beats hands-on experience and familiarity when it comes to understanding the questions you're likely to encounter on a certification test. Book learning is essential, but hands-on experience is the best teacher of all!

The Citrix Certification Program

Passage of the CCA exam demonstrates the ability to install and administer Citrix MetaFrame or WinFrame server-based, thin-client software. Until the CCEA certification was recently introduced, the CCA was the only comprehensive training/certification program for Citrix system administrators and resellers. The Citrix MetaFrame 1.8 Certification Exam consists of 10 unequally weighted sections. The 10 sections are: Introduction to MetaFrame, Windows Terminal Server Overview, Implementing and Installing MetaFrame, Installing and Configuring ICA Clients, Creating a Seamless User Experience, Configuring ICA Client Features,

Administering MetaFrame, Implementing Load Balancing, Configuring Web Connectivity and Using Performance Monitor and Troubleshooting. Because the CCA exam consists of only 40 questions, most of the sections are only briefly covered. A passing grade is 68 percent correct answers. Most questions are multilple choice, but there are also some true/false questions. Note that the multiple choice questions can have one or several correct answers.

The following information is available at **www.citrix.com/training/**:

The CCA certification is offered in three different versions:

➤ *CCA for MetaFrame 1.8 (Windows)*—Course CTX-302.2 and Exam 218 Citrix MetaFrame 1.8 for Windows Administration. Also visit the **www.citrix.com/training/testing.htm** page and click on the MetaFrame 1.8 Exam Guide link to view some sample test questions and answers.

➤ *CCA for MetaFrame 1.0 (UNIX)*—Course CTX-3020 and Exam 310 Citrix 1.0 for Unix Administration.

➤ *CCA for WinFrame 1.8*—Course CTX-181 and Exam 118 for Citrix WinFrame Administration.

Citrix also offers the CCEA, CCSP and CCI certifications:

➤ *Citrix Certified Enterprise Administrator (CCEA)*—As mentioned in the Self-Assessment Chapter, the CCEA is designed for networking professionals who manage large server farms that require the use of Citrix's optional add-on enterprise products. Candidates must already have their CCA certification and must pass four of seven advanced Citrix exams. The CCEA exams cover various aspects of Citrix Load Balancing, RMS, IMS, SecureICA, and NFuse.

➤ *Citrix Certified Sales Professional (CCSP)*—This is an online exam designed to ensure that Citrix sales professionals understand the benefits and advantages of Citrix's server-based, thin-client computing. The economic justifications and Return on Investment (ROI) of the various Citrix products are covered in detail. A CCSP self-study course (CTX-5081) is available from Citrix; alternately, the course is also available from one of the Citrix Authorized Learning Centers (CALCs).

➤ *Citrix Certified Instructor (CCI)*—CCIs must complete the Citrix instructional method course and have the CCA certification. CCIs are available for MetaFrame 1.8 for Windows, MetaFrame 1.1 for Unix, and WinFrame 1.8. For MetaFrame 1.8 (Windows). Applicants must complete course CTX-302.2, MetaFrame Administration, at a Citrix Authorized Learning Center. The candidate must also have passed the CCA exam with a score of 80 percent

Table 1   Citrix CCA and CCEA Requirements

CCA

You must pass one of the following exams:

Exam 118	Citrix WinFrame 1.8 Administrator
► Exam 218	Citrix MetaFrame 1.8 Administrator
Exam 220	Citrix MetaFrame XP 1.0 for Windows Administrator
Exam 310	Citrix MetaFrame 1.0 or 1.1 Administrator for Unix Operating Systems

CCEA

You must first be a CCA, then pass four of the following exams:

Exam 910	Citrix Resource Management Services
	OR
Exam 911	Citrix Resource Manager
Exam 920	Citrix Installation Management Services
	OR
Exam 921	Citrix Installation Manager
Exam 930	SecureICA and Security
Exam 940	Load Balancing Services/Citrix Program Neighborhood
Exam 950	Citrix NFuse Administration

(regular CCA candidates need to score only 68 percent to pass the exam). Prospective CCIs must also have Microsoft Product Specialist status for NT Server 4.0 and an approved industry trainer certification (e.g. Microsoft MCT, Novell CNI or equivalent). Finally, candidates must have completed the new Citrix Train the Trainer course to earn the CCI.

The Citrix training Web page (**www.citrix.com/training/**) contains all of the relevant information on the Citrix courses and exams. The **www.citrix.com/partners/calc page** contains contact information and pricing for the Citrix Authorized Learning Centers (CALCs) where you can take the various certification courses. There is also information on how to contact the Prometric testing center near you where you can take the certification exams.

Taking a Certification Exam

Once you've prepared for your exam, you need to register with a testing center. Each computer-based CCA exam costs $100, and if you don't pass, you may retest for an additional $100 for each additional try. In the United States and Canada, tests are administered by Prometric. You can sign up for a test through the company's Web site at **www.prometric.com**. Or, you can register by phone at 800-755-3926 (within the United States or Canada) or at 410-843-8000 (outside the United States and Canada).

To sign up for a test, you must possess a valid credit card, or contact Prometric for mailing instructions to send them a check (in the U.S.). Only when payment is verified, or a check has cleared, can you actually register for a test.

To schedule an exam, call the number or visit the Web page at least one day in advance. To cancel or reschedule an exam, you must call before 7 P.M. pacific standard time the day before the scheduled test time (or you may be charged, even if you don't appear to take the test). When you want to schedule a test, have the following information ready:

➤ Your name, organization, and mailing address.

➤ Your Citrix Test ID. (Inside the United States, this means your Social Security number; citizens of other nations should call ahead to find out what type of identification number is required to register for a test.)

➤ The name and number of the exam you wish to take.

➤ A method of payment. (As we've already mentioned, a credit card is the most convenient method, but alternate means can be arranged in advance, if necessary.)

Once you sign up for a test, you'll be informed as to when and where the test is scheduled. Try to arrive at least 15 minutes early. You must supply two forms of identification—one of which must be a photo ID—to be admitted into the testing room.

All exams are completely closed-book. In fact, you will not be permitted to take anything with you into the testing area, but you will be furnished with a blank sheet of paper and a pen or, in some cases, an erasable plastic sheet and an erasable pen. We suggest that you immediately write down on that sheet of paper all the information you've memorized for the test. In *Exam Cram* books, this information appears on a tear-out sheet inside the front cover of each book. You will have some time to compose yourself, record this information, and take a sample orientation exam before you begin the real thing. We suggest you take the orientation test before taking your first exam, but because they're all more or less identical in layout, behavior, and controls, you probably won't need to do this more than once.

When you complete a Citrix certification exam, the software will tell you whether you've passed or failed. If you need to retake an exam, you'll have to schedule a new test with Prometric and pay another $100.

How to Prepare for an Exam

Preparing for any Citrix certification exam (including the MetaFrame 1.8 for Windows NT exam) requires that you obtain and study materials designed to provide comprehensive information about the product and its capabilities that will appear on the specific exam for which you are preparing. The following list of books and Web sites will help you study and prepare (these resources and others are also listed in the "Need to Know More?" sections found at the end of the book chapters):

➤ Mathers, Todd and Shawn Genoway. *Windows NT Thin Client Solutions: Implementing Terminal Server and Citrix Metaframe.* Macmillan Technical Publishing, Indianapolis, IN, 1999. ISBN 1-57870-065-5. Extensive information on installing and administering TSE and Metaframe networks.

➤ Keele, Allen (series Editor). *CCA Certified Administrator for MetaFrame 1.8.* Osborne/McGraw Hill, Berkeley, CA, 2000. ISBN 0-07-212439-3. A good source for both exam related materials and for general MetaFrame 1.8 administration information.

➤ Minasi, Mark. *Mastering NT Server 4, 7th Edition.* Sybex Inc., 1151 Marina Village Parkway, Alameda, CA 94501. ISBN 0-7821-2693-6. Chapter 12 has very good coverage of NT Domains and Trust Relationships.

➤ **www.citrix.com/support** has a great deal of information in the Solution KnowledgeBase(KB). From the KB, select Additional KB Resources, then Product Documentation, then *MetaFrame 1.8 for Windows NT Terminal Server.* This large .pdf manual offers in-depth coverage of all aspects of MetaFrame. For an excellent ICA overview, search the KnowledgeBase for *Citrix ICA and Server Based Computing.* This smaller .pdf file presents a good overview of ICA.

➤ The help files in MetaFrame 1.8 are extensive and very helpful. From the server desktop ICA Administration Toolbar, click on the book icon to launch the Books On-line reference. The MetaFrame Administration Guide (located under the Contents tab) is useful for exam related issues as well as for actual MetaFrame administration.

➤ Search the **www.thethin.net** site for *MetaFrame* or *CCA.* Very good source for links to Citrix issues—including the CCA exam. Try the **http://thethin.net/links.cfm** link and look under the Training and Certification section.

➤ Visit the **www.ccaheaven.com** site for good Citrix and CCA related articles and links. Be sure to check out their CCA cramsession.

➤ Also visit the **www.thinplanet.com** site. This is one of the major Web sites for server-based and thin-client industry news.

➤ *Study Guides*—Several publishers—including The Coriolis Group—offer Citrix titles. The Coriolis Group series includes the following:

➤ *The Exam Cram series*—These books give you information about material you need to know to pass the tests.

➤ *The Exam Prep series*—These books provide a greater level of detail than the Exam Cram books and are designed to teach you everything you need to know from an exam perspective. Each book comes with a CD that contains interactive practice exams in a variety of testing formats.

Together, the two series make a perfect pair.

➤ *Multimedia*—These Coriolis Group materials are designed to support learners of all types—whether you learn best by reading or doing:

➤ *The Exam Cram Personal Trainer*—Offers a unique, personalized self-paced training course based on the exam.

➤ *The Exam Cram Personal Test Center*—Features multiple test options that simulate the actual exam, including Fixed-Length, Random, Review, and Test All. Explanations of correct and incorrect answers reinforce concepts learned.

About this Book

Each topical *Exam Cram* chapter follows a regular structure, along with graphical cues about important or useful information. Here's the structure of a typical chapter:

➤ *Opening hotlists*—Each chapter begins with a list of the terms, tools, and techniques that you must learn and understand before you can be fully conversant with that chapter's subject matter. We follow the hotlists with one or two introductory paragraphs to set the stage for the rest of the chapter.

➤ *Topical coverage*—After the opening hotlists, each chapter covers a series of topics related to the chapter's subject title. Throughout this section, we highlight topics or concepts likely to appear on a test using a special Exam Alert layout, like this:

This is what an Exam Alert looks like. Normally, an Exam Alert stresses concepts, terms, software, or activities that are likely to relate to one or more certification test questions. For that reason, we think any information found offset in Exam Alert format is worthy of unusual attentiveness on your part. Indeed, most of the information that appears on The Cram Sheet appears as Exam Alerts within the text.

➤ Pay close attention to material flagged as an Exam Alert; although all the information in this book pertains to what you need to know to pass the exam, we flag certain items that are really important. You'll find what appears in the meat of each chapter to be worth knowing, too, when preparing for the test. Because this book's material is very condensed, we recommend that you use this book along with other resources to achieve the maximum benefit.

➤ In addition to the Exam Alerts, we have provided tips that will help you build a better foundation for Citrix MetaFrame knowledge. Although the information may not be on the exam, it is certainly related and will help you become a better test-taker.

 This is how tips are formatted. Keep your eyes open for these, and you'll become a MetaFrame guru in no time!

➤ *Practice questions*—Although we talk about test questions and topics throughout the book, a section at the end of each chapter presents a series of mock test questions and explanations of both correct and incorrect answers.

➤ *Details and resources*—Every chapter ends with a section titled "Need to Know More?" This section provides direct pointers to Citrix and third-party resources offering more details on the chapter's subject. In addition, this section tries to rank or at least rate the quality and thoroughness of the topic's coverage by each resource. If you find a resource you like in this collection, use it, but don't feel compelled to use all the resources. On the other hand, we recommend only resources we use on a regular basis, so none of our recommendations will be a waste of your time or money (but purchasing them all at once probably represents an expense that many network administrators and would-be CCAs might find hard to justify).

The bulk of the book follows this chapter structure slavishly, but there are a few other elements that we'd like to point out. Chapter 10 includes a sample test that provides a good review of the material presented throughout the book to ensure you're ready for the exam. Chapter 11 is an answer key to the sample test that appears in Chapter 10. In addition, you'll find a handy glossary and an index.

Finally, the tear-out Cram Sheet attached next to the inside front cover of this *Exam Cram* book represents a condensed and compiled collection of facts and tips that we think you should memorize before taking the test. Because you can dump this information out of your head onto a piece of paper before taking the exam, you can master this information by brute force—you need to remember it only long enough to write it down when you walk into the test room. You might even want to look at it in the car or in the lobby of the testing center just before you walk in to take the test.

How to Use this Book

We've structured the topics in this book to build on one another. Therefore, some topics in later chapters make more sense after you've read earlier chapters. That's why we suggest you read this book from front to back for your initial test preparation. If you need to brush up on a topic or you have to bone up for a second try, use the index or table of contents to go straight to the topics and questions that you need to study. Beyond helping you prepare for the test, we think you'll find this book useful as a tightly focused reference to some of the most important aspects of MetaFrame 1.8.

Given all the book's elements and its specialized focus, we've tried to create a tool that will help you prepare for—and pass—Citrix Exam 218. Please share your feedback on the book with us, especially if you have ideas about how we can improve it for future test-takers. We'll consider everything you say carefully, and we'll respond to all suggestions.

Send your questions or comments to us at **learn@examcram.com**. Please remember to include the title of the book in your message; otherwise, we'll be forced to guess which book you're writing about. And we don't like to guess—we want to *know*! Also, be sure to check out the Web pages at **www.examcram.com**, where you'll find information updates, commentary, and certification information.

Thanks, and enjoy the book!

Self-Assessment

The reason we included a Self-Assessment in this *Exam Cram* book is to help you evaluate your readiness to tackle Citrix CCA certification. It should also help you understand what you need to know to master the topic of this book—Exam 218, "Citrix MetaFrame 1.8 Administrator." But before you tackle this Self-Assessment, let's talk about concerns you may face when pursuing a CCA for MetaFrame 1.8.

CCAs in the Real World

Increasing numbers of people are attaining Citrix certifications, so the goal is within reach. You can get all the real-world motivation you need from knowing that many others have gone before, so you will be able to follow in their footsteps. If you're willing to tackle the process seriously and do what it takes to obtain the necessary experience and knowledge, you can take—and pass—all the certification tests involved in obtaining an CCA. Besides CCA, other Citrix certifications include:

➤ Citrix Certified Enterprise Admininstrator (CCEA), which is aimed at networking professionals who administer large server farms that dictate the use of Citrix's optional add-on enterprise products. Candidates must already have their CCA and must pass four of seven advanced Citrix exams. The CCEA exams cover various aspects of Citrix Load Balancing, RMS, IMS, SecureICA, and NFuse.

➤ Citrix Certified Sales Professional (CCSP) is designed to ensure that your sales staff knows how to properly present Citrix solutions to prospective clients. The open book, on-line exam grills candidates on MetaFrame benefits - especially on favorable Return on Investment (ROI) calculations.

In addition to the above, Citrix also offers Citrix Certified Instructor (CCI) certifications plus individual courses and exams for the enterprise add-on products mentioned in the CCEA section.

➤ Citrix also offers standalone certification on their Nfuse portal product.

The Ideal CCA Candidate

Citrix MetaFrame 1.8 is an enhancement or add-on to the Windows NT/Windows 2000 operating system. Therefore, the first qualification for the ideal CCA candidate is a good working knowledge of the underlying Windows NT/2000 network operating system. Prospective CCAs who have experience administering Windows NT/2000 networks or candidates with any of the following Microsoft certifications should have the necessary knowledge to tackle the Citrix certification path:

➤ Microsoft Certified Professional (MCP) – MCPs who are certified on Windows NT or Windows 2000 Server.

➤ Microsoft Certified Systems Engineer (MCSE) – The MCSE is an advanced certification which requires a thorough knowledge of Windows NT/2000 operating systems and of Windows based networks in general. MCSEs with networking experience are excellent candidates for Citrix certification.

Although the certification process can be both educational and profitable for the successful candidate, hands on experience is necessary for anyone who plans to actually manage and administer real world computer networks.

For the CCA exam, you should have a working knowledge of the following Windows NT network topics:

➤ Windows NT domain trust relationships.

➤ Windows NT user profiles and profiles.

➤ The User Manager for Domains (UMD) utility as used to manage users and groups.

➤ Windows 95/98/NT client software.

➤ Windows NT installation issues.

Basically, Windows NT/2000 administrators with some real world experience have the necessary prerequisites and knowledge to study for the CCA MetaFrame 1.8 exam. Citrix does not mandate any previous certifications or experience of CCA candidates. In short, if you have experience administering Windows NT/2000 networks, you are ready to start on the MetaFrame certification path.

Testing Your Exam-Readiness

Whether you attend a formal class on a specific topic to get ready for an exam or use written materials to study on your own, some preparation for the Microsoft certification exams is essential. At $100 a try, pass or fail, you want to do everything you can to pass on your first try. That's where studying comes in.

We have included a practice exam in this book, so if you don't score that well on the test, you can study more and then tackle the test again. We also have exams that you can take online through the **ExamCram.com** Web site at **www.examcram.com**. If you still don't hit a score of at least 70 percent after these tests, you'll want to investigate the other practice test resources we mention in this section.

For any given subject, consider taking a class if you've tackled self-study materials, taken the test, and failed anyway. The opportunity to interact with an instructor and fellow students can make all the difference in the world, if you can afford that privilege. For information about Citrix classes, visit the Training and Certification page at **www.citrix.com/training**.

Onward, through the Fog!

Once you've assessed your readiness, undertaken the right background studies, obtained the hands-on experience that will help you understand the products and technologies at work, and reviewed the many sources of information to help you prepare for a test, you'll be ready to take a round of practice tests. When your scores come back positive enough to get you through the exam, you're ready to go after the real thing. If you follow our assessment regime, you'll not only know what you need to study, but when you're ready to make a test date at Prometric. Good luck!

Citrix Certification Exams

Term you'll need to understand:

✓ Multiple-choice question formats

Techniques you'll need to master:

✓ Assessing your exam-readiness
✓ Practicing (to make perfect)
✓ Making the best use of the testing software
✓ Budgeting your time
✓ Guessing (as a last resort)

Exam taking is not something that most people anticipate eagerly, no matter how well prepared they may be. In most cases, familiarity helps offset test anxiety. In plain English, this means you probably won't be as nervous when you take your fourth or fifth IT certification exam as you'll be when you take your first one.

Whether it's your first exam or your tenth, understanding the details of taking the exams (how much time to spend on questions, the environment you'll be in, and so on) and the exam software will help you concentrate on the material rather than on the setting. Likewise, mastering a few basic exam-taking skills should help you recognize—and perhaps even outfox—some of the tricks and snares you're bound to find in some exam questions.

This chapter, besides explaining the exam environment and software, describes some proven exam-taking strategies that you should be able to use to your advantage.

Assessing Exam-Readiness

We strongly recommend that you read through and take the Self-Assessment included with this book (it appears just before this chapter, in fact). This will help you compare your knowledge base to the requirements for obtaining CCA, and it will also help you identify parts of your background or experience that may be in need of improvement, enhancement, or further learning. If you get the right set of basics under your belt, obtaining Citrix certification will be that much easier.

Once you've gone through the Self-Assessment, you can remedy those topical areas where your background or experience may not measure up to an ideal certification candidate. But you can also tackle subject matter for individual tests at the same time, so you can continue making progress while you're catching up in some areas.

Once you've worked through an *Exam Cram*, have read the supplementary materials, and have taken the practice test, you'll have a pretty clear idea of when you should be ready to take the real exam. Although we strongly recommend that you keep practicing until your scores top the 75 percent mark, 80 percent would be a good goal to give yourself some margin for error in a real exam situation (where stress will play more of a role than when you practice). Once you hit that point, you should be ready to go. But if you get through the practice exam in this book without attaining that score, you should keep taking practice tests and studying the materials until you get there. You'll find more pointers on how to study and prepare in the Self-Assessment. But now, on to the exam itself!

The Exam Situation

When you arrive at the testing center where you scheduled your exam, you'll need to sign in with an exam coordinator. He or she will ask you to show two forms of identification, one of which must be a photo ID. After you've signed in and your time slot arrives, you'll be asked to deposit any books, bags, or other items you brought with you. Then, you'll be escorted into a closed room.

All exams are completely closed book. In fact, you will not be permitted to take anything with you into the testing area, but you will be furnished with a blank sheet of paper and a pen or, in some cases, an erasable plastic sheet and an erasable pen. Before the exam, you should memorize as much of the important material as you can, so you can write that information on the blank sheet as soon as you are seated in front of the computer. You can refer to this piece of paper anytime you like during the test, but you'll have to surrender the sheet when you leave the room.

You will have some time to compose yourself, to record this information, and to take a sample orientation exam before you begin the real thing. We suggest you take the orientation test before taking your first exam, but because they're all more or less identical in layout, behavior, and controls, you probably won't need to do this more than once.

Typically, the room will be furnished with anywhere from one to half a dozen computers, and each workstation will be separated from the others by dividers designed to keep you from seeing what's happening on someone else's computer. Most test rooms feature a wall with a large picture window. This permits the exam coordinator to monitor the room, to prevent exam-takers from talking to one another, and to observe anything out of the ordinary that might go on. The exam coordinator will have preloaded the appropriate Citrix certification exam— for this book, that's Exam 218—and you'll be permitted to start as soon as you're seated in front of the computer.

All Citrix certification exams allow a certain maximum amount of time in which to complete your work (this time is indicated on the exam by an on-screen counter/ clock, so you can check the time remaining whenever you like). All Citrix certification exams are computer generated. Although this may sound quite simple, the questions are constructed not only to check your mastery of basic facts and figures about Citrix MetaFrame 1.8, but they also require you to evaluate one or more sets of circumstances or requirements. Often, you'll be asked to give more than one answer to a question. Likewise, you might be asked to select the best or most effective solution to a problem from a range of choices, all of which technically are correct. Taking the exam is quite an adventure, and it involves real thinking. This book shows you what to expect and how to deal with the potential problems, puzzles, and predicaments.

In the next section, you'll learn more about how Citrix test questions look and how they must be answered.

The types of question formats are:

➤ Multiple choice, single answer

➤ Multiple choice, multiple answers

➤ True and false

Multiple-Choice Question Format

Some exam questions require you to select a single answer, whereas others ask you to select multiple correct answers. The following multiple-choice question requires you to select a single correct answer. Following the question is a brief summary of each potential answer and why it is either right or wrong.

Question 1

ICA PassThrough can be used to do which of the following:

○ a. Enable users to access servers on different networks or subnets

○ b. Allow Win16 clients to access published applications

○ c. Allow Mac clients to use the features available in Program Neighborhood

○ d. Allow DOS clients to access network printers

The correct answer is c. None of the other options involve ICA PassThrough.

This sample question format corresponds closely to the Citrix certification exam format—the only difference on the exam is that questions are not followed by answer keys. To select an answer, you would position the cursor over the radio button next to the answer. Then, click the mouse button to select the answer.

Let's examine a question where one or more answers are possible. This type of question provides checkboxes rather than radio buttons for marking all appropriate selections.

Question 2

> Where can administrators can shadow users? [Check all correct answers]
>
> ❏ a.   Only in the domain they are currently logged onto
>
> ❏ b.   Across domains
>
> ❏ c.   Across domains and across subnets
>
> ❏ d.   On both WinFrame and MetaFrame servers

Answers a and d are the correct answers. Answers b and c are incorrect because an administrator cannot shadow across domains.

For this particular question, two answers are required. For Question 2, you have to check the boxes next to items a and d to obtain credit for a correct answer. Notice that picking the right answers also means knowing why the other answers are wrong!

Exam-Taking Basics

A well-known principle when taking exams is to first read over the entire exam from start to finish while answering only those questions you feel absolutely sure of. On subsequent passes, you can dive into more complex questions more deeply, knowing how many such questions you have left.

There's at least one potential benefit to reading the exam over completely before answering the trickier questions: Sometimes, information supplied in later questions sheds more light on earlier questions. At other times, information you read in later questions might jog your memory about MetaFrame facts, figures, or behavior that helps you answer earlier questions. Either way, you'll come out ahead if you defer those questions about which you're not absolutely sure.

Here are some question-handling strategies:

➤ When returning to a question after your initial read-through, read every word again—otherwise, your mind can fall quickly into a rut. Sometimes, revisiting a question after turning your attention elsewhere lets you see something you missed, but the strong tendency is to see what you've seen before. Try to avoid that tendency at all costs.

➤ If you return to a question more than twice, try to articulate to yourself what you don't understand about the question, why answers don't appear to make sense, or what appears to be missing. If you chew on the subject awhile, your subconscious might provide the details you lack, or you might notice a "trick" that points to the right answer.

As you work your way through the exam, another counter that Citrix provides will come in handy—the number of questions completed and questions outstanding. It's wise to budget your time by making sure that you've completed one-quarter of the questions one-quarter of the way through the exam period, and three-quarters of the questions three-quarters of the way through.

If you're not finished when only five minutes remain, use that time to guess your way through any remaining questions. Remember, guessing is potentially more valuable than not answering, because blank answers are always wrong, but a guess may turn out to be right. If you don't have a clue about any of the remaining questions, pick answers at random, or choose all as, bs, and so on. The important thing is to submit an exam for scoring that has an answer for every question.

 At the very end of your exam period, you're better off guessing than leaving questions unanswered.

Question-Handling Strategies

For those questions that take only a single answer, usually two or three of the answers will be obviously incorrect, and two of the answers will be plausible—of course, only one can be correct. Unless the answer leaps out at you (if it does, reread the question to look for a trick; sometimes those are the ones you're most likely to get wrong), begin the process of answering by eliminating those answers that are most obviously wrong.

Almost always, at least one answer out of the possible choices for a question can be eliminated immediately because it matches one of these conditions:

➤ The answer does not apply to the situation.

➤ The answer describes a nonexistent issue, an invalid option, or an imaginary state.

After you eliminate all answers that are obviously wrong, you can apply your retained knowledge to eliminate further answers. Look for items that sound correct but refer to actions, commands, or features that are not present or not available in the situation that the question describes.

If you're still faced with a blind guess among two or more potentially correct answers, reread the question. Try to picture how each of the possible remaining answers would alter the situation. Be especially sensitive to terminology; sometimes the choice of words ("remove" instead of "disable") can make the difference between a right answer and a wrong one.

Only when you've exhausted your ability to eliminate answers, but remain unclear about which of the remaining possibilities is correct, should you guess at an answer. An unanswered question offers you no points, but guessing gives you at least some chance of getting a question right; just don't be too hasty when making a blind guess.

Numerous questions assume that the default behavior of a particular utility is in effect. If you know the defaults and understand what they mean, this knowledge will help you cut through many Gordian knots.

Mastering the Inner Game

In the final analysis, knowledge breeds confidence, and confidence breeds success. If you study the materials in this book carefully and review all the practice questions at the end of each chapter, you should become aware of those areas where additional learning and study are required.

After you've worked your way through the book, take the practice test in the back of the book. Taking this test will provide a reality check and help you identify areas to study further. Make sure you follow up and review materials related to the questions you miss on the practice exam before scheduling a real exam. Only when you've covered that ground and feel comfortable with the whole scope of the practice test should you set an exam appointment. Only if you score 80 percent or better should you proceed to the real thing (otherwise, obtain some additional practice tests so you can keep trying until you hit this magic number).

Armed with the information in this book and with the determination to augment your knowledge, you should be able to pass the certification exam. However, you need to work at it, or you'll spend the exam fee more than once before you finally pass. If you prepare seriously, you should do well. We are confident that you can do it!

Additional Resources

A good source of information about Citrix certification exams comes from Citrix itself. Because its products and technologies—and the exams that go with them—change frequently, the best place to go for exam-related information is online. Go to **www.citrix.com/training** for information about the MetaFrame 1.8 Administration for Windows course #CTX-302.2 and the associated #218 exam. Adobe Acrobat PDFs are available with information on all of the Citrix certification courses and exams.

Also search the **www.thethin.net** site for *MetaFrame* or *CCA*, which contains very good links to Citrix issues, including the CCA exam. Try the **http://thethin.net/links.cfm** link and look under the Training and Certification section.

Finally, feel free to use general search tools—such as **www.search.com**, **www.altavista.com**, and **www.excite.com**—to look for related information.

Introduction to Citrix MetaFrame

Terms you'll need to understand:

✓ Thin-client computing
✓ Multiwin
✓ Server-based computing
✓ Independent Computing Architecture (ICA) protocol
✓ Program Neighborhood
✓ WinFrame
✓ Load Balancing
✓ Installation Management Services (IMS)
✓ Resource Management Services (RMS)

Techniques you'll need to master:

✓ Understanding IMS
✓ Understanding RMS
✓ Knowing the features of SecureICA

This introductory chapter begins with a list of the various topics covered on the Citrix Certified Administrator (CCA) exam. Next, we briefly discuss the architecture and functionality of Citrix MetaFrame 1.8 for Windows NT 4 Terminal Server Edition (TSE) and present an overview of thin-client computing. Then, we introduce some of the optional add-on products designed to extend the reach and versatility of MetaFrame, including Load Balancing, Installation Management Services (IMS), Resource Management Services (RMS), SecureICA, and NFuse. The importance of these tools is twofold: First, the reader will encounter them when working on MetaFrame networks; second, they are covered on the (CCA) exam. Load Balancing and SecureICA are covered in greater depth in Chapters 8 and 10, whereas IMS and RMS are discussed in this chapter only. The CCA exam focuses on MetaFrame, so you need only a general knowledge of the IMS and RMS components for certification. Another product discussed below is WinFrame, Citrix's predecessor to MetaFrame. WinFrame is similar to MetaFrame but has fewer features and employs the Windows 3.51 interface. The Citrix MetaFrame 1.8 certification exam consists of 10 unequally weighted sections:

➤ Introduction to MetaFrame

➤ Windows Terminal Server Overview

➤ Implementing and Installing MetaFrame

➤ Installing and Configuring ICA Clients

➤ Creating a Seamless User Experience

➤ Configuring ICA Client Features

➤ Administering MetaFrame

➤ Implementing Load Balancing

➤ Configuring Web Connectivity

➤ Using Performance Monitor and Troubleshooting

The CCA exam is a brief, 40 question multiple-choice test. Since some of the above exam sections receive more attention than the others on the test, this book will focus more on those topics. Therefore, extra attention will be devoted to the topics of Installing and Configuring ICA Clients, Implementing Load Balancing and MetaFrame Administration.

If you have a solid Windows NT networking background, you will have little trouble with the Windows NT and Terminal Server test questions. A quick survey of Chapters 4 and 5 should provide a sufficient overview of the Windows NT issues covered on the CCA exam.

MetaFrame 1.8 and Thin-Client Computing

Citrix MetaFrame 1.8 is a server-based, thin-client solution that installs on top of Microsoft NT 4 Terminal Server Edition TSE; Microsoft Windows 2000 Server with Terminal Services installed; or on Solaris, Sun's Unix operating system. As of this writing, the Citrix CCA certification exam is based on MetaFrame installed on Windows NT 4 TSE. Although MetaFrame for Windows 2000 Server is available, we will focus on the NT 4 TSE version because our task is to prepare you for the current CCA exam.

With Citrix MetaFrame's server-based approach, all applications are installed, managed, executed, and supported on the server(s). Server-based computing allows all processing to be done on the server, with only the keystrokes, mouse clicks, and screen images passing between the server and the client workstation. Applications are installed, managed, and executed 100 percent on the server. Server-based computing requires the use of a multiuser operating system like Windows Terminal Server for distributing the presentation of a user interface (UI) to a client workstation. The client hardware—be it a PC, Network Computer (NC), Unix or DOS workstation, or even a Personal Digital Assistant (PDA)—needs only the Citrix ICA client installed locally to be able to access published applications offered via the Citrix MetaFrame servers. Supported applications include DOS and Windows 16- and 32-bit programs. *Application publishing* is the term Citrix uses for applications that are made available to the network users and that run 100 percent on the server rather than on the client workstations. This approach offers network administrators a simple method of pushing server-installed applications to the users' desktops.

With MetaFrame, multiple users can run traditional Windows and Java-based applications simultaneously, utilizing the ICA client on virtually any terminal (even on old, slow PCs). Unlike NCs, ICA clients do not download the applications from the server. ICA client devices can be either thin or fat. *Thin clients* are terminal devices that are generally without hard drives, floppy drives, or CD-ROMs, similar to Java terminals in the Network Computing Model. *Fat clients* are PCs or Macs that use their own memory, CPUs, and hard drives. The client device's processing power is not an important factor because the processing for the application is done on the server. The client receives screen shots of the application that is running on the server; to the client, it appears as if the application is running locally. The client offloads all the work to the server, allowing for centralized management of data and for all software upgrades to be done on the server rather than on each client. Applications are run entirely on the server; this qualifies ICA as a 100 percent thin client.

Core Features of Citrix MetaFrame

Multiwin is the core of the multiuser technology, which Microsoft licensed from Citrix to create Windows NT 4 TSE. The Multiwin component allows multiple, concurrent users to run separate, protected application sessions on a TSE, MetaFrame, WinFrame, or Sun Solaris server. The ICA protocol (covered in more detail in Chapter 6) separates the application's logic from its user interface, so only keystrokes, mouse clicks, and screen updates travel the local area network (LAN), wide area network (WAN), or wireless network. Therefore, application performance does not depend on the network bandwidth. ICA is the heart of MetaFrame's server-based, thin-client computing architecture and includes both server and client software components. Citrix's ICA protocol has become the industry standard in the thin-client computing world.

Citrix describes MetaFrame as a networking platform that centralizes application- and client-management tools. This centralization allows information technology (IT) staffers to deploy, upgrade, and troubleshoot applications from the server (rather than having to visit all of the client workstations). This is possible because the client offloads all the work to the server, which allows for centralized management of data and for all software upgrades to be done on the server rather than on each client.

As you will discover while reading this book, MetaFrame runs virtually any DOS or Windows application over any LAN, WAN, or wireless network, on virtually any client hardware device.

Key Features of Citrix's Server-Based, Thin-Client Networks

The following list of features offers you a quick overview of some key MetaFrame tools and networking concepts. These MetaFrame tools and strategies serve as an introduction to terms and ideas that will recur throughout the upcoming chapters, as well as on the CCA exam:

➤ *Centralized network management*—Means that application installs and upgrades are performed at the server rather than at the workstations. This centralized administration is also designed to reduce workstation hardware and software support.

➤ *Program Neighborhood (named after Windows Network Neighborhood)*—Is a tool that allows network administrators to provide user access to server-based applications. You can place program icons in the Program Neighborhood window on the users' desktops. Alternatively, administrators can place shortcut icons directly onto client desktops or *push* the applications to a user's Start menu.

➤ *Session shadowing*—Allows administrators to remotely take over single or multiple user sessions for support, troubleshooting, or training. You can initiate shadowing from either the Shadow button in the Citrix Server Administration tool or from the Shadow taskbar. The Shadow button lets administrators shadow one user at a time, whereas the Shadow taskbar enables them to shadow one or several clients simultaneously. Administrators can view sessions and even take control of the client's keyboard and mouse.

➤ *Server farm*—Is a term Citrix uses to designate a group of connected MetaFrame/WinFrame servers that share a common user database and can be jointly managed from a central location. You can add servers to a server farm without making any changes to the client desktop.

➤ *Data security and data integrity*—Are addressed in two ways. In a server-based, thin-client environment, data is not downloaded from the server to the clients. It is easier to safeguard the data if it is housed in a single location. The second method that MetaFrame employs to ensure security is by using the SecureICA client. This optional client encrypts all data while it is traveling the network, phone lines, or the Internet.

➤ *Low bandwidth requirements*—Mean that ICA clients enable high-speed computing over *thin pipes*. As mentioned above, the ICA client and the server exchange only mouse clicks, keystrokes, and screen updates. Because of the minimal client-to-server traffic, an ICA client workstation consumes only between 10 and 20K of LAN or WAN bandwidth to attach to applications on a MetaFrame server. This allows remote users and branch offices to access the company's servers over inexpensive dial-up phone connections or via the Internet. These remote clients will perform like local network clients. ICA clients also use less LAN bandwidth than conventional network clients.

➤ *Mixed environment support*—Is provided by MetaFrame in two ways. First, Citrix ICA client software is designed to run on almost all available clients, including Windows (16 or 32 bit), DOS, Mac, Java or Unix workstations, PDAs, and wireless devices. Second, MetaFrame supports diverse network protocols, including Transmission Control Protocol/Internet Protocol (TCP/IP), Internetwork Packet Exchange (IPX), Sequence Packet Exchange (SPX), and NetBIOS, as well as direct asynchronous connections.

➤ *Scalability*—Is one of the main enhancements that MetaFrame adds to the underlying Terminal Server software. Citrix's Load Balancing option dynamically routes network traffic to the least busy server (Load Balancing is discussed briefly later in this chapter and in more detail in Chapter 8). MetaFrame's centralized management model is also useful for IT staffs that administer large-scale networks.

➤ *Seamless desktop integration*—Is a term Citrix introduced to indicate that MetaFrame clients can access network and local resources while working in a familiar desktop environment. Although the applications run on the server, they appear to run locally. Users can access both server-based and local programs by clicking on desktop icons or from the Start menu. Local and network printers are available through the regular File/Print menu option.

Additional Citrix Products

Citrix offers additional products that are designed to enhance MetaFrame manageability, scalability, and Web publishing capabilities. These products are Load Balancing, IMS, RMS, SecureICA, and NFuse. Load Balancing and the SecureICA client are discussed briefly here and in detail in Chapters 6 and 8. IMS and RMS are covered in the following sections only. Although NFuse is an important Citrix product with its own exam and certification, it is not covered in the CCA exam, although we discuss it briefly here.

As stated above, the CCA exam will focus on core MetaFrame components along with Load Balancing and SecureICA. IMS and RMS will be represented on the CCA exam, although not in depth. These optional products are used in large networks that contain tens or hundreds of servers, and hundreds or thousands of users. Because of the central importance of the products, they are covered in the CCA exam. The importance of these tools is further illustrated by the fact that the new Citrix Certified Enterprise Administrator (CCEA) certification tests are based on these optional add-on packages. Load Balancing, IMS, RMS, and SecureICA represent the four exams that comprise the CCEA exam track.

WinFrame

Citrix WinFrame is not a MetaFrame enhancement. Rather, it is a legacy product and the predecessor of MetaFrame. Even with the success of MetaFrame, there is still a large, installed base of WinFrame networks worldwide. WinFrame includes the Windows NT 3.51 operating system (that's right—Windows NT 3.51!). MetaFrame, unlike WinFrame, is installed on top of Windows NT TSE. This means that MetaFrame purchasers must buy the Microsoft NT 4 TSE software package separately, whereas NT 3.51 comes bundled with WinFrame. Although only superficially covered on the CCA exam, WinFrame is occasionally referred to with regard to the backward compatibility of MetaFrame and other Citrix products.

Load Balancing

Load Balancing is an optional system service that dynamically and automatically routes ICA clients to the least busy server. It allows you to balance the loads of multiple WinFrame and MetaFrame servers into a single server farm. This facilitates the delivery of applications to hundreds, or even thousands, of concurrent users. It also promotes network scalability because you can add servers at any time.

Load Balancing is not considered a fault-tolerant solution because a server crash disconnects any connected users. However, it does offer some redundancy because disconnected users are routed to one of the other servers when they log back onto the network. Load Balancing is a core Citrix technology; it will be covered in greater detail in Chapter 8.

IMS

With IMS, administrators can avoid the time and complexity involved in manually installing applications on every WinFrame and/or MetaFrame server in a server farm. IMS allows an administrator to install an application simultaneously onto servers in a load-balanced server farm. This tool is composed of three elements:

➤ *IMS Packager*—Readies the application files for installation. The IMS Packager component must be installed onto a dedicated computer; this is where the packages are created and distributed to a network file server.

➤ *Application Publishing Enhancements*—Loads the prepared files onto the servers.

➤ *Installer*—Executes the installed files and represents the only licensed component.

IMS is a valuable tool for large networks. It ensures that exactly the same version of an application is installed onto all of the load-balanced servers in a server farm. This is important given the variety of service packs and patches available for current enterprise-level applications. IMS also makes it easy to uninstall an application from all of the servers by simply deleting the software from within the Published Application Manager tool.

RMS

As with the other optional management tools, RMS must be purchased, licensed, and installed separately from other Citrix products. RMS provides in-depth application and system management for WinFrame, MetaFrame, and TSE on Windows NT networks. It works in conjunction with an open database connectivity (ODBC) database like Microsoft SQL to monitor user connections and accessed applications. Tracking application usage helps you plan capacity. The System Monitoring tools include the ability to enable pager or email alerts if certain usage thresholds are exceeded.

Billing reports allow departmental-level billing based on CPU time (in $.00 per minute), Session time (in $.00 per hour), Application active time (in $.00 per minute) and on Memory usage. You can use the application usage statistics to track Web browser activity, which enables organizations to monitor employee Internet use. Figure 2.1 shows the RMS Billing Fees screen.

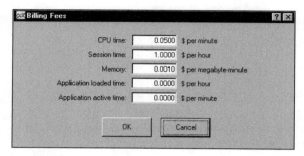

Figure 2.1   The RMS Billing Fees screen.

Like IMS, RMS is made up of three components:

➤ *Data Collection Agen*—Is installed on each monitored MetaFrame server and collects information on user access and application usage (note that Excel and text files are not compatible with RMS). The Data Collection Agent is the only component of RMS that must be licensed.

➤ *Data Source*—Is any ODBC-compliant database. It can be a client/server database or a desktop database like Access. Even though you can run the Data Source locally on a MetaFrame server, it is not recommended to do so due to resource utilization. You should run this component on a remote database server.

➤ *Analysis Tools*—Can be installed on any Windows 9.x or NT machine on the network. This component gets the data from the Data Source and then presents it to the administrator. The Analysis Tools offer detailed monitoring for applications, users, and fees and can display system snapshots and current system status. Unlike the Data Collection Agent, Citrix does not require the Analysis Tools to be licensed. Figure 2.2 shows one of the RMS Analysis Tools screens.

RMS works with Microsoft NT 4 TSE as well as with MetaFrame and WinFrame servers.

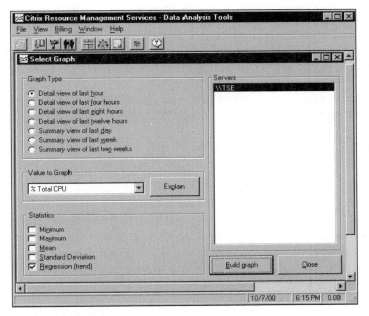

Figure 2.2 An Analysis Tools screen from RMS.

SecureICA

This optional enhancement provides a high level of security for all traffic between the servers and clients. SecureICA services must be installed and licensed on the MetaFrame server, and an unlicensed component must be installed on the client workstation. The standardICA client uses simple encryption, which is not secure enough for sensitive government or corporate data. SecureICA services use the RC5 encryption algorithm, developed by RSA to encrypt the ICA session data. The North American version of SecureICA employs up to 128-bit encryption both for the handshake (authentication) and for the session data, which is considered extremely secure. The SecureICA services use four keys during each ICA session. When the user logs on to the MetaFrame server, SecureICA uses two 40-, 56-, or 128-bit keys for the handshake. A third key encrypts the ICA packets that the MetaFrame server sends to the client. The fourth key is used for client-to-server communication. SecureICA clients are available for 16- or 32-bit Windows, DOS, and contemporary Web clients like the Netscape plug-in and the Internet Explorer (IE) ActiveX control. The client works with all of the MetaFrame-supported network protocols and connections.

When the CCA exam was written, U.S. regulations stated that products that employ an encryption key length greater than 40 bits could not be exported. Although these restrictions no longer exist, the CCA exam has not been updated to reflect the changes. For the CCA exam, there are two versions of SecureICA:

North American and International. The North American version offers the client 40-, 56-, or 128-bit encryption for both the handshake and session data. The International version offers the client a 128-bit handshake and a 40-bit session encryption. Secure ICA is covered in more detail in Chapter 6.

 For the exam, remember that 40-bit encryption is the most secure version of SecureICA that can be exported outside of North America.

NFuse

NFuse is a free tool that extends the capabilities of Citrix MetaFrame and Program Neighborhood. It is an easy-to-use Web portal wizard that allows an administrator to create an HTML Web portal that is front-end compatible with many of today's leading Web servers. NFuse supports Microsoft Internet Information Servers (IIS), Netscape, and Apache Web servers. Via the Web portal, NFuse offers network users a completely secure, single logon to all published applications within a Citrix server farm. NFuse extends the Web browser integration first introduced in Citrix's Application Launching and Embedding (ALE), a feature of Program Neighborhood. In short, NFuse allows access to corporate information over the Internet or an intranet using a standard Web browser. Although NFuse is not included in the CCA exam, Citrix does offer a 40-question certification exam for the product. NFuse is an extremely important product for Citrix's future success in the Internet environment.

Practice Questions

Question 1

> With MetaFrame 1.8, what percentage of the processing work is done on the server(s)?
>
> ○ a. 10
>
> ○ b. 25
>
> ○ c. 75
>
> ○ d. 100

Answer d is correct. With Citrix server-based computing, all of the processing is done on the server(s). This is possible because the client offloads all the work to the server, which allows for centralized management of data and for all software upgrades to be done on the server rather than on each client.

Question 2

> What two network operating systems can be used on a MetaFrame server? [Check all correct answers]
>
> ❑ a. Windows NT 4 TSE
>
> ❑ b. Sun Solaris
>
> ❑ c. Linux
>
> ❑ d. Apple

Answers a and b are correct. Currently, MetaFrame supports only these two operating systems. It does not support Linux and Apple, so answers c and d are incorrect.

Question 3

What is the name of the multiuser component used in TSE, MetaFrame, and WinFrame?

○ a. Winview

○ b. Multiwin

○ c. ASP

○ d. IMS

Answer b is correct. Multiwin was developed by Citrix to allow multiple, server-based user sessions to co-exist on a single Citrix server. The product was later licensed by Microsoft for use with Terminal Server. Winview was an early Citrix server-based product based on OS/2. Therefore, answer a is incorrect. ASP is a network model used in delivering applications over the Internet. Therefore, answer c is incorrect. IMS is a Citrix tool for installing applications on Citrix servers. Therefore, answer d is incorrect.

Question 4

With the ICA protocol, what two pieces of information are exchanged by the local client and the MetaFrame server(s)? [Check all correct answers]

❏ a. Mouse clicks and keystrokes

❏ b. Screen updates

❏ c. Application processing calls

❏ d. Application data

Answers a and b are correct. The ICA protocol separates the application's logic from its user interface, so only mouse clicks, keystrokes, and screen updates travel the LAN, WAN, or wireless network. Answer c is incorrect as processing calls have nothing to do with the ICA protocol. Answer d is incorrect as application data remains on the Citrix server.

Question 5

In what two locations can an administrator manage a MetaFrame network? [Check all correct answers]

❑ a. At a client workstation

❑ b. At the server(s)

❑ c. From a network share

❑ d. From the Citrix administration terminal

Answers a and b are correct. One of the main advantages of MetaFrame is that administrators can perform all management chores at the server or via an ICAclient. Answer c is incorrect as a network share is not a location from which you can administer the network. Answer d is incorrect as it does not exist.

Question 6

Clients supported by MetaFrame 1.8 include which of the following? [Check all correct answers]

❑ a. DOS

❑ b. 16- and 32-bit Windows

❑ c. Unix workstations

❑ d. Macs

❑ e. PDAs

Answers a, b, c, d, and e are correct. MetaFrame supports all of the listed clients.

Question 7

What three network protocols does MetaFrame 1.8 support? [Check all correct answers]

❑ a. ARP

❑ b. TCP/IP

❑ c. ODBC

❑ d. IPX

❑ e. NetBIOS

Answers b, d, and e are correct. MetaFrame can use the TCP/IP, IPX/SPX, and NetBIOS (NetBIOS is also referred to as NetBEUI) protocols to establish network connectivity. ARP is a routing protocol rather than a network protocol. Therefore, answer a is incorrect. ODBC is a database standard. Therefore, answer c is incorrect.

Question 8

What optional MetaFrame product can you use for greater network scalability?

- O a. Clustering
- O b. Load Balancing
- O c. Program Neighborhood
- O d. SecureICA

Answer b is correct. Load Balancing promotes scalability by making it (relatively) easy for the administrator to add more MetaFrame servers to handle increased user load. Server clustering is a technique used by Microsoft and others for greater scalability. Therefore, answer a is incorrect. Program Neighborhood is included with MetaFrame and is used for publishing applications for use by the network clients. Therefore, answer c is incorrect. SecureICA is the encrypted, secure version of the ICA client. Therefore, answer d is incorrect.

Question 9

What two features are available in RMS? [Check all correct answers]

- ❏ a. System resources monitoring and management
- ❏ b. Data replication services
- ❏ c. Management of NT 4 Terminal Server
- ❏ d. Generation of application installation scripts

Answers a and c are correct. RMS provides in-depth system monitoring and management of WinFrame, MetaFrame, and TSE on Windows NT networks. It works in conjunction with an ODBC-compliant database like Microsoft SQL to monitor user connections and applications accessed. Data replication and installation-script generation are not available in RMS. Therefore, answers b and d are incorrect.

Question 10

How much bandwidth is required for an ICA LAN or WAN connection?

○ a. 10 to 20K

○ b. 20 to 40K

○ c. 60 to 80K

○ d. 80 to 100K

Answer a is correct. The Citrix MetaFrame server-based network model with the ICA client offers remote access to corporate networks via a 56K dial-up connection. The client offers LAN-like performance using only 10 to 20K of bandwidth. ICA is a truly *thin* client. Therefore, answers b, c, and d are incorrect.

Need to Know More?

 Kanter, Joel. *Understanding Thin-Client/Server Computing*. Microsoft Press, Redmond, WA, 1998. ISBN 1-57231-744-2. This is a good introduction to Microsoft TSE and MetaFrame server-based, thin-client solutions. It offers in-depth case studies of thin-client solutions for different industries.

 Mathers, Todd and Shawn Genoway. *Windows NT Thin Client Solutions: Implementing Terminal Server and Citrix MetaFrame*. Macmillan Technical Publishing, Indianapolis, IN, 1999. ISBN 1-57870-065-5. This book offers extensive information on installing and administering TSE and MetaFrame networks. There is also a later version of the book that covers Windows 2000 Server/MetaFrame networks.

 See **www.networkmagazine.com** for the April 2000 article on "Decreasing TCO with Thin Clients" by Jonathan Angel. This is an excellent, balanced article on reducing the total cost of ownership (TCO) of corporate networks by using TSE and MetaFrame.

Network Models

Terms you'll need to understand:

✓ Peer-to-Peer Network Model

✓ Traditional Network Model

✓ Client/Server Computing Model

✓ Network Computing Model

✓ Server-Based Computing Model

✓ Application Service Provider (ASP) Model

Techniques you'll need to master:

✓ Identifying the different network models

✓ Knowing in which network model MetaFrame and WinFrame will be used

This chapter presents a brief survey of the common network models and client workstations that work within them. We will examine the various network types, starting with the Peer-to-Peer Network Model and progressing to the Application Service Provider (ASP) Model. By the end of this chapter, you should also understand the role of the Server-Based Computing Model that Citrix MetaFrame and WinFrame use.

Our discussion will focus on how the differing network types that make company resources (such as shared data files, email, and networked printers) available to employees' desktops.

Although this chapter is not specific to the Citrix Certified Administrator (CCA) exam, per se, the network model information found here is essential to understanding MetaFrame's server-based computing. If you are already familiar with the various types of networks, you may want to skip to the next chapter.

Until the 1980s, the Mainframe Networking Model was the only way of sharing information among users. In the early days of computing, mainframe computers represented the only available network model. Mainframes are associated with centralized computing, where all the applications and computer processing are located on the mainframe and the client workstations are nothing more than dumb terminals with limited processing capabilities (similar to today's server-based models).

With the advent of the PC, new ways of networking computers became possible. Our discussion will begin with the simplest network type, the Peer-to-Peer Network Model, which households and small businesses use. Next comes the Traditional Network Model, which introduces the use of dedicated file and print server computers to improve both performance and data security. We then progress to the client/server approach, which can distribute processing tasks among clients and multiple specialized server computers. The discussion then moves on to the more recent Network Computing Model, which involves downloading Java applications from servers to stripped-down network computers. After network computing, we examine the Server-Based Computing Model, which moves all of the processing tasks onto the server(s). This model is used both in mainframe environments as well as in Citrix MetaFrame and WinFrame networks. The final networking model discussed is the new ASP approach, whereby organizations outsource their information technology (IT) infrastructure. ASPs deliver applications directly to user desktops over phone lines or via the Internet.

Peer-to-Peer Network Model

The Peer-to-Peer Network Model is popular with families with multiple computers and with small businesses with limited IT needs and budgets. An office with a small user population may choose to use a peer-to-peer network, due in part to the quick setup and minimal daily maintenance. This type of network is cheap and easy to set up but offers limited functionality.

A peer-to-peer network can be effective in an environment where the following conditions exist:

➤ The user population does not exceed 10.

➤ Users are located in the same area.

➤ Users need to share files and a printer.

➤ Security is not a concern.

➤ Ease of use is a higher priority than customization.

➤ All of the client workstations have an operating system that is capable of peer-to-peer networking (e.g., Windows 9 and Mac).

In a peer-to-peer network, each client machine is a PC or Mac; there are no dedicated servers. Each individual PC is considered equal and is referred to as a *peer*. Every PC in the network acts as its own server and is responsible for its local file security and user authentication. This allows each user to determine what data on the computer is shared on the network, and what remains private.

 In a peer-to-peer network, each PC can be used as a standalone system, not connected to the network. This differs from other network models, in which dedicated servers provide file and print services, as well as other tasks.

The peer-to-peer network becomes difficult to manage as the user population increases. There is no central management of users and shared data. And, as shown in Figure 3.1, there is no central file server for data storage. Users do not store data files on a file server, so mission-critical data can easily be lost. The users and data can become hard to administer when this type of network grows too large (i.e., over 10 PCs).

Note: The Peer-to-Peer Network Model is essentially a stripped-down version of the Traditional Network Model, without centralized management.

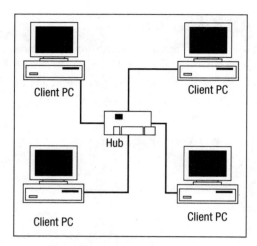

Figure 3.1 A peer-to-peer network.

Pros and Cons Comparison

As with all the network models, peer-to-peer networks have both strengths and weaknesses in a business environment. This section contains a general listing of some of the pros and cons of this network model.

The pros of the Peer-to-Peer Network Model are:

➤ It's easy to set up.

➤ No expensive network operating system is required (Windows 9x or Mac OS will suffice).

➤ You can share files and printers over the network.

➤ It's cost effective in a small environment.

The cons of the Peer-to-Peer Network Model are:

➤ It has limited scalability.

➤ There is no central management of network resources and users.

➤ Client software and hardware must be upgraded on every PC.

➤ It offers moderate security.

Traditional Network Model

At the heart of the Traditional Network Model is the network server that stores data files or functions as a centrally located print server for the entire network. These data files and print services are available to the client workstations (generally PCs or Macs) located on the local area network (LAN). With the Traditional Network Model, the processing is distributed between the user system and the server. The Traditional Network Model is suitable for small and mid-size businesses where the user population starts at 11 and scales up to 100 networked users.

Client workstations can either download data files from a network server or open a data file on the file server. When the client accesses a file located on the server, the server's file system locks the file and makes it read only. This mechanism protects the data from being changed by more than one client at a time while it is being accessed. The client workstations run applications locally using local memory, processing, and hard drives. Clients essentially use the network server as a remote hard drive or network printer. This allows a systems administrator to back up mission-critical data in one location rather than at each client workstation.

The Traditional Network Model is common in small and mid-sized business environments due to its relative simplicity and minimal maintenance requirements. However, when the user population exceeds 100, performance decreases. This is a result of the file server maintaining client connections via a "keep-alive" message service, even when no work is being performed. Figure 3.2 shows the components found in the Traditional Network Model.

Note: The Traditional Network Model is also referred to as the two-tier model.

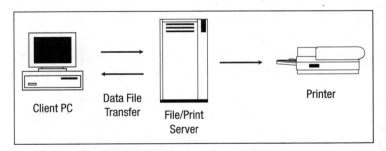

Figure 3.2   A Traditional Network Model with a file/print server.

Pros and Cons Comparison

The Traditional Network Model works well for organizations with between 11 and 100 users. This section contains some of the advantages and disadvantages of this approach.

The pros of the Traditional Network Model are:

➤ It offers centralized storage and printing.

➤ Minimum maintenance is required.

➤ No expensive network operating system is required (any operating system with networking capabilities will work).

➤ It's cost effective in a small environment.

The cons of the Traditional Network Model are:

➤ It has limited scalability.

➤ Client software and hardware must be upgraded on every PC.

➤ As the user population approaches 100, performance decreases.

Client/Server Computing Model

The Client/Server Computing Model has been in use since the late 1980s and has been widely adopted in corporations and the military. It distributes the processing of applications among different servers in the network. In this model, there is a client workstation, usually a PC or Mac, and front- and back-end servers (in most cases, the back-end server houses a database like Oracle, SAP, People Soft, or SQL). The client makes a request to the front-end server and then the front-end server acts as an intermediary between the client and the back-end server. The front-end server passes the query to the back-end server, and then the back-end server retrieves the requested information, formats it, and sends it back to the client. Figure 3.3 illustrates the components of a client/server network.

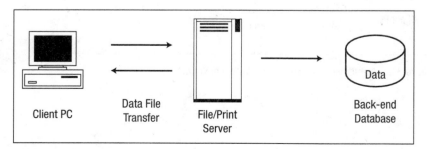

Figure 3.3   A diagram of the Client/Server Computing Model.

When the client accesses a data file in the Client/Server Computing Model, the database locks individual records rather than the entire data file. This differs from the Traditional Network Model approach, where the data file is locked. This is due to the fundamental difference between the methods of housing data. In a database, a record is composed of fields, with each field containing one item of information. A group of records make up a file. In a client/server network, clients can access and use data records that other users aren't using.

A back-end server can run on any machine on the network that the front-end server can communicate with. The front- and back-end servers handle the data-access functions, whereas the client workstation handles the presentation service and the business logic functions of the application running on the client.

The front- and back-end server components have fundamentally different requirements for computing resources, including processor speeds, memory, disk speeds, and input/output devices. In addition, the hardware and operating system of the client and server does not have to be the same. This means that a PC or Java client can co-exist on a network with a Unix, Linux, Windows, or Mac server. The client and server communicate with a well-defined set of standard network protocols such as Transmission Control Protocol/Internet Protocol (TCP/IP), NetBIOS, or Internetwork Packet Exchange/Sequence Packet Exchange (IPX/SPX).

An important characteristic of the Client/Server Computing Model is scalability. You can scale networks horizontally or vertically. Horizontal scaling requires adding or removing client workstations, which may impact performance. Vertical scaling means upgrading to a larger and faster server.

Note: The Client/Server Computing Model is also referred to as a three-tier model or multi-tier architecture.

Pros and Cons Comparison

Once the number of users goes beyond 100 or an organization needs to use a sophisticated database (e.g., Oracle and SQL), a client/server network becomes a viable option. This section lists some of the strengths and weaknesses of client/server networks.

The pros of the Client/Server Computing Model are:

➤ It offers centralized storage and administration.

➤ It requires less software on the client than the Traditional Model.

➤ It is scalable to accommodate larger networks than the Traditional Network Model.

The cons of the Client/Server Computing Model are:

➤ Additional hardware is required.

➤ Additional administration is necessary.

Network Computing Model

The Network Computing Model works within a Java environment. The Java-based server stores all of the Java applications and the client data. The client downloads the requested Java-based application from the central server and then runs it on its local Java virtual machine (VM). The data always stays on the server while the applications can run wherever a VM is running on a client workstation.

The client is referred to as a Java terminal or Network Computer (NC). The Java terminal has a CPU, RAM, a network, and a video card onboard, but it does not include a hard drive. NCs are designed with the network, the Internet, and intranets in mind and are not like PCs that can operate independently of a network. An NC must have a Java VM installed and must support both network-based and standalone applications.

The Network Computing Model has inherent limitations. First and foremost is that traditional Windows-based applications do not run well in a Java environment. Applications must be specifically written in Java. Also, the applications are downloaded from a central application server to each client on a per-use basis, so network traffic can be negatively affected. Figure 3.4 shows a typical Network Computing Model environment.

Pros and Cons Comparison

The Network Model has generated a lot of interest in recent years but its high bandwidth requirements and lack of applications have slowed its acceptance. This section lists the advantages and disadvantages of the Network Computing Model.

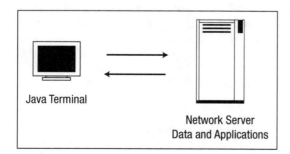

Java Terminal

Network Server
Data and Applications

Figure 3.4   A diagram of the Network Computing Model.

The pros of the Network Computing Model are:

➤ Java terminals require little maintenance.

➤ It offers centralized data and application storage.

The cons of the Network Computing Model are:

➤ It is bandwidth intensive.

➤ Not many Java applications are available.

Server-Based Computing Model

The Server-Based Computing Model allows all processing to be done on the server, with only the keystrokes, mouse clicks, and screen images passing between the server and the desktop. Applications are installed, managed, and executed 100 percent on the server. The Server-Based Computing Model uses a multiuser operating system like Windows Terminal Server for distributing the presentation of a user interface (UI) to a client device. This model has the look and feel of the old dumb terminal-mainframe model, with the added benefit of presenting a Windows interface to the client. The client can be located anywhere on a LAN, wide area network (WAN), wireless network, or the Internet. The server-based network products that we will focus on are Window NT TSE and Citrix MetaFrame 1.8.

The client devices can be either thin or fat. *Thin clients* are terminal devices that are generally without hard drives, floppy drives, or CD-ROMs, similar to Java terminals in the Network Computing Model. *Fat clients* are PCs or Macs that use their own memory, CPUs, and hard drives. The client device's processing power is not an important factor because the processing for the application is done on the server. The client receives screen shots of the application that is running on the server. To the client, it appears as if the application is running locally. The client offloads all the work to the server, allowing for centralized management of data and for all software upgrades to be done on the server rather than on each client.

The Server-Based Computing Model appeared several decades ago with the dumb terminal-mainframe model. Centralized applications ran on mainframes and minicomputers. Like current server-based approaches, the mainframe model offered centralized control over the use of the application and avoided using the client's processing power. With centralized applications and data storage, connectivity was all that a network had to supply.

There are fundamental differences between contemporary server-based computing models and the dumb terminal-mainframe model. The current client terminals (either *thin* windows terminals or *fat* PC clients) can access Internet- and Windows-based applications, whereas the old mainframe dumb terminals could not. Also, PC server hardware costs have decreased dramatically. This makes server-based computing affordable by allowing multiple inexpensive servers to do the job of a single million-dollar mainframe computer. Figure 3.5 shows a diagram of the Server-Based Computing Model.

Pros and Cons Comparison

This section covers the pros and cons of the Server-Based Computing Model. As you can see, server-based computing has more pluses than minuses.

The pros of the Server-Based Computing Model are:

➤ It offers centralized storage and administration.

➤ It is scalable; it can accommodate the largest networks.

➤ It requires minimal LAN or WAN bandwidth.

➤ It employs off-the-shelf software applications with little or no modification. Custom applications may also be deployed (assuming the custom applications are compatible with TSE).

➤ It can run the latest Windows applications on legacy PCs.

➤ You upgrade user software from a central location.

➤ It allows non-PC machines to run Windows applications.

➤ It allows remote users to access applications over a WAN, wireless links, or the Internet with LAN-speed performance.

The cons of the Server-Based Computing Model are:

➤ It requires additional server hardware.

➤ Server administration requirements increase as servers are added.

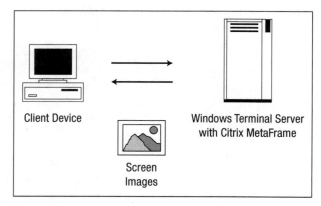

Figure 3.5 A diagram of the Server-Based Computing Model.

ASP Model

The term ASP is currently used to describe a company that hosts applications and offers data storage on its servers, located at secure data centers. Corporations pay a subscription or per-user fee for their employees to access predefined applications and corporate data via the Internet or a private network. Essentially, ASPs offer a solution for companies who wish to outsource parts of their IT infrastructure.

Most current and many legacy applications can be delivered via the ASP model. Applications as varied as enterprise resource planning (ERP) systems, office productivity suites, customer relationship management (CRM) solutions, sales force automation (SFA) solutions, and full desktop and printing emulation services can be provided.

Along with data and application hosting to corporate and individual customers, ASPs offer Independent Software Vendors (ISVs) a way of delivering their products to customers via the Internet. ISVs can showcase new products or update older versions of software immediately through the ASP and make the products available over the Internet. This new paradigm offers an attractive alternative to current software-distribution methods.

This model is still in its infancy and has not yet gained widespread acceptance. Security and access issues need to be resolved before corporations will adopt this new technology. Even so, the ASP model is changing the way we look at networking models, network management, and software distribution. Figure 3.6 shows a representation of the ASP model.

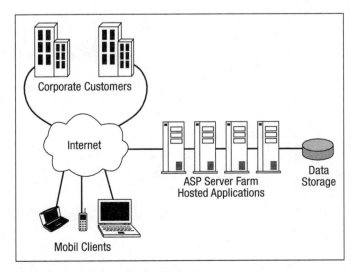

Figure 3.6   A diagram of the ASP Model.

Pros and Cons Comparison

Because the ASP model is so new, there is still some disagreement about its virtues and shortcomings. This section covers the current consensus of the pros and cons of the ASP approach.

The pros of the ASP Model are:

➤ It allows organizations to outsource IT needs.

➤ It offers centralized data and application storage.

The cons of the ASP Model are:

➤ It has perceived security limitations.

➤ It offers limited global user management.

➤ It offers limited global file security.

Practice Questions

Question 1

> Which network model is considered to be the most bandwidth intensive?
>
> ○ a. Peer-to-Peer Network Model
>
> ○ b. Traditional Network Model
>
> ○ c. Client/Server Computing Model
>
> ○ d. Network Computing Model
>
> ○ e. Server-Based Computing Model

Answer d is correct. In the Network Computing Model, all applications are down-loaded from a central application server to each client on a per-use basis. In peer-to-peer networks, all applications and data are located on the individual workstations. Usually, network traffic is limited to the occasional sharing of files or printers. Therefore, answer a is incorrect. In the Traditional Network and Client/Server Computing models, only data traffic is carried across the network.. Therefore, answers b and c are incorrect. In server-based networks, the applications and data remain on the server(s) so network traffic is reduced to sending mouse clicks and keystrokes to the server(s) and screen updates to the clients. Therefore, answer e is incorrect.

Question 2

> Of the listed network models, which one uses the Internet exclusively as a way for users to access services?
>
> ○ a. Peer-to-Peer Network Model
>
> ○ b. Traditional Network Model
>
> ○ c. Client/Server Computing Model
>
> ○ d. Network Computing Model
>
> ○ e. Server-Based Computing Model
>
> ○ f. ASP Model

Answer f is correct. An ASP is a remote service; users access the ASP via the Internet using the TCP/IP protocol. The other network models listed normally use a LAN or WAN to provide users with access to network resources. Therefore, answers a through e are incorrect.

Question 3

Which network model uses a multiuser operating system, like Windows NT Terminal Server Edition (TSE)?

- ○ a. Peer-to-Peer Network Model
- ○ b. Traditional Network Model
- ○ c. Client/Server Computing Model
- ○ d. Network Computing Model
- ○ e. Server-Based Computing Model

Answer e is correct. The Server-Based Computing Model uses a multiuser operating system like Windows Terminal Server for distributing the presentation of a UI to a client device. None of the other models employs a multiuser operating system. Therefore, answers a through d are incorrect.

Question 4

What is ISV an acronym for?

- ○ a. Internet Software Version
- ○ b. Internet System Vendor
- ○ c. Independent System Version
- ○ d. Independent Software Vendor

Answer d is correct. ISVs like Microsoft and Sun Microsystems can now use ASPs as a way of delivering their products to customers via the Internet. Therefore, answers a, b, and c are incorrect.

Question 5

What network model is synonymous with a three-tier model?

○ a. Peer-to-Peer Network Model

○ b. Traditional Network Model

○ c. Client/Server Computing Model

○ d. Network Computing Model

Answer c is correct. The Client/Server Computing Model has three components: clients, front-end servers, and back-end servers; thus, it's a three-tier model. Peer-to-peer networks do not use servers. Therefore, answer a is incorrect. Although the other network types often deploy multiple servers, they do not use the front-end server/back-end data store model used by client/server networks. Therefore, answers b and d are incorrect. Refer to Figure 3.3 for an illustration of the front-end and back-end servers employed in client/server networks.

Question 6

Which model is reminiscent of the dumb terminal-mainframe model?

○ a. Peer-to-Peer Network Model

○ b. Traditional Network Model

○ c. Client/Server Computing Model

○ d. Network Computing Model

○ e. Server-Based Computing Model

○ f. ASP Model

Answer e is correct. The Server-Based Computing Model first appeared several decades ago with the dumb terminal-mainframe model. Centralized applications ran on mainframes and minicomputers. This architecture also describes the basic structure of the Server-Based Computing Model. In a peer-to-peer network, applications are loaded onto the individual workstations, so answer a is incorrect. Unlike mainframe networks, the Traditional, Client/Server Computing, and Network Computing approaches place at least some of processing load on the client workstations. Therefore, answers b, c, and d are incorrect. ASPs also require more than dumb terminals to access the central server(s). Therefore, answer f is incorrect.

Question 7

In which network model would you see a database product like Oracle, SAP, People Soft, or SQL?

○ a. Peer-to-Peer Network Model

○ b. Traditional Network Model

○ c. Client/Server Computing Model

○ d. Server-Based Computing Model

Answer c is correct. The Client/Server Computing Model distributes the processing of applications among different servers in the network. In this model, there are client workstations (usually PCs or Macs) and front- and back-end servers. The back-end server in most cases is a database like Oracle, SAP, People Soft, or SQL. With the other network types listed, there is no inherent division of the servers into database and file servers. Therefore, answers a, b, and d are incorrect.

Question 8

Which network model locks data files, allowing only one user at a time to make changes?

○ a. Peer-to-Peer Network Model

○ b. Traditional Network Model

○ c. Client/Server Computing Model

○ d. Network Computing Model

○ e. Server-Based Computing Model

Answer b is correct. In the Traditional Network Model, when the client accesses a file located on the file server, the server's file system locks the file and makes it read only. This mechanism protects the data from being changed by more than one client at a time while it is being accessed. In peer-to-peer networks, the users store their data on their own hard drives. Therefore, answer a is incorrect. Client/server, network computing, and server-based networks allow different users to simultaneously modify different records within the same data file. Therefore, answers c, d, and e are incorrect.

Question 9

> Thin clients are terminal devices that are generally without hard drives, floppy drives, or CD-ROMs.
>
> ○ a. True
>
> ○ b. False

Answer a is correct. Thin-client devices do not need hard drives, floppy drives, or CD-ROM drives. They do not require hard drives because they access applications that run on the application server and data that is stored remotely on a file or database server. PCs need hard drives, floppies, or CD-ROM drives to install software or store data. A thin-client device accesses applications and data remotely, eliminating the need for hard drives, floppy drives, or CD-ROMs.

Question 10

> Which network model is most likely to deploy Java VM software on the client terminals?
>
> ○ a. Peer-to-Peer Network Model
>
> ○ b. Traditional Network Model
>
> ○ c. Client/Server Computing Model
>
> ○ d. Network Computing Model
>
> ○ e. Server-Based Computing Model
>
> ○ f. Application Service Provider Model

Answer d is correct. The Network Computing Model is the model most identified with Java. Although Java programs can run in some of the other network types, they are most commonly associated with the Network Computing Model. Thus, answers a, b, c, e, and f are incorrect.

Need to Know More?

 Derfler, Frank. *Practical Networking*. Que/Macmillan Press, Indianapolis, IN, 1999. ISBN 0-7897-2252-6. This book offers an in-depth discussion of client/server networking and different server types (e.g., file, application, and database).

 Hallberg, Bruce. *Networking: A Beginner's Guide*. Osbourne/McGraw Hill, Berkeley, CA, 2000. ISBN 0-07-21226-9. Page 4 of this book offers a good introduction to several of the network models discussed in this chapter.

 Tittle, Ed and David Johnson. *Networking Essentials*. Certification Insider Press, Scottsdale, AZ, 1998. ISBN 0-57610-237-8. Chapter 1 contains information on peer-to-peer versus client/server computing.

Installing Microsoft NT 4 Terminal Server Edition (TSE) and Citrix MetaFrame 1.8

Terms you'll need to understand:

✓ Scalability

✓ Microsoft Hardware Compatibility List (HCL)

✓ Command-line switches

✓ Software activation

✓ Anonymous user accounts

✓ Resource monitoring

Techniques you'll need to master:

✓ Understanding how and why to use drive mapping

✓ Understanding the issues regarding preinstallation of MetaFrame 1.8

✓ Understanding anonymous user accounts

Citrix's Certified Citrix Administrator (CCA) exam requires a basic knowledge of Windows NT 4 Terminal Server Edition (TSE), including an understanding of NT 4 networking concepts and administrative tools. One example of a core concept is NT's domain model with Primary Domain Controllers (PDCs) and Backup Domain Controllers (BDCs). An example of an important administrative tool is NT's User Manager for Domains. MetaFrame 1.8 installs on top of TSE, so it uses NT's underlying domain-management architecture. Although the exam focuses primarily on MetaFrame, you should be somewhat familiar with TSE installation and configuration issues.

You must install Terminal Server before MetaFrame, so we include the TSE installation process for your convenience. As with the MetaFrame install, covering the Terminal Server installation process will help you review some of the TSE features, functionality, and configuration options. As already mentioned, a basic knowledge of Terminal Server installation and setup is needed to prepare for the test.

Following the coverage of the Terminal Server installation, we detail the MetaFrame installation procedures. Installing the software exposes you to several important issues that are important to network administration and to test success. The installation process is brief and fairly uncomplicated. The chapter concludes by covering some TSE/MetaFrame configuration and optimization procedures.

Introduction to Microsoft Server NT 4 TSE

Windows NT 4 TSE is a separate, standalone multiuser version of NT 4 Server. Although TSE is a standalone product, it installs and looks very much like NT 4. The management tools also look similar, excluding the addition of the Terminal Server tools.

Terminal Server, like WinFrame and MetaFrame, is a server-based, thin-client, multiuser solution that emulates the old mainframe-dumb terminal model. But unlike mainframe clients, TSE, WinFrame, or MetaFrame clients can access Windows and Web applications from the network server or from the Internet via their desktops. And, as with MetaFrame or WinFrame, all applications are installed, managed, executed, and supported on the server(s) with only the Remote Desktop Protocol (RDP) client installed on the client workstations. Note that TSE will not support Independent Computing Architecture clients unless MetaFrame/WinFrame is also installed.

To achieve Terminal Server's multiuser functionality, Microsoft licensed Multiwin from Citrix. Multiwin is the multiuser technology used in both WinFrame and MetaFrame to allow multiple concurrent users to log on and run applications in separate, protected sessions running in the NT kernel on the TSE server.

Like MetaFrame, Terminal Server supports all Windows clients, including 16-bit/Windows 3.x, 32-bit/Windows 9.x/NT, and Windows-based terminals. However, TSE does *not* support DOS, Mac, or Unix clients unless MetaFrame is also deployed.

Scalability and Sizing

Scalability is a major consideration in a Terminal Server environment, where applications run 100 percent on the server(s). *Scalability* describes how a hardware or software system can adapt to increased demands. A scalable network is one that can start off with just a few client workstations and servers and then easily expand to hundreds or thousands of client workstations and servers. The scalability of a Terminal Server-based server farm depends on the user load, the type of applications running on the server, the server configuration, and the network bandwidth. When one or more servers in the server farm is running out of resources, an administrator can simply add a server (or servers).

In a Terminal Server network environment, users share the server's resources. Essentially, multiple users are sharing a common Windows NT system simultaneously. This environment requires a TSE server to have sufficient CPU, memory, and disk resources to handle multiple client demands and to support the installed applications. All of the processing occurs on the Terminal Server, so the CPU and memory requirements are much more extensive than on a workstation. The sizing of a server is loosely based on user and application system demand.

User Demand

Calculating the user demand of a network is not an exact science. For this book, we will categorize user demand based on two types of users:

➤ *Typical users (task oriented)*—These users generally access only one application and one data file per user session. Typical users do not consume excessive resources.

➤ *Power users (administrators)*—These users run multiple applications and access multiple data files simultaneously. Power users consume a fair amount of server resources and have more extensive data-access requirements than typical users.

Application Demand

Application demand is calculated on a per-application basis. Therefore, testing an application is a critical step in demonstrating that the application will install and run efficiently in a Terminal Server environment. Testing also allows you to establish the application's system demand requirements.

It is important to test the environment with your expected user load, with varying numbers of user sessions running one or more applications for a time period that simulates real usage. Using a mixture of typical users (task oriented) and power users (administrators) gives you a fair evaluation of the system requirements.

You may place applications that require significant system resources on a separate server within the server farm. This strategy may favor the deployment of a larger number of smaller servers as opposed to using only a few very large servers.

Below are some general application considerations:

➤ 16-bit applications require a minimum of 25 percent more processing power than 32-bit applications.

➤ 16-bit text-based applications may not be compatible in a Terminal Server environment.

➤ All users who access a 16-bit application run within their own separate application session. 16-bit applications differ from 32-bit applications, which can share components running in memory. This helps explain why 16-bit applications are more resource hungry than 32-bit programs.

Server Sizing and Accessibility

Although there are no absolute, one-size-fits-all server-sizing criteria, the following information can help you design your TSE network. One major consideration is that dual/multiple processor servers maximize CPU availability and should be considered as a minimum requirement for TSE servers. Terminal Server supports up to four CPUs out of the box. Up to 32 processors can be accommodated with third-party add-ons. Purchasing a multiprocessor-capable server, even if you start with only one CPU, allows you to easily add capacity as your requirements grow. However, while adding a second CPU can double the processing capacity of a server, adding additional CPUs will not achieve the same level of performance improvement. Thus, adding a third CPU will impact performance much less than will the addition of a second CPU.

Installing additional memory also maximizes accessibility. When a server runs out of memory, things run very slowly and users may be dropped. Microsoft states that the minimum memory requirements for a TSE server are 32MB of memory plus an additional 4 to 12MB for each user. These are the absolute minimum requirements for a TSE server to run and should not be considered as base setup parameters.

Typically, a network with a single TSE server that is serving an office with 50 typical and 50 power users that access multiple 32-bit applications would require a Terminal Server with:

➤ Dual Pentium III 550 MHz CPUs

➤ 512K of cache

➤ 1GB of memory

➤ A 10,000-rpm Small Computer System Interface (SCSI) hard drive

This is a general sizing scenario and varies greatly in virtually every environment. Most hardware manufacturers offer sizing charts for servers that come bundled with Terminal Server. Always check with the manufacturer before buying a TSE server to ensure that it will meet your requirements.

Terminal Server Hardware Requirements and Preinstallation Issues

This section covers Microsoft's minimum hardware requirements for a TSE installation. As always, it is preferable to use components that exceed the suggested minimum specifications. Before starting the install, determine the manufacturer and model number of the Network Interface Card (NIC) and of the SCSI drives and controllers to verify that the components are compatible with Terminal Server. For a complete list of components that are compatible with TSE, see the Microsoft Hardware Compatibility List (HCL) for Windows NT 4 (the HCL is available on the Microsoft Web site). Fortunately, MetaFrame 1.8 is also compatible with the hardware shown on the NT HCL.

Following are Microsoft's minimum hardware requirements for a TSE server:

➤ 32-bit x86 microprocessor (such as Intel Pentium or higher).

➤ 32 MB of RAM, plus 4 to 8MB for each typical connected user (8 to 12MB for each power user).

➤ VGA or higher-resolution monitor with a maximum of 256 colors.

➤ 3.5-inch floppy disk.

➤ CD-ROM drive.

➤ NIC: An NT-compatible, 100MB network adapter is recommended.

Note: Before you start the installation, have the NIC driver on a floppy or CD–ROM because it may not be on the installation media. This is a common installation stumbling block and often causes problems.

➤ A network protocol, preferably Transmission Control Protocol/Internet Protocol (TCP/IP).

➤ One or more hard disks, with 128MB minimum of free hard disk space on the partition that will contain the Terminal Server system files. This is the absolute minimum space needed according to Microsoft, but 300MB minimum is recommended.

 If a server has multiple hard drives that use a "stripe set" configuration—e.g., Redundant Array of Independent Disks (RAID) 0 or RAID 5—for improved performance and/or fault tolerance, the Performance Monitor utility might indicate a high reading for the Disk Queue Length counter. This counter shows the amount of data waiting to be transferred to the disk(s) and should read no greater than 1.5 to 2 times the number of spindles on the physical disk(s). For the CCA exam, remember that a reading higher than 2.0 indicates that the disk subsystem should be replaced.

Terminal Server Licensing

Microsoft requires you to have several licenses to implement Terminal Server. This section discusses Microsoft licensing issues. Citrix licensing is discussed in the "Citrix MetaFrame Preinstallation Issues" section later in this chapter. It is important to understand the Microsoft and Citrix licensing requirements so that you set up a server correctly.

The first required license is a Windows NT 4 server license, sometimes referred to as a *base license*. This is included with the operating system. The next required license is an NT Client Access License (CAL). A separate CAL is required for each client device that accesses network resources such as a shared network printer or a file server. These two licenses are for the base NT 4 component of Windows NT 4 TSE; additional licensing is required for the TSE component.

Terminal Server requires that, except for NT Workstation and Windows 2000 Professional clients, each client workstation accessing the TSE server have an additional Terminal Server CAL. This TSE CAL is in addition to the NT 4 client CAL. These licenses must be installed in Per Seat, not Per Server, mode (see Step 15 in the "Microsoft NT 4 TSE Installation Procedure" section later in this chapter). The Per Seat licensing option requires one CAL for each client computer that will access a TSE server (or servers). This option allows clients to log on to multiple servers. With Per Server licensing, the quantity of CALs you purchase is applied to a particular server computer and clients can connect only to the licensed server. The Per Server option is not a valid option for a TSE server.

Note: Microsoft contends that since Terminal Server delivers a virtual NT desktop to each attached Windows desktop, all non-NT Workstation clients must be licensed. Therefore, all non-NT clients must have both a Windows NT CAL and a Terminal Server CAL.

Microsoft NT 4 TSE Installation Procedure

An administrator who has experience installing Windows NT will find the Terminal Server installation very familiar. The installations for NT and TSE are virtually identical. We will outline the common installation methods and then proceed to the installation using a CD-ROM.

If you have experience installing Windows NT, skip to the "Citrix MetaFrame Preinstallation Issues" section later in this chapter. As with the MetaFrame install, the Terminal Server installation process will help you review some of TSE's features, functionality, and configuration options. A basic knowledge of TSE installation and setup is needed to prepare for the test.

Note: During installation, you should configure the Terminal Server as a standalone or member server. Making it a Domain Controller (PDC or BDC) will drain processor and memory resources because Domain Controllers must handle user authentication and other chores. Also, users effectively log on locally to the Terminal Server, so there are security issues when users are allowed to log on to a Domain Controller.

Here is a brief outline of the two common installation methods used to install TSE:

1. You can directly install Terminal Server from the CD-ROM, if the computer BIOS provides support for the El Torito bootable CD-ROM standard. This is the most common method.

2. If the server has network connectivity, you can install Terminal Server from the Terminal Server installation files stored on a network server's hard drive. For a network install, boot the server using DOS, format the hard drive partition, and then install Terminal Server via the network. If you install TSE from the DOS prompt using the winnt.exe or winnt32.exe command from the i386 directory, you can use the command-line switches detailed in Table 4.1.

A TSE installation is no more time-consuming than a standard NT installation. However, the time required to complete a TSE installation will vary depending on the selected installation method and the server's hardware.

 If you install Terminal Server over an existing Windows 3.51; Windows NT 4; or WinFrame 1.6, 1.7, or 1.8 installation, the local user database—Security Access Manager (SAM)—will be saved, but you will have to reinstall all of the applications. However, it is normally easier and less complicated to install TSE on a clean hard drive partition.

Table 4.1	The winnt.exe and winnt32.exe command-line switches.
Switch	**Action**
/S[:]*source*	Identifies the source location of the TSE files. Use a full path description or the Uniform Naming Convention (UNC) path (i.e., \\server\sharename\path).
/T[:]*tempdrive*	Identifies the drive that is temporarily used to hold the setup files.
/OX	Creates the setup floppy diskettes.
/X	Specifies that the setup diskettes will not be created.
/B	Installs Terminal Server without employing the setup diskettes.
/F	Avoids the verification of files copied during the install.
/C	Negates the inspection of the hard drives for available free space.
/W	Allows TSE to be installed from the Windows 95/98 operating system.

Here are the steps to perform a complete TSE installation using the CD-ROM disk. Except for Steps 1 and 2, the procedure is basically the same for all three installation methods.

1. Insert the CD-ROM and start the server.

2. From the Welcome To Setup window, press Enter to continue.

3. Allow the install program to autodetect the mass storage devices (e.g., IDE, SCSI, and CD-ROM drives). It is recommended that you avoid manually choosing the storage devices unless doing so is absolutely necessary. When prompted, insert the Terminal Server setup CD-ROM into the CD-ROM drive. Press Enter to continue. The CD-ROM files are now copied to the hard drive partition.

4. Press Page Down and then F8 to agree to the license agreement.

5. Review the Detected Hardware and press Enter if it is correct.

6. Select Unpartitioned Space or the partition you created and then press Enter.

7. If you have not yet partitioned the drive, press C to make a partition in the unpartitioned area. Just remember that NT or Terminal Server can recognize only a 2GB partition; the installation will fail if the partition size is larger. Also, it is preferable to install TSE on its own partition and use a separate partition or drive for applications and data.

8. Select the default location, \wtsrv, unless you have a custom setup requirement, and then select Enter to continue.

9. Press Esc to bypass the exhaustive hard drive check or press Enter to run the drive check; then wait for the additional files to be copied.

10. Remove any floppy diskette and CD-ROM and then press Enter to reboot.

11. Re-insert the CD-ROM when prompted, and then click on OK and wait for the additional files to be copied.

12. From the Windows NT Setup window, click on Next to begin the first of three phases of the installation process, which are: gathering information about your server, installing Windows NT networking, and finishing setup.

13. Enter the name of the registered software owner and an organization or company name.

14. Enter the CD-ROM key license number, located on the Terminal Server CD-ROM case.

15. The next step allows you to select the Per Seat or the Per Server License Option. Select Per Seat and enter the total number of desktops that will connect to the TSE server.

16. Type in a server name. The name can be from 1 to 15 characters long and must be different than any other computer name in your network (this is the NetBIOS name).

17. Select Member Server for the server type. Citrix recommends that Terminal Server not be installed on a PDC or BDC.

18. Enter an administrator password.

19. You now have the option of creating an Emergency Repair Disk (ERD).

20. Select Accessories and accept the default setting (you can add or remove accessories later).

21. You now have the option to install Microsoft Internet Explorer (IE) 4. As with most of the optional components of TSE, IE can be installed later.

22. Now you begin the second part of the installation, installing Windows NT networking. Select the This Computer Will Participate In A Network and the Wired To The Network options. Do not select the Remote Access Service (RAS) option unless the server will connect to the network using a dialup connection.

23. You now have the option to install Microsoft Internet Information Server (IIS) 3. You can also install it after the TSE installation.

24. Select Start Search to autodetect the installed NIC, and then click on Next if the correct NIC was located. If not, insert the NIC manufacturer's driver disk to install the driver. Select TCP/IP as the network protocol.

Note: TCP/IP is the only network protocol that Terminal Server's RDP client uses. If you will also be installing MetaFrame, you can select additional protocols—e.g., Novell NetWare's NWLink Internet Protocol Exchange/Sequence Packet Exchange (IPX/SPX). To minimize resource usage, install only those network protocols that will be used on the network.

25. You now have the option to install network services. Accept the default services displayed. After the install is complete, you can add other network services using the Network applet, available in the Terminal Server Control Panel.

26. Click on Next to install the selected networking components.

27. Click on No for using Dynamic Host Configuration Protocol (DHCP). Terminal Server will always use a fixed or static IP address instead of using DHCP.

28. Configure the TCP/IP address.

29. Click on Next on Show Bindings For window. Accept the defaults unless you have special requirements.

30. Click on Next on the Windows NT Setup window, and then click on Finish to complete the third phase of the setup.

31. Select whether the server should be part of a domain or workgroup based on the intended role of the Terminal Server. If in doubt, choose Workgroup because you can add the server to a domain at any time.

32. Set the time zone information.

33. Set the display, test it, and then select OK.

34. Remove any diskettes and the CD-ROM, and reboot the Terminal Server.

Congratulations! You now have a TSE server that is ready for the Citrix MetaFrame installation. Before installing MetaFrame, please note that you should not install any programs on your Terminal Server until you complete the MetaFrame installation. This is due to the option of remapping the server drive letters during the MetaFrame installation. Therefore, it is necessary to wait to install any program or application until after MetaFrame is installed (this includes service tools and soft packs). Programs that were installed to run from the C: drive on the server will not operate correctly once the drive mapping is altered. We will discuss drive mapping in detail in the next section.

Before proceeding with the MetaFrame installation, you must be fully aware of the preinstallation issues, which are addressed in the next section.

Citrix MetaFrame Preinstallation Issues

Installing Citrix MetaFrame is both quick and simple. If the Terminal Server installation was completed properly, the MetaFrame installation will be straightforward. As mentioned in the "Terminal Server Hardware Requirements and Preinstallation Issues" section earlier in this chapter, it is important to make sure that the server has adequate resources to support MetaFrame 1.8. A MetaFrame server needs 32MB of memory plus 4 to 12MB for each user. In addition, the install requires at least 30MB of hard drive space. As always, it is better to err on the generous side when it comes to memory and hard drive resources.

Also, be aware that even if the Terminal Server has a modem configured to use RAS, it does not support dial-up asynchronous ICA connections.

Remapping

Another factor to consider is if you will remap the server's drive letters during the MetaFrame installation. MetaFrame allows you to remap the hard drives so that users can continue to use the traditional C and D drive letters to access their local drives when connected to the MetaFrame server. If you choose not to remap the servers drives from C: and D:, the local drives of clients that connect to the MetaFrame server show up as V: and U: rather than C: and D:. During the installation of MetaFrame, you are presented with two drive mapping windows. Figure 4.1 shows the first window, which explains the drive mapping features and ramifications.

The second drive mapping window, shown in Figure 4.2, allows you to select the new server drive letters. Citrix MetaFrame defaults to M: as the first default reassigned drive letter, although you can select any letter that works in your network environment. If you select Next from this window, you cannot revert back to the original drive letters (even if you uninstall MetaFrame).

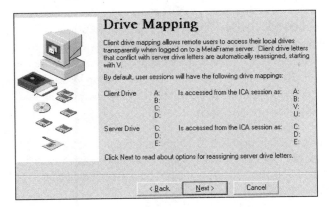

Figure 4.1   The first of two drive mapping windows.

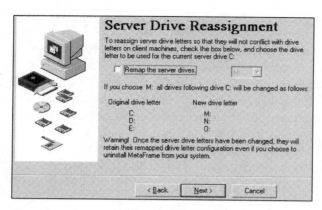

Figure 4.2 The second drive mapping window.

Citrix License Activation

Citrix licensing is unlike most software licensing, whereby a serial number is entered and the software is then licensed. All Citrix software—including MetaFrame, Resource Management Services (RMS), Installation Management Services (IMS), Load Balancing, and client license packs—must be activated after you have entered the serial number. You manage Citrix licensing using the Citrix Licensing utility and the Activation Wizard. Simply entering the serial number or original license number in the Citrix Licensing utility does not activate the license(s). You are given a grace period, usually 30 days, before you must activate a license. If a Citrix license is not activated before the grace period runs out, the installed software or client license will stop working.

During the installation of MetaFrame, you are prompted to enter the serial number located on the CD-ROM jewel case (see Step 4 in the "Citrix MetaFrame Installation" in the next section). The serial number is a 21-character string that starts with 3 letters. After you type in the serial number, an eight-character machine code is added. This combination number will be unique to the server and is required for you to activate the license. To activate a Citrix license, you must obtain an activation code from Citrix. The process of entering this activation code in the Citrix Licensing utility is what activates the license. You can use the Activation Wizard or call Citrix to obtain the code. The Activation Wizard gives you the option of activating one or more licenses over the Internet, via the telephone, by fax, or by using a dial-up connection.

 MetaFrame's serial number is a 21-character string that starts with 3 letters. After you type in the serial number, an eight-character machine code is added. This combination number is then used to obtain an activation number from Citrix.

Citrix MetaFrame Installation

Once you have a completed the Terminal Server installation, you can proceed to the installation of MetaFrame 1.8. for Windows NT 4 TSE. Citrix MetaFrame can be installed only on a TSE operating system; you cannot install it directly over Windows NT 3.51; Windows NT 4; or WinFrame versions 1.6, 1.7, or 1.8. However, you can install MetaFrame directly over MetaFrame 1 as an upgrade (this is not recommended, but it's supported). Be sure that no applications or programs are installed on the Terminal Server before you install MetaFrame.

 A complete installation of MetaFrame, including the support, help files, and the online documentation, requires 30MB of disk space.

Here are the steps involved in installing MetaFrame using the CD-ROM:

1. Before you begin the installation, make sure all users remain logged off during the install. From the DOS prompt, use the command: **change logon /disable**.

2. Insert the MetaFrame CD-ROM. The Welcome window automatically appears. If the window does not appear, use the command **D:\i386\setup.exe** from the Run option on the Start menu, or browse to the D:\i386 folder from the Add/Remove Program utility (located in the Control Panel) and execute the setup.exe program.

3. From the Setting Up MetaFrame window, click on Next to continue.

4. From the MetaFrame 1.8 Licensing window, add your Citrix license number by clicking on the Add License Packs button. Please note that it is not necessary to install the licenses during the installation; you can do this after the MetaFrame installation. If you choose to install the licenses, locate the serial number on the CD-ROM jewel case (the serial number is a 21-character string that starts with 3 letters). After you type in the serial number, an eight-character machine code is added. This combination number is unique to the server and is required for you to activate the license.

5. From the Network ICA Connection window, select the network protocols. TCP/IP is the default protocol; it should already be selected and grayed out. Deselect any protocols that you will not use (e.g., IPX or NetBIOS).

6. From the TAPI Modem Setup window, you can add modems and their associated drivers.

7. The Asynchronous ICA Connection dialog box appears. Select any desired devices.

8. The Drive Mapping window displays the current server and client drive mappings and shows the available reassignment options. You do the actual drive reassignment in the subsequent Server Drive Reassignment dialog box. To use the existing drive mapping scheme, click on the Next button.

Note: If you do not remap the server drives, the user's local drives will be changed to V:, U:, and so on (working backwards through the alphabet). The server drives will then appear to the client as C:, D:, and so on. This can be confusing to users, so drive remapping is recommended.

9. From the System Reboot window, click on Finish and then remove the MetaFrame CD-ROM. The install program automatically creates 15 anonymous user accounts (discussed in the next section), remaps the server drives (providing you chose to re-map them), and then reboots the computer.

Congratulations! You have now successfully installed Citrix MetaFrame.

Anonymous User Accounts

It is important to understand why anonymous user accounts were created and how MetaFrame employs them. Anonymous user accounts are local user accounts that belong to the MetaFrame server's Guest and Anonymous user groups. They are similar to the anonymous users that access file transfer protocol (FTP) sites. Anonymous users are allowed access without an explicit logon (an explicit logon requires both a username and password).

Anonymous accounts are useful when large numbers of guest users need to access published applications over the Internet. In most situations, requiring an explicit logon for hundreds or even thousands of users would be impractical. Therefore, Citrix introduced anonymous user accounts as a way to manage these anonymous user logons.

If a MetaFrame server is set up as a PDC or BDC, you cannot create anonymous user accounts on that server. This is due to the Windows NT authentication process (covered in the Chapter 5), whereby all clients must be authenticated by a PDC or BDC to log on to a domain (Microsoft characterizes an authenticated logon as *explicit* access).

When MetaFrame is installed as a member server, anonymous users log on using a local guest account rather than an NT domain account. Although these local guest accounts are inherently less secure than authenticated domain accounts, they are very useful for facilitating Internet access. Anonymous accounts are local, non-authenticated accounts, not global domain accounts.

Uninstalling MetaFrame

If you need to uninstall MetaFrame from a server, use the Add/Remove Programs tool, located in the Control Panel. Before you uninstall MetaFrame, make sure all users are logged off during the uninstall. From the DOS prompt, use the **change logon /disable** command (note the space after **change** and after **logon**). You can uninstall MetaFrame at any time; doing so removes the ICA functionality from the TSE server as well as uninstalls all of the Citrix licenses and published applications.

Optimizing Terminal Server

This section covers some optimization and monitoring strategies to help improve the performance and reliability of your MetaFrame server. Although not mandatory, these strategies will help prevent some of those mysterious problems and slowdowns that can occur in large, complex networks. The following steps will assist you in improving the performance and reliability of your TSE MetaFrame server:

➤ Reboot the server monthly.

➤ Make sure the server is set up as a member or standalone server. Do *not* use it as a PDC/BDC, Web server, or database server.

➤ Use roaming profiles and place the profiles on a separate server. When using User Manager for Domains to create a new user, use the Profile button to set up the UNC path to the roaming profiles directory.

  In the User Profile path, enter the UNC to the shared folder on the file server. If there is no existing folder for the user, you can employ the %username% variable and the folder will be created. The Shared Users folder must be available on the server before you can utilize the %username% variable.

➤ To avoid eating up all of the server's hard drive space, set the log files to periodically overwrite the log contents. The overwrite options are to Overwrite Events As Needed (i.e., overwrite whenever the log files exceed a specified maximum size) or Overwrite Events Older Than Days.

➤ Keep up on Microsoft's Terminal Server Service Packs and Hot Fixes. The first line of defense against mysterious application glitches (after trying the obvious Internet/Usenet Tech searches) are the Service Packs and Hot Fixes. On a similar theme, make sure you are using the latest version of Terminal Server (version 419.3h6 at the time of this writing).

➤ After setting up a new user, log into and out of the new account at least once. This allows TSE to release the memory assigned when a user first logs into a new account.

➤ Delete any extraneous bitmap files. Look in the %systemroot% directory for likely prospects (e.g., Startup or Background bitmaps).

Once administrators have completed the optimization strategies, they can use one of several Windows NT management utilities (e.g., Performance Monitor) to monitor system resources. Monitoring allows administrators to look at resource usage for selected components and processes. Performance Monitor enables you to view resource usage via charts and reports to determine your TSE MetaFrame server's efficiency. With the collected data, it is possible to identify and troubleshoot possible system bottlenecks, and to plan for future hardware needs.

Practice Questions

Question 1

> MetaFrame can be installed on an NT 3.51 or NT 4 server.
>
> ○ a. True
> ○ b. False

Answer b is correct. MetaFrame can be installed only on an NT 4 TSE or Windows 2000 Server computer.

Question 2

> Which client protocol is supported on a TSE application server?
>
> ○ a. TCP
> ○ b. ICA
> ○ c. IPX
> ○ d. RDP
> ○ e. All of the above

Answer d is correct. TSE uses the multichannel RDP client protocol. TCP and IPX are network protocols. Therefore, answers a and c are incorrect. ICA is the Citrix thin-client protocol. Therefore, answer b is incorrect. Answer e is incorrect because only one answer is correct.

Question 3

> What is TSE's base memory requirement?
>
> ○ a. 32MB
> ○ b. 16MB
> ○ c. 64MB
> ○ d. 128MB

Answer a is correct. Microsoft recommends 32MB of RAM for the server and 4 to 8MB for each typical connected user (8 to 12MB for each power user). Answers b through d are incorrect as they do not match the Microsoft recommendations.

Question 4

Which of the listed hardware components can be added to maximize client access to the TSE server?

- ○ a. 32MB video card
- ○ b. Universal Serial Bus (USB) port
- ○ c. Faster CD-ROM
- ○ d. Additional memory

Answer d is correct. Installing additional memory maximizes accessibility. When a server runs out of memory, things run very slowly and users may be dropped. Video cards, USB ports, and cooling fans will have little impact on server availability. Therefore, answers a, b, and c are incorrect.

Question 5

According to Microsoft, what is the absolute minimum free hard disk space required to install TSE?

- ○ a. 528MB
- ○ b. 300MB
- ○ c. 128MB
- ○ d. 98MB

Answer c is correct. Microsoft recommends one or more hard disks, with 128MB minimum of free hard disk space on the partition that will contain the Terminal Server system files. This is the absolute minimum space needed according to Microsoft. Answer b is wrong as 300MB is the recommended minimum drive space (rather than the absolute minimum). Answers a and d are incorrect as they do not reflect TSE's drive space requirements.

Question 6

How many processors does TSE support out of the box?

○ a. 2

○ b. 4

○ c. 8

○ d. 32

Answer b is correct. Terminal Server supports up to four CPUs out of the box. Answer d is incorrect as third-party add-ons are required to support 32 processors. Answers a and c are incorrect as they do not describe the number of CPUs supported by TSE.

Question 7

MetaFrame requires server drives to be remapped to provide client access.

○ a. True

○ b. False

Answer b is correct. Server drive remapping is optional and is used to allow clients to keep C:, D:, and so on as their local hard drive letters.

Question 8

Which of the following three answers reflect how MetaFrame enhances TSE? [Check all correct answers]

❏ a. MetaFrame has management tools that allow the installation and administration of very large networks from a single server desktop.

❏ b. MetaFrame supports Unix clients.

❏ c. MetaFrame supports the IPX/SPX protocol.

❏ d. MetaFrame allows for remote administration by enabling remote access to the service display console.

Answer a is correct as centralized administration is one of the strengths of MetaFrame. Answer b is correct as Unix clients are supported. Answer c is correct since MetaFrame does support the IPX/SPX network protocol. An administrator can remotely manage a MetaFrame server by accessing the server desktop, not the service display console. Therefore, answer d is incorrect.

Question 9

RDP supports Mac, DOS, and 16- and 32-bit Windows clients.

○ a. True

○ b. False

Answer b is correct. RDP supports only 16-bit and 32-bit Windows clients.

Question 10

Terminal Server should be configured as:

○ a. A PDC

○ b. A BDC

○ c. A standalone server

○ d. An IIS server

Answer c is correct. Due to server load and security issues, TSE should be set up as a standalone server rather than as a Domain Controller. Therefore, answers a and b are incorrect. IIS is Microsoft's Web server. Therefore, answer d is incorrect.

Need to Know More?

 Keele, Allen (series editor). *CCA Certified Administrator for MetaFrame 1.8*. Osborne/McGraw Hill, Berkeley, CA., 2000. ISBN 0-07-212439-3. Chapter 4 covers MetaFrame installation options in great detail.

 www.microsoft.com/ntserver/terminalserver/deployment/default.asp has extensive information on Windows NT TSE deployment, licensing, capacity planning, and more.

 www.citrix.com/support/ is a good source for information on all aspects of deploying and configuring MetaFrame and WinFrame servers. Several useful options are located in Citrix support. Try the Product Documentation button.

Windows NT Domains, User Logons, and Policies

Terms you'll need to understand:

✓ Windows NT domain
✓ Server Directory Services
✓ Security Account Manager (SAM), or security accounts database
✓ Primary Domain Controller (PDC)
✓ Backup Domain Controller (BDC)
✓ Trust relationship
✓ Trusted domain
✓ Account domain
✓ Trusting domain
✓ Resource domain
✓ Domain account
✓ Policy
✓ Profile

Techniques you'll need to master:

✓ Identifying trust relationships and the domain models
✓ Understanding the user logon process
✓ Understanding how profiles and policies are applied

Domain Models Introduction

This chapter reviews the Windows NT domain models, logon process, user profiles, and policies. It is important to understand these central NT issues so that you can administer users and servers in a domain. Although the Citrix Certified Citrix Administrator (CCA) exam is focused on MetaFrame 1.8 for Terminal Server Edition (TSE), fundamentally, the test is based on an NT domain model with authenticated domain users.

The domain is the core on which Microsoft designed the Windows NT Server Directory Services. A directory service offers a way of managing the storage and distribution of shared information. This information could be names, addresses, and phone numbers of a company's employees or the system configuration information for a suite of applications. Essentially, the Windows NT domain model is a logical grouping of individual user accounts, user groups, network servers, client workstations, and network printers.

A domain structure allows an administrator to centrally manage the access to network resources located across several network servers, based on the users' domain membership. When users want to access a domain resource, like a shared file, published application, or network printer, they must be validated as authorized domain users for the desired network resource. A Windows NT domain can contain groups of servers with various operating systems—including Windows NT, Unix, Mac, and Novell NetWare—that offer different services to the domain users. Some of the main services offered to domain users are: user authentication, application hosting, data storage, network printing, and email services.

A Windows NT domain offers the following functionality:

➤ *Centralized administration*—A domain structure allows an administrator to centrally manage domain users and network resources located across several network servers, from one centralized location.

➤ *Security Account Manager (SAM), or security accounts database*—The data that is stored within the SAM database, located on the Primary Domain Controller (PDC), is periodically replicated to all Backup Domain Controllers (BDCs) within the Windows NT domain. This secures the SAM database if a server fails because the BDCs store a backup version of information about the domain user accounts, resources, and security. The SAM is covered in more detail later in this chapter.

➤ *Single logon to access network applications and file and print services*—This allows users to log on to a domain once, eliminating the need to log on to individual servers to gain access to domain resources. Once authenticated from a PDC or BDC, users do not have to type in additional logon IDs or passwords to access domain resources on a different server.

The SAM and Domain Controllers

The SAM contains the security and account information for all objects in the domain as well as provides user validation. The SAM database provides a security identifier for domain users and groups. This information is maintained in Windows Registry key files, referred to as *hives*. The master hive files are located on a designated Windows NT server called a PDC. Copies of the SAM are stored on BDCs. Along with storing the master SAM, a PDC is responsible for domain-wide user authentication. The BDC contains a read-only copy of the master SAM database, and it is regularly replicated to other BDCs. Table 5.1 shows the functions of PDCs and BDCs and Table 5.2 shows the disk space used for objects contained in the SAM database.

Table 5.1	Domain Controllers and their primary functions.
Type	**Function**
PDC	An NT domain can contain only one PDC. The PDC stores the master copy of the Registry hive file. The PDC authenticates domain users by verifying the username and password.
BDC	The BDC stores a copy of the master hive files and may authenticate users when they log on to the domain. Microsoft recommends at least one BDC, even for a small network.

Table 5.2	How much disk space is used in the SAM database for various objects.
Object in the SAM Database	**Size of the Object**
User account	1K
Computer account	512K
Global group account	512K for the group plus 12K for each user in the group
Local group account	512K for the group plus 36K for each user in the group

Windows NT Trust Relationships

Windows NT domains may participate in trust relationships with other NT domains. *Trusts* are directional one-way relationships that allow domain resources in one domain to be accessed by the users of other domains. Using a trust relationship with another NT domain extends the physical and corporate boundaries of both networks. A domain is generally established to allow access to network resources and to share a common SAM database with its common user and file security policies. This allows an administrator to establish a domain-wide security policy that extends physical and corporate boundaries. The domain where the user is located is called the *trusted* or *account domain*. The trusted domain is where the user's account resides. The domain that contains the network resource is referred to as the *trusting domain*. A trusting domain can contain groups of servers that offer various network resources to the domain users. Figure 5.1 shows the direction of a trust relationship, pointing to the user. The arrow depicts the direction of the trust. The resource *trusts* the user, and the user is considered as trusted. The arrow always points to the user, or account domain.

 The CCA exam focuses on the network resources offered from the Citrix MetaFrame server. The MetaFrame server is an application server that offers hosted applications to domain users. The applications that the MetaFrame server offers are considered network resources, and in most cases the MetaFrame server is located in the trusting domain. You should understand the domain models and trust relationships when taking the CCA exam.

The Four Windows NT Domain Models

This section provides a brief overview of the four Windows NT domain models. We will begin with the Single Domain Model and then move on to the Master Domain Model, Multiple Master Model, and Complete Trust Model. The Citrix CCA exam is focused on MetaFrame 1.8 for TSE, so the Citrix MetaFrame servers referred to in the exam will be in a Windows NT domain, and the domain may have a trust relationship with other domains.

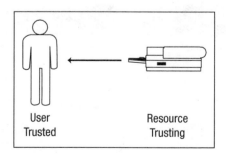

Figure 5.1 A one-way trust relationship.

The Single Domain Model

The Single Domain Model is the most basic of the domain models and is the dominant model for use in small networks. The advantages of the model are that it has only one PDC in the entire network, and there are no trust relationships to manage. A single domain is completely isolated from other domains. It may contain several servers that offer domain resources available to domain members. This approach provides the most centralized administration of the four domain models. Figure 5.2 shows the Single Domain Model.

The Master Domain Model

This domain model offers mid-sized corporations a way to centralize their security administration. All of the user accounts are centralized and managed in the master domain. The master domain, also referred to as the *account domain*, can support a maximum of 40,000 users in the SAM database. In this model, the resource domain's administrators decentralize and manage the network resources in the resource domain. This allows each department within a corporation to manage its own resources. The resource domain trusts the master domain and is, in turn, the trusting domain. The master domain maintains domain-wide security for all of the domains within this structure and is referred to as the *trusted domain*. There is one trust relationship for each resource domain that trusts the master domain. Figure 5.3 shows the Master Domain Model and the trust relationships between the account and resource domains.

The Multiple Master Domain Model

The Multiple Master Domain Model is appropriate for large organizations that need centralized security administration. This approach was designed for organizations with over 40,000 users (a single SAM database cannot support more than 40,000 users). With multiple master domains, the network administration overhead increases. This is due to the addition of trust relationships and the necessity to maintain, synchronize, and control multiple domain user accounts located in

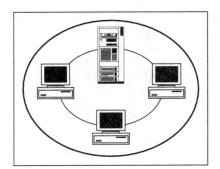

Figure 5.2   Diagram of the Single Domain Model.

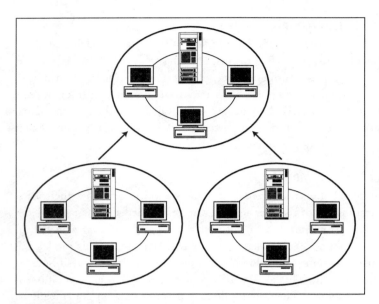

Figure 5.3 Diagram of the Master Domain Model.

each master domain. The master domains trust each other, and the resource domains have a trust relationship with the master domains. The master domains control domain-wide security and are the trusted domains. The resource domains are the trusting domains. Figure 5.4 shows the trust relationships among the account and resource domains.

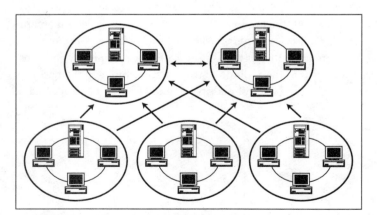

Figure 5.4 Diagram of the Multiple Master Domain Model.

The Complete Trust Model

The Complete Trust Model is a way of sharing resources among separate domains, where each domain has its own user accounts and resources. This model essentially provides peer-to-peer domains. The Complete Trust Model is appropriate for large companies that allow each corporate department/domain to administer its own resources and users. This approach decentralizes domain and resource administration. The trust relationships in this model can become very complicated and difficult to manage when there are multiple trusts among several domains. The complexity and administrative overhead are the greatest drawbacks of the Complete Domain Model. Figure 5.5 shows the trust relationships among the domains.

Example of a Simple Trust Relationship

A user named Bill is a member of domain A and needs to access a network share in domain B. The shared directory is called Bill's Stuff and is located on File Server in domain B. The first step is to establish a trust relationship between domains A and B whereby domain B trusts domain A. In this example, domain B is the trusting domain, and domain A is the trusted domain. Figure 5.6 shows the direction of the trust between the two domains.

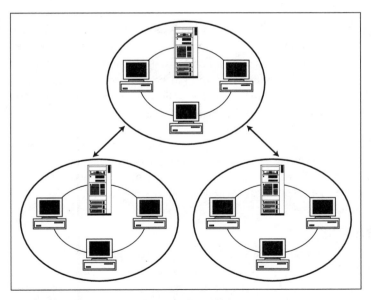

Figure 5.5   Diagram of the Complete Trust Model.

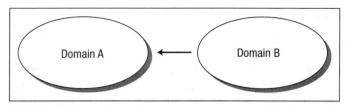

Figure 5.6   The direction of the trust between domains A and B.

User Authentication and the Logon Process

It is important for you to know the basics of the Windows NT user authentication and logon process and how profiles and system policies affect user authentication, because all users who access resources on a MetaFrame server are authenticated by the NT logon process. To cover thoroughly, this topic would require several chapters, however, we will briefly cover the major parts of the authentication process that affect MetaFrame users because the CCA exam is focused on Citrix MetaFrame. If you feel that you need additional information on this subject, refer to the "Need to Know More?" section at the end of this chapter.

User authentication is how NT determines a user's identity. It is the core of Windows NT security. Before domain users are granted access to any network resource, they must first log on to the server. The NT domain logon process requires that users type in both an account name and password in the Network Logon dialog box. After users have been validated as valid domain members, they receive access to the appropriate shared network resources.

 Anonymous user accounts are local accounts created during a Citrix MetaFrame installation. These accounts can only be created on a member server, not on a domain controller. Know the difference between an anonymous user and a domain user.

Logon Process

When users log on to an NT network, there is a pre-defined order in which the policies and profiles are applied before the users get control of their desktops. First, the user profile is loaded and then the user policy is applied. Next, the computer policy is applied. If the administrator did not set a policy for the users, they receive the default user policy. Similarly, if there is not a policy for the users' machines, the default computer policy is applied.

After a Domain Controller authenticates a user, Windows NT first loads the user profile and then loads the system policy. The complete logon process occurs in this order: User Profile, User Policy, Group Policy, Computer/System Policy.

When an administrator makes a change to a user profile or system policy, the changes do not go into effect until after the user logs off and then back on to the network. System policies are not dynamically updated; the changes occur as the user logs off and then back on to the network.

User Profiles and System Policies

Administrators can not only allow users to access shared network resources, but they can also apply a system, group, or user policy, which establishes a user's access rights. A system, group, or user policy controls the method in which a user interacts with the network system; it is a way for an administrator to fine-tune network security. A policy affects the user after successful authentication by restricting access to certain network resources.

 In the NT environment, policies take precedence over profiles. Individual policies take precedence over group policies. Machine policies take precedence over all policies i.e. the order of precedence is:

✓ Policies over profiles

✓ Individual policies over group policies

✓ Machine policies over all policies

In a Windows NT network, an administrator can modify policies by using the System Policy Editor, a standard Windows NT Server tool.

User Profiles

A user profile contains the user settings that load when a user logs on. Depending on the type of user, profiles may contain various desktop and Start menu preferences. The actual user profile file can be stored locally on the user's machine or on a network server that has been mapped on the PDC with the User Manager for Domains administration tool.

The user profile is a combination of both files and Registry entries. The profile settings reside in specific locations in the file system and Registry. When users are logged on interactively, the system Registry entries are located in the HKEY_CURRENT_USER (HKCU) Registry hive. This Registry hive is dedicated to storing user-specific configuration information. When users log off their workstations, the Registry information is updated and written to a file called ntuser.dat.

The information files contained in a user profile are comprised of the shortcuts and folders in the user's desktop and Start menu and are stored in the %systemroot%\Profiles folder. These files represent the user interface (UI) and are essentially what a user sees on the desktop. On the other hand, the Registry settings determine how the user interacts with the underlying computing environment.

Note: When a user is accessing applications that are hosted on a Citrix MetaFrame server, the user is logged on locally to the server. The server loads the user's specific configuration information in the system Registry. These entries are located in the HKCU Registry hive on the MetaFrame server.

User Profiles Compared to System Policies

A user profile controls the UI; i.e., the interface between the user and the desktop. The profile can contain desktop, Start menu, and display preferences. The actual user profile file is located either locally on the user's machine or on a network server that has been mapped on the PDC with the User Manager for Domains administration tool. A system or group policy allows a systems administrator to fine-tune user access to network resources. The access restrictions go into effect only after a Domain Controller has successfully authenticated users.

Practice Questions

Question 1

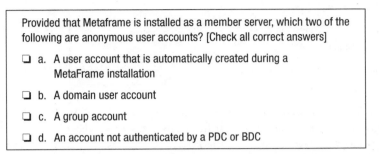

Provided that Metaframe is installed as a member server, which two of the following are anonymous user accounts? [Check all correct answers]

❏ a. A user account that is automatically created during a MetaFrame installation

❏ b. A domain user account

❏ c. A group account

❏ d. An account not authenticated by a PDC or BDC

Answer a is correct because 15 (or more) anonymous user accounts are automatically created during the MetaFrame installation. Answer d is also correct because MetaFrame servers are configured as member servers rather than as PDCs or BDCs. Note: Also remember that PDCs and BDCs require a username and password for logon. By definition, anonymous users do not have usernames or passwords. Answer b is incorrect since the Anonymous user accounts created during a MetaFrame installation are local user accounts, not domain accounts. Also, an anonymous account is a local, rather than a group, account. Therefore, answer c is incorrect.

Question 2

What is the difference between a user profile and a system policy?

○ a. A system policy controls the UI, whereas a user profile controls security.

○ b. A systen policy can be stored on a separate network server, but a profile cannot.

○ c. A profile controls the UI; a system policy controls security.

○ d. A profile controls security.

Answer c is correct. A user profile controls the UI, which is the interface between the user and the desktop whereas a system or group policy is a method for a systems administrator to fine-tune a user's security restrictions. Answer a is incorrrect as it is the opposite of the correct answer. A roaming profile, not a system policy, can be stored on a network file server, so answer b is incorrect. Answer d is incorrect as security is controlled via a system policy, not with a user profile.

Question 3

> Where is the user profile Registry information updated when a user logs off the network?
>
> ○ a. %systemroot%\Profiles
>
> ○ b. %systemroot%\system32
>
> ○ c. ntconfig.pol
>
> ○ d. ntuser.dat

Answer d is correct. When a user logs off a workstation, the Registry information is updated and written to the ntuser.dat file Each user's ntuser.dat file contains registry settings which are mapped to the HKEY_CURRENT_USER portion of the registry. While a user is logged on, the ntuser.dat registry hive maintains the user's environment preferences. It stores unique user settings that maintain network connections, Control Panel settings and application specific configurations. Answer a is incorrect, the %systemroot%\Profiles directory is the location where user profiles are stored. Answer b is incorrect, the %systemroot%\system32 directory is where many system dlls and executable files are stored. Answer c is incorrect, the ntconfig.pol policy file is stored on the PDC in the Netlogon share and is used to distribute domain policy.

Question 4

> You edit system policies using the User Manager for Domains administration tool.
>
> ○ a. True
>
> ○ b. False

Answer b is correct. You edit system policies using the System Policy Editor. You use the User Manager for Domains administration tool to create and manage user accounts.

Question 5

XYZ Inc. has two departments located in the same building, each with separate domains. The two domains are named A and B. There is no trust relationship between the two domains. The CEO has decided that the users in network A should be allowed to access two Citrix MetaFrame application servers located on network B. Domain B has 150 users, 1 PDC, 1 BDC, 1 print server, 1 file server, and 2 MetaFrame application servers. Domain A has _00 users, 1 PDC, _BDCs, 1 Oracle database, 2 print servers, 1 Exchange server, and 1 Internet Information Server (IIS) Web server. The CEO has assigned the task to Bob, the systems administrator for domain A. Bob must establish the trust relationship between the two domains. He made domain B the trusting domain and domain A the trusted domain. Has Bob set up the trust correctly? Figure 5.7 shows the direction of the trust relationship.

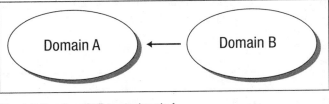

Figure 5.7   Domain B trusts domain A.

○ a. True

○ b. False

Answer a is correct. The domain where the users are located (in this case, domain A) is called the trusted or account domain. The domain with the network resource (in this case, domain B) is referred to as the trusting domain. A trusting domain can contain groups of servers that offer various network resources to the domain users. The arrow depicts the direction of the trust relationship. The resource *trusts* the user. The user is designated as trusted, whereas the resource is called trusting.

Question 6

> The XYZ domain has 50 users. The administrator has established a group policy for each group in his domain. At what point are policies activated?
>
> ○ a. When a user requests a network resource
>
> ○ b. When a user prints a document
>
> ○ c. Once a user is authenticated
>
> ○ d. After a user enters the correct username and password in the NT Logon dialog box

Answer c is correct. When a user is authenticated on an NT network, policies and profiles are applied before the user gets control of the desktop. Answers a and b are incorrect as they have nothing to do with the activation of the policies. Answer d is wrong as policies are not activated until after the server verifies the username and password (i.e. until after the server authenticates the user).

Question 7

> Company Z has two domains on the same network located in the same building. The two domains are domains A and B. There is a trust relationship between the two domains. Domain B is the trusting domain, and domain A is the trusted domain (domain B trusts domain A). Domain A has 100 users, 1 PDC, 2 BDCs, 1 file server, 1 print server, and 1 Exchange email server. Domain B has 70 users, 1 PDC, and 1 MetaFrame application server that is hosting office productivity tools. There are resources in domain A that users in domain B need to access. What trust relationship must be added or modified for domain B users to access domain A resources? Figure 5.8 shows the direction of the existing trust relationship.

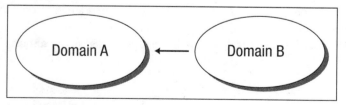

Figure 5.8   Domain B trusts domain A.

> ○ a. Move all the users to domain A.
>
> ○ b. Move all the users to domain B.
>
> ○ c. Have domain B trust domain A.
>
> ○ d. Have domain A trust domain B.

Answer d is correct. If you establish a trust where domain A trusts domain B, the users in domain B will gain access to the resources in domain A. The question asks, "What trust relationship must be added or modified for domain B users to access domain A resources?" so moving the users to a different domain as suggested in answers a and b is not an option. Answer c reflects the existing situation (where domain B trusts domain A), which is the reverse of what is required. Therefore, answer c is incorrect.

Question 8

Of the four domain models, which model does not use trust relationships?

O a. Single Domain Model

O b. Master Domain Model

O c. Multiple Master Domain Model

O d. Complete Trust Model

Answer a is correct. The Single Domain Model has one PDC and no trust relationships to manage. The other three models all use trust relationships. Therefore, answers b, c, and d are incorrect.

Question 9

XYZ Inc. has two corporate locations, one in Los Angeles and the other in San Jose, each with completely separate domains. The two domains are named LA and SJ. The two locations have never had network connectivity and share information by sending it as email attachments and via mail. The owners of XYZ Inc. have decided they need to share information and network resources, so they have established a wide area network (WAN) link between the LA and SJ locations. The owners want to allow the LA users access to resources in the SJ domain but do not want to allow SJ domain users access to LA. The LA domain has _00 users, 1 PDC, 2 BDCs, 1 print server, and 1 SQL database. The SJ domain has 400 users, 1 PDC, _BDCs, 1 SQL database, 2 print servers, 1 Exchange server, and 1 IIS Web server. The CEO has assigned the task to Jennifer, the systems administrator for the LA domain. Jennifer must establish the trust relationship between the two domains. She has established a trust whereby the SJ domain trusts the LA domain. Has Jennifer set up the trust correctly? Figure 5.9 shows the direction of the trust relationship.

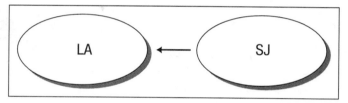

Figure 5.9   The SJ domain trusts the LA domain.

○ a. True

○ b. False

Answer a is correct. The domain where the users are located (in this case, the LA domain) is called the trusted or account domain. The domain with the network resource (in this case, the SJ domain) is referred to as the trusting domain. A trusting domain can contain groups of servers that offer various network resources to the domain users. The arrow depicts the direction of the trust relationship. The domain where the resource is trusts the domain with the users. The account domain is designated as trusted, whereas the resource domain is called trusting.

Question 10

> The SAM database stores user files.
>
> ○ a. True
> ○ b. False

Answer b is correct. The SAM database stores the security identifiers for domain users and groups. This information is maintained in Windows Registry key files, referred to as hives. The master hive files are located on a designated Windows NT server called a PDC. Copies of the SAM are stored on BDCs. Along with storing the master SAM, a PDC is responsible for domain-wide user authentication.

Need To Know More?

 Donald, Lisa and James Chellis. *MSCE: NT Server 4 in the Enterprise Study Guide, 3rd Edition.* Sybex Inc., Alameda, CA, 1999. ISBN 0-7821-2697-9. Chapters 1, 3, and 5 offer information on the NT domain model, the management of users and groups, and on user profiles and system policies.

 Ivens, Kathy. *Managing Windows NT Logons.* O'Reilly & Associates, Sebastopol, CA, 2000. ISBN 1-56592-637-4. This is a comprehensive guide to managing Windows NT logons. Chapters 1, 4, and 6 are especially pertinent to issues involving user profiles and controlling user access to network resources.

 Jennings, Roger. *Using Windows NT Server 4, 2nd Edition.* Que Corp., Indianapolis, IN, 1997. ISBN 0-7897-1388-8. Take a look at Chapter 17, "Understanding Windows NT's Domain Models"—the chapter title says it all.

 Minasi, Mark. *Mastering NT Server 4, 7th Edition.* Sybex Inc., Alameda, CA, 2000. ISBN 0-7821-2693-6. Chapter 12 has very good coverage of NT domains and trust relationships.

 The Microsoft web site (**www.microsoft.com**) offers a tremendous amount of information on Windows NT domains, profiles and policies. From the home page, access the Support tab and choose the Knowledge Base option. Select Windows NT Server 4 from the dropdown box then enter a keyword(s) to research a topic. For example, a search on *user profile* yields several articles including, *Guide to Windows Profiles and Policies (document #Q185589)*.

Independent Computing Architecture (ICA) Features and Client Configurations

6

. . . .

Terms you'll need to understand:

✓ Citrix's Independent Computing Architecture (ICA)

✓ Microsoft's Remote Desktop Protocol (RDP)

✓ SpeedScreen 2

✓ Remote Access Service (RAS)

✓ Asynchronous ICA connection

✓ DirectICA

✓ Shadowing

✓ Program Neighborhood

✓ Published application

✓ Application sets

✓ Remote Application Manager (RAM)

✓ ICA PassThrough

✓ Client caching

✓ Seamless window

Techniques you'll need to master:

✓ Knowing the network protocols and clients that ICA supports

✓ Knowing the various connection types that ICA supports

✓ Understanding the components of the ICA packet

✓ Understanding how shadowing works and what it is used for

✓ Understanding the functions and features of Program Neighborhood

A Tale of Two Clients: Citrix ICA vs. Microsoft RDP

Instead of using Citrix's ICA, Microsoft created its own thin-client protocol, called RDP. RDP is a multichannel protocol. Like ICA, RDP carries mouse clicks and keystrokes from the client to the server and screen refreshes from the server to the client.

Compared to Citrix's ICA, RDP uses more bandwidth and does not support non-Windows clients. According to tests done by Tolly Research, RDP consumes four to six times more bandwidth than ICA. Although Microsoft contends that RDP functions well using a dial-up 56K connection (with 44K actual throughput), tests reveal slow application performance and choppy screen updates while typical office programs are run. MetaFrame employs a server-side agent called SpeedScreen 2, which can lower bandwidth consumption by 60 percent.

 SpeedScreen 2 works by transmitting only the areas of the client screen that have changed since the last screen refresh. This can provide performance up to four times faster over low-bandwidth (i.e., dial-up) connections.

Also, RDP currently supports only Transmission Control Protocol/Internet Protocol (TCP/IP). To use Internetwork Packet Exchange (IPX), NetBIOS (also referred to as NetBEUI), or any of the other standard protocols, you must use MetaFrame along with the ICA client. And, as mentioned in Chapter 2, ICA supports Macintosh, DOS, and Unix clients, whereas RDP supports only 16- and 32-bit Windows clients.

To provide users with access to applications, Terminal Server uses RDP to provide users with a virtual NT desktop (the desktop from the TSE server). The desktop is delivered as a window within the local desktop or full screen. In addition to delivering applications as desktops, WinFrame and MetaFrame allow applications to be served up in the form of desktop icons, as selections on the Start menu, or as icons in Citrix's Program Neighborhood (PN) window. (PN is covered in more detail later in this chapter.) These Citrix options allow the network administrator to provide users with a local desktop environment whereby local or server-based programs can be accessed within the local desktop, not via the server's virtual desktop. This avoids user confusion over which desktop (i.e., local or server) is being used, as well as some of the security issues inherent in providing users with access to the Terminal Server desktop. Of course, the administrator locks down the Terminal Server virtual desktop using profiles and policies, but a knowledgeable user might still gain access to the administrative tools, Control Panel, command prompt, or secured files and folders.

Citrix ICA Protocol and Client Overview

ICA is the core of MetaFrame's server-based, thin-client computing architecture. It is a combination of both server and client software components, as well as the ICA protocol. As we learned in Chapter 3, a typical client/server network distributes the processing between the client workstations and the servers. The servers and client workstations are sharing the processing burden and continually exchange data across the local area network (LAN) or wide area network (WAN). As a result, network traffic bottlenecks can become an issue. Another drawback to having the servers and workstations share the processing load is that older, slower workstations further slow network traffic. Thus, client/server networks require periodic workstation upgrades to maintain acceptable workstation and network performance.

With the Citrix MetaFrame server-based model, the ICA component separates the application's logic from the user interface (UI), allowing the ICA protocol to send only the UI to the ICA client. The workstations send only keystrokes and mouse clicks to the server, whereas the server sends only screen refreshes via SpeedScreen 2 back to the clients.

Server-based architecture not only reduces the network traffic but also enables old, slow workstations (e.g., 386 PCs with 2MB of RAM) to work like Pentium III PCs. The LAN or WAN bandwidth that the ICA client needs is only 10 to 20Kbps, which means no LAN bandwidth bottlenecks. This also allows remote access to the network via Remote Access Service (RAS) or an asynchronous ICA connection at LAN-equivalent speeds.

The ICA protocol supports the use of 32 "virtual channels." Table 6.1 lists the seven currently utilized channels. These channels can accommodate different types of LAN or WAN traffic such as audio, port, and printer data. It's important to be familiar with the functions of these channels because they are a core feature of ICA. We will go into greater detail about some of the individual channels later in the chapter.

Citrix has designed ICA to assemble the data from all the channels into a single ICA packet rather than sending separate packets for each virtual channel. This avoids excessive server-to-client traffic on the network.

Table 6.1 The seven currently employed virtual channels and their functions.	
ICA Virtual Channel	**Channel Function**
Thinwire	The most widely employed virtual channel. Is responsible for sending screen updates to the ICA clients and mouse clicks and keystrokes to the MetaFrame server.

(continued)

Table 6.1	The seven currently employed virtual channels and their functions *(continued)*.
Audio	Provides the audio feed from the server applications to the clients.
Serial port	Allows server applications or print spoolers to send data to the client serial ports.
LPT port	Has the same functionality as the serial port channel except that data is sent to the client's parallel port.
Drive mapping	Allows client hard drives to be remapped to avoid user confusion over whether the C: and D: drives belong to the server or to the local workstation (see Chapter 4 for a detailed overview of drive mapping).
Clipboard	Allows clients to cut and paste between the client and server applications. Note that RDP does not support clipboard mapping.
Printer Spooling	Sends printer data from server applications to the client.

ICA Clients and Network Protocols

Citrix offers ICA client software that supports virtually all the major computer platforms, like Windows, Unix, Macintosh, and Java. The Citrix ICA client also offers support for the major connection types (discussed later in this chapter) and network protocols. This is a major advantage for a Citrix-based network, allowing effortless network integration between dissimilar networks and client workstations. Table 6.2 shows a complete list of ICA clients and the protocols they support.

 For the exam, you should be familiar with the protocols that the various clients support.

As the table demonstrates, Windows and DOS ICA clients support all of the major network protocols, including TCP/IP, IPX/SPX, and NetBIOS. Windows CE, Unix, Macintosh, Java, and Web clients use only TCP/IP. You can transport the above network protocols using Point-to-Point Protocol (PPP), Asynchronous dial-up, Integrated Services Digital Network (ISDN), Frame Relay, and Asynchronous Transfer Mode (ATM).

ICA Connection Types

ICA supports three connection types: network, asynchronous ICA (Dial-Up Networking), and DirectICA connections. As will be discussed in Chapter 7, ICA network and asynchronous connections are virtual connections that trans-

Table 6.2	ICA clients and the protocols they support.
Client	**Supported Protocols**
16-bit Windows (Win 3.x)	NetBIOS, Internetwork Packet Exchange/Sequence Packet Exchange (IPX/SPX), TCP/IP
32-bit Windows (Windows 9x, NT, and 2000)	NetBIOS, IPX/SPX, TCP/IP
Windows CE client	TCP/IP
Web clients (Netscape Navigator plug-in or Microsoft Internet Explorer—IE—with an ActiveX control)	TCP/IP
DOS 16 and 32-bit	NetBIOS, IPX/SPX, TCP/IP
Unix	TCP/IP
Macintosh	TCP/IP
Java	TCP/IP

port data via network protocols like TCP/IP. DirectICA connections, however, are physical connections that require a cable connection between a server and a client.

 You must manually download the Navigator plug-in and install it. On the other hand, the IE client uses an ActiveX control. You can automatically download and install the IE client by connecting to a Web site that contains content from a Citrix server.

Network Connection Types

The network connection types that ICA supports are LAN and WAN, which include intranet and Internet connectivity. ICA network and asynchronous connections can use the TCP/IP, NetBIOS, IPX/SPX, PPP Dial-up, and PPTP protocols to establish network connectivity. The protocol that will be used depends on the underlying network; i.e., Windows NT and Novell support multiple network protocols unlike Unix networks that generally use TCP/IP only.

For example, consider a client that accesses network resources located on a corporate intranet. Let us assume that the network runs Windows NT and uses the NetBEUI protocol. This would require that all network clients be configured with the NetBEUI protocol to have network connectivity to access the corporate intranet. The same would be true for remote users who access the network over PPP; clients must be configured not only with PPP but also with the protocol that is used within the network. Also, all remote clients must have TCP/IP configured to dial in to the network (after authentication, clients may use NetBIOS/NetBEUI within the network).

Asynchronous ICA Connections and Remote Network Access

The Citrix MetaFrame server-based network model also offers clients remote access to a corporate network via a 56K dial-up connection or a Web page, with LAN-like performance. This is commonly referred to as Dial-Up Networking. Common methods of offering remote access are to deploy a RAS server, an NT component, or a Citrix solution called an asynchronous ICA connection. Remote access allows users to dial in to the corporate RAS server or asynchronous ICA connection and access network resources (e.g., published applications from a MetaFrame server). An asynchronous ICA connection allows direct dial-in access to a MetaFrame server without the additional overhead required for RAS-based connections.

 An asynchronous ICA connection is a standalone remote access solution and does not use RAS. You cannot configure a modem or serial port as both a RAS service port and an ICA connection port.

Here is the procedure to create an asynchronous ICA connection using the Citrix Connection Configuration (CCC) utility (for more information about this utility, see the "CCC Utility" section later in this chapter and refer to Chapter 7):

1. Open the CCC utility, which is accessible from the MetaFrame toolbar or from the Start menu.

2. At the Connection menu, click on New. The New Connection dialog box appears.

3. Enter a unique name for the new connection, and then click on Citrix ICA 3.0 from the Type list.

4. In the Transport list, click on async.

5. From the Device list, click on the modem or COM port for this connection. If no modem is configured, click on Install Modem. The Windows Install New Modem Wizard guides you through the installation process.

6. Click on OK.

You have just successfully configured an asynchronous ICA connection. Now, clients can dial in from home or from the road to gain access to shared network resources.

DirectICA

Citrix's ICA client has one major drawback: It does not support high speed, high resolution, or high color for clients using graphically rich applications. Currently, ICA supports only 256 colors and a maximum screen resolution of 1,280×800.

To address this need, Citrix MetaFrame ships with DirectICA, a combination software and hardware solution for users of programs like AutoCAD or PhotoShop. The software component is included with MetaFrame but you must purchase the hardware components separately.

The required hardware includes a multi-VGA adapter card for the MetaFrame server and thin-client terminals, called *DirectICA stations*. A DirectICA connection is actually a server console connection that runs locally on the server. Essentially, DirectICA provides connectivity between physically connected server and client devices. The physical connection is a cable that runs directly from the DirectICA station into the multi-VGA card that must be installed in the MetaFrame server. A major limitation is the cable distance, which varies from vendor to vendor.

 DirectICA runs locally on the server. You cannot use it across a LAN or WAN. DirectICA workstations do not support drive mapping, COM port mapping, or printer mapping.

The DirectICA software is available in the DrctICA directory on the MetaFrame CD-ROM or from the %SystemRoot%\System32\DrctICA directory on the server drive. To install DirectICA, just double-click on the setup.exe file and respond to the prompts.

ICA Packet Architecture

An ICA packet is made up of a mandatory 1-byte command and optional data. Figure 6.1 shows a diagram of the required and optional components of an ICA packet. The CCA exam will require you to have only a cursory knowledge of each individual component. Table 6.3 provides a brief description of the individual ICA components shown in Figure 6.1.

CCC Utility

The CCA exam places heavy emphasis on the various Citrix administration tools; we cover these in detail in Chapter 7. However, this is a good place to briefly examine the CCC utility. This chapter focuses on ICA client issues, but it is difficult to discuss client configuration without some explanation of the server-side client administration tools. You can use the CCC tool to add, change, or delete client-to-server connections. You might recall that during the MetaFrame installation, there was an option to enable the various transport protocols that MetaFrame supports. By default, one ICA and one RDP connection were automatically created for each installed protocol (also remember that ICA supports TCP/IP, IPX, SPX, NetBIOS, and asynchronous connections, whereas Microsoft's

Table 6.3 The ICA packet components.	
Component	**Description**
Frame head	Optional preamble that is used with the Reliable protocol to support error-free streaming communications such as asynchronous and TCP/IP.
Reliable	Optional preamble used with IPX and asynchronous sessions for error detection and correction.
Encryption	Optional encryption preamble for use with the basic encrypted ICA packet.
Compression	Optional preamble used to manage compressed data traffic.
Command	Required ICA command byte that must precede any command data. Command is the only required ICA packet component.
Command data	Optional data tied to the specified command. It can transport the virtual channel protocol packets.
Frame trailer	Optional trailer used with TCP/IP and asynchronous connections.

RDP client supports only TCP/IP). After the MetaFrame installation, you can use the CCC tool to create additional protocol-specific ICA connections. You can use CCC to configure ICA connection settings, connection security, audio bandwidth settings, and shadowing.

Connection Settings

The Client Settings dialog box in the CCC tool , shown in Figure 6.2, allows an administrator to manage a connection's drive and printer mapping options. You can connect client drives and printers at logon, have the client's print mapping

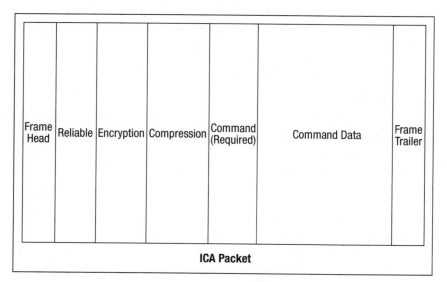

ICA Packet

Figure 6.1   The required and optional elements of an ICA packet.

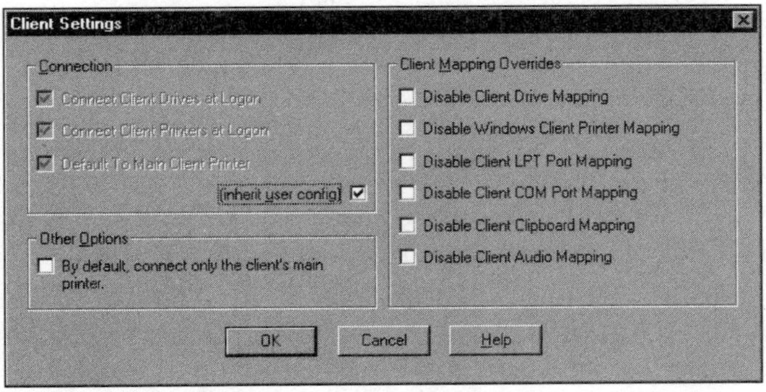

Figure 6.2   The Client Settings dialog box in the CCC utility.

default to the server's printer, or even require that the client use the server's default printer only. The settings shown in the right side of the dialog box allow an administrator to disable any of the client-side device mappings.

The Inherit User Config checkbox in the middle of the screen is an option in the Citrix administration tools that you commonly encounter. When this is checked, the user or group configurations set in Terminal Server's User Manager for Domains utility override the displayed connection settings. However, the Client Mapping Overrides options displayed on the right side of the screen allow you to disable any of the individual mappings shown.

Connection Security

When initially created, an ICA connection is available to anyone who can log on to the MetaFrame server. This includes the Everyone and Guests Groups. Administrators can access the Security/Permissions menu in CCC to configure the permissions available on each connection. Figure 6.3 shows the Connection Per-

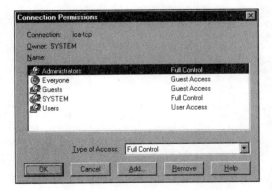

Figure 6.3   The Connection Permissions window.

missions window, which you can access from the CCC utility. The Type Of Access drop-down menu presents different security options ranging from No Access, Guest Access, and User Access to Full Control.

Audio Bandwidth

You can use the CCC utility to set the audio level of an ICA connection. Only DOS or Windows clients with sound cards can receive audio traffic. MetaFrame has three audio levels that you can specify, depending on the available LAN or WAN bandwidth. To set the audio level, highlight an ICA connection in the CCC utility. Next, right-click on the connection and choose Edit to display the Edit Connection screen. Click on the ICA Settings option to bring up the ICA Settings window, shown in Figure 6.4. For low-bandwidth dial-up connections, select the Low (16Kbps) setting; for normal LAN audio, use the default Medium (64Kbps) compression level; and for very high-quality sound reproduction where network bandwidth is plentiful, select the High (1.3Mbps) option.

Shadowing

Session shadowing is an important tool for MetaFrame administrators. Shadowing allows administrators to remotely take over single- or multiple-user sessions for support, troubleshooting, or training. Instead of having to visit client workstations, IT staffers can resolve many user problems from any network workstation. Additionally, the staffers can employ shadowing to train one or more users on new applications or features.

The default settings allow administrators to take over a user's keyboard and mouse while viewing the user session. Also, by default, the user is notified and given the option to refuse the session shadowing. You can initiate shadowing from either

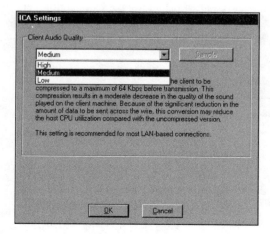

Figure 6.4   The ICA Settings window.

the Shadow button in the Citrix Server Administration tool or from the Shadow taskbar, located on the ICA Administrator toolbar. The Shadow button lets an administrator shadow one user at a time, whereas the Shadow taskbar enables you to shadow one or several clients simultaneously.

Only an administrator can initiate or end a shadowing session. Another limitation to keep in mind is that the window size and number of colors of the client session must be equal to or less than those of the session doing the shadowing. Also, audio is not available for use when you are shadowing.

Although you can initiate session shadowing only from the Shadow button in the Server Administration tool or from the Shadow taskbar located on the ICA Administrator toolbar, you can configure the shadowing settings from within CCC. Pressing the Advanced button in this utility displays the Advanced Connections Settings screen. The drop-down menu on this screen allows the administrator to enable/disable shadowing over the ICA connection. Other options include whether to notify the user that she is being shadowed and if the administrator's keystrokes and mouse clicks will be sent to the client workstation. Shadowing is covered in more detail in Chapter 7.

ICA Client Installation

You can install an ICA client in several ways. The steps involved in each of the various methods are similar, excluding the Java and Web clients (these methods are covered in detail in Chapter 9). You should be familiar with the methods because they may be covered on the CCA exam.

The available ICA clients that Citrix MetaFrame supports are located on the Citrix MetaFrame CD-ROM or in the %SystemRoot%\System32\Clients\ICA directory of any MetaFrame server. To install a client with the CD-ROM, follow these steps:

1. Put the CD-ROM in the client's CD-ROM drive.

2. Once you see the Citrix MetaFrame CD-ROM splash screen (shown in Figure 6.5), select Setup ICA Client and follow the commands to install the client (see the "Installing Win32 Clients" section later in this chapter for details on a Win32 client install).

Installing a client from the %SystemRoot%\System32\Clients\ICA directory is virtually identical to installing it from a CD-ROM installation. Follow these steps:

1. Once in the %SystemRoot%\System32\Clients\ICA directory, select the directory corresponding to the desired client.

2. Then, from within that directory, run setup.exe. You must reboot the client machine after the installation.

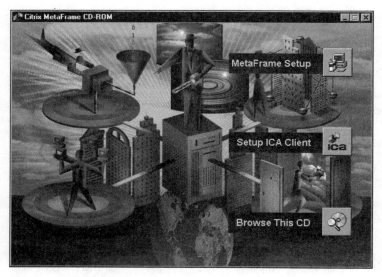

Figure 6.5   The Citrix MetaFrame CD-ROM splash screen.

 You may share the %SystemRoot%\System32\Clients\ICA directory and use it as a central installation point.

The ICA Client Creator, a Citrix utility located on the MetaFrame toolbar or acessible from the Start menu, allows an administrator to create ICA client installation floppy diskettes. Once the utility is started, simply select the desired client and the destination drive letter, and then click on OK. Figure 6.6 shows the ICA Client Creator interface.

 Do not confuse the ICA Client Creator with the ICA Client Update utility.

Figure 6.6   The ICA Client Creator.

Installing Win32 Clients

Citrix's Win32 client has become the most widely deployed ICA client in contemporary MetaFrame networks. During the client installation, you are prompted to provide a destination directory on the client workstation in which to store the client files. Accept the default location in the Program Files\Citrix\ICA Client directory. Next, select a destination directory for the client's program icons. Finally, choose a client name (make sure the name is unique on the network). The local machine name is chosen by default.

You should install the Win32 client on a Windows 95, 98, NT, or 2000 workstation, not on a Java, DOS, or Macintosh workstation. During the install procedure, you are asked to accept or modify the default locations for the client files and for the program icons. You are also prompted to either accept or change the current workstation name.

Use the following procedure to install the Win32 client:

1. Run setup.exe from the installation location (i.e., from the CD-ROM, network share, or installation diskettes). On the CD-ROM, setup.exe is located in the ICACLNT\ICA32\Disk 1 folder.

2. To accept the license terms, click on Yes.

3. Click on Next to accept the default destination, or use the Browse option to place the files in a different directory.

4. Click on Next to place the ICA client icons in the Start menu program folder, or choose a different location for the icons.

5. Click on Next to use the workstation's name (i.e., the NetBIOS name) as the client name. This name must be unique on the network.

6. Click on OK to copy the client files.

7. Click on OK to finish the setup.

8. Reboot the workstation.

Program Neighborhood (PN)

Along with the introduction of MetaFrame 1.8 came the new ICA client tool, Program Neighborhood (PN). PN, shown in Figure 6.7, is a client-side Citrix utility that allows users and administrators to access and configure published applications, application sets, and server desktops via a single logon. It is essential to know all the features of PN because it is a core component of Citrix and a tool that Citrix administrators use daily. Citrix uses the term *published applications* to refer to programs that have been configured on a MetaFrame server and are available to authorized network users and groups via PN, Remote Application Manager (RAM), NFuse, or a Web page. RAM is discussed later in this chapter.

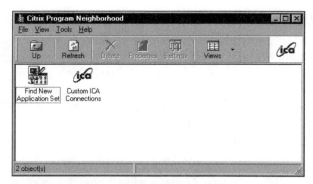

Figure 6.7   The Program Neighborhood utility.

PN can be broken down into three main components: application sets, custom ICA connections, and the Add ICA Connection icon.

Application Sets

Aside from presenting the icons that provide a direct link to the published applications, PN is a full-featured tool that allows users and administrators to configure several types of connections to application sets, individual servers, and applications. You access one of the features via the Find New Application Set icon. This wizard enables you to find other application sets on other server farms or on remote networks. The term *application set* defines a grouping of published applications located within a Citrix MetaFrame server farm that are available via PN. Each server farm has only one application set. If more than one server farm is available, there is an additional application set for each farm. You can make one of the application sets the default set by right-clicking on its icon and selecting the default option. Users then see this default set in their desktop PN window. Users may also have available multiple application sets that are published from different server farms.

Custom ICA Connections

The Custom ICA Connection feature available in PN is virtually identical to the one offered in the older RAM utility. You can configure a custom ICA connection to access a specific server or a published application within a server farm, but you cannot use it to access an application set. PN supports only Win32 ICA clients; all other clients must use the RAM tool, ICA PassThrough (discussed later in this chapter), NFuse, or a Web page to access and configure applications.

Know which ICA clients Program Neighborhood supports and how Citrix PassThrough technology enhances client support.

The Custom ICA Connections tool is represented as a folder that runs a wizard that allows the client to configure both published and server applications. If users have already set up any custom ICA connections, their icons will also appear in the Custom ICA Connection window. Before PN was introduced, the only way to access server applications was by setting up custom connections to the programs using the RAM tool. You can configure the following ICA connection settings for applications that appear in the Custom ICA Connections folder:

➤ *Compress the Data Stream*—This option is enabled by default. It improves performance for dial-up and other limited-bandwidth connections.

➤ *Bitmap Caching*—This is another option that improves performance over low-bandwidth connections. Bitmap caching allows you to cache often-used graphical objects on a local hard drive, decreasing the amount of bandwidth needed. Bitmap caching is enabled on any connection that was originally set up for low-bandwidth connections.

➤ *Queuing of mouse movements and keystrokes*—This is never enabled by default. It is another option provided for low-bandwidth connections. One drawback is that the user's keystrokes may be delayed slightly before displaying.

➤ *Encryption level*—This is automatically set at the highest encryption available on the workstation. If the optional SecureICA option is not used, the level is set to basic (low-level) encryption.

Add ICA Connection Icon
The final component of PN is the Add ICA Connection icon. The Add ICA Connection Wizard enables a user to set up a custom ICA connection to server applications that have not been published. The major parameters that you must set for a custom connection are Connection Type (LAN, WAN, or dial-up), Description (a unique name for the application), Network Protocol (TCP/IP, IPX, NetBIOS, and so on), and Application (the executable name of the application to be accessed). A user can also specify the window color and size, whether to enable sound, and if a password and username will be required.

RAM
As mentioned earlier in this chapter, PN supports only Win32 clients. For Win16, DOS, Unix, or Macintosh ICA clients, you use RAM to make connections to published applications and servers. RAM is an older Citrix tool that originates with WinFrame and requires users to manually find and configure the application connections. The important connection parameters in RAM are very similar to those discussed in the "Add ICA Connection Icon" section earlier in this chap-

ter. The connection parameters are Connection Type (network or dial-up), Description (a unique application title), Network Protocol, Application Executable Name, Window Size and Color, and whether to enable sound.

ICA PassThrough Technology

An alternative to using RAM to configure non-Win32 clients is to use ICA PassThrough technology. This approach enables Win16, DOS, Unix, and Macintosh clients to utilize all of the Program Neighborhood features and avoids having users configure their own connections/applications.

 ICA PassThrough enables non-Win32 clients to take advantage of Program Neighborhood features.

To set up PassThrough, an administrator installs the ICA client on a MetaFrame server. When non-Win32 clients access the server, they can pass through the server's client to enable an ICA-over-ICA connection. Although the PassThrough component uses more network resources than a standard connection, Citrix has modified the technology to improve performance. PassThrough supports drive/printer mapping and audio, but not COM or LPT port mappings.

Additional ICA Client Features

Several other ICA enhancements and options are important to MetaFrame administrators as well as to Citrix CCA test takers. These features are primarily concerned with improving performance and network security.

Client Caching

As mentioned earlier in this chapter, ICA clients can use bitmap caching to improve performance over low-bandwidth connections. MetaFrame client/server traffic consists of mouse clicks, keystrokes, and screen refreshes. Although it makes little sense to try to cache client mouse clicks and keystrokes, caching screen updates can significantly lower LAN, WAN, or Internet bandwidth requirements. Citrix SpeedScreen 2 updates the changed portions of the screen images, but the unchanged elements can be cached on the client's hard drive. Bitmap images are normally large files, and caching portions of the images greatly improves performance. This improvement is especially noticeable over dial-up connections, the Internet, or on overloaded networks.

You can configure caching from the Tools/ICA Settings menu in PN. From within the Settings window, you can configure the percentage of disk space to allocate to the cache, the local drive folder where the cached images will be stored, and the minimum bitmap size to be cached. Figure 6.8 shows the Bitmap Cache tab of the ICA Settings dialog box, which you access from the Tools/ICA Settings menu in PN.

Here is the procedure to change the client cache settings:

1. From the Tools/ICA Settings menu, click on the Bitmap Cache tab.

2. Adjust the slide bar to specify the percentage of disk space to dedicate to caching. The default is 1 percent.

3. Click on the Change Directory button to select the local drive directory where the cached images will be stored.

4. Adjust the slide bar to specify the minimum image size that will be cached. The default image size is 8k.

5. Right-click in the blank area of the PN window, click on Properties, and then click on the Default Options tab.

6. Confirm that the Use Disk Cache For Bitmaps box is checked.

SecureICA

The SecureICA client is an optional upgrade that secures the traffic between clients and servers using the industry standard RC5 encryption. The standard ICA client uses what Citrix calls *basic encryption*. Although this low level of encryption is better than sending network traffic in clear text, it is not secure enough for many business or government environments. SecureICA is available in two versions:

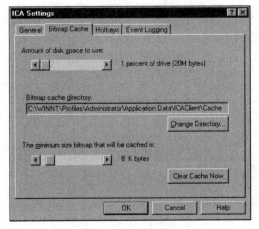

Figure 6.8 The Bitmap Cache tab.

➤ *North American*—This version offers 40-, 56-, and 128-bit encryption levels. As mentioned in Chapter 2, when the user logs on to the MetaFrame server, North American SecureICA uses two 40-, 56-, or 128-bit keys for the handshake and session data. One key encrypts the server-to-client traffic; the second key encrypts all client-to-server packets. With the exception of a small encryption header, all packet commands and data are encrypted.

➤ *International*—This version offers 40-bit encryption. And, like the North American version, the international version can use a 128-bit key for the handshake, but it can use only a maximum 40-bit encryption for the session data. Thus, the international version is considered a 40-bit solution. Just as in the North American version, one key encrypts the server-to-client traffic; the second key encrypts all client-to-server packets.

 Although the U.S. government has removed all restrictions on exporting 128-bit encryption products, you should know the difference between the North American and international encryption levels.

You must install and license SecureICA services on the MetaFrame server as well as install an unlicensed component on the client workstation. You cannot establish client-to-server connections unless both the server- and client-side components are present. Also, be aware that the minimum encryption level of basic is set as a default for the connection on the server. Clients must have encryption levels equal to or greater than the level on the server connection that the client will access. If the server connection encryption is set to 56 bit, for example, all clients must have 56-bit or higher encryption installed on the workstations. If a client has a higher encryption level configured than that on the server connection, the resulting connection will support the higher encryption level (i.e., a client with 128-bit encryption can open a 128-bit session with a server connection that is configured at a lower encryption level).

SecureICA Features

SecureICA is a versatile, cross-platform solution. When the CCA exam was created, SecureICA was an extra cost option, like Load Balancing, Installation Management Services (IMS), and Resource Management Services (RMS). Citrix recently announced that SecureICA will be bundled with MetaFrame at no extra cost. Just remember that for the exam, SecureICA is considered an optional component. Here are some features of SecureICA:

➤ SecureICA supports DOS, Win16/32, and Web clients (Netscape plug-in or IE ActiveX) and all of the network protocols these clients support.

➤ SecureICA also supports all standard LAN and WAN connection types, including RAS and asynchronous dial-up.

➤ Different encryption levels can be configured for each client connection.

➤ Different encryption levels can be set for different applications.

In terms of the CCA exam, there are two drawbacks to using SecureICA. First, it is an extra cost option. Second, SecureICA uses 60K more memory than the standard ICA client.

To install SecureICA, first install the SecureICA Option Pack on the MetaFrame server. Then, install the client software via the installation diskettes created with the ICA Client Creator.

Seamless Window

A *seamless window* is a feature that allows an ICA client to run hosted applications via a MetaFrame server seamlessly on the client desktop. Although the application is running on the MetaFrame server, it appears to be running locally on the user's workstation. A seamless window enables users to transparently multitask between local and hosted applications. You can minimize, maximize, or resize windows, just as in a standalone PC session. Users can run remote applications from desktop icons, the Start menu, Program Neighborhood, or NFuse. They can print to local or network printers that they can access from the client's local File/Print menu (i.e., no additional software or user configuration is required). In addition, multiple programs can run from within a single ICA connection.

Win32 clients that run applications in a seamless window can use a Citrix utility called the ICA Connection Center, which you access from an icon in the System Tray. You use this utility to monitor active connections and currently active applications. It allows users to close a window or log off of all active windows. They can also see whether open applications are local or server based.

Although seamless windows are a powerful feature, they do have some limitations you should keep in mind:

➤ Only Win32 ICA clients can take advantage of seamless windows.

➤ Licensing issues can arise if the network is not carefully designed.

➤ Seamless windows can consume additional client licenses if application settings vary between servers in a server farm. Also, additional licenses can be used if a server runs low on resources and a client is disconnected and then reconnected to a different server.

To avoid using extra client licenses, two conditions must be met. The first is that all published applications must have the same encryption level, bitmap caching, disk compression, window colors, audio, queuing mouse movements, and keystroke settings. The second condition is to avoid having users access applications from different, non-load-balanced servers as this can consume multiple client licenses. Essentially, users have multiple ICA connections established with different servers, and each connection to a server requires a license.

 For the CCA exam, make sure you understand the limitations of seamless windows.

Client Printing in a Seamless Desktop Environment

Client printer mapping is an important benefit of working in a seamless desktop environment. After logging on to a MetaFrame server, users can have access to local and network printers that have been configured for their use. Clients can use their local printers to print information from applications that run on the MetaFrame server. Once the print shares are established, the client printer mappings automatically enable clients to print to all configured local and network printers. By default, the client printer mappings are enabled for all supported network protocols.

You can modify client printer mappings for all configurable ICA connections using the CCC tool or by using Terminal Server's User Manager for Domains utility. Refer back to Figure 6.2 to see the Client Settings screen, which you access from the CCC utility.

Note that you can configure printer configurations for ICA and RDP clients with the User Manager for Domains utility on a TSE machine but not on a standard NT 4 server. The TSE machine has an additional Config button in the User Properties area where you can modify the printer mapping and other settings. Figure 6.9 shows the User Configuration window, which you access via the Terminal Server's User Manager for Domains Config button.

Citrix uses its own naming convention for both Windows and DOS printer mappings. Windows clients must name printers using the clientname#printername naming convention. This allows multiple printers to share a port without problems. DOS mappings use the clientname#portname convention to name printers. This approach dictates that only one printer can be used on the specified port.

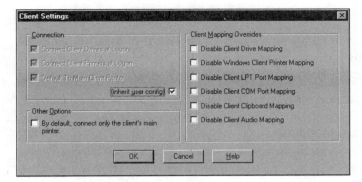

Figure 6.9   Terminal Server's client settings screen.

 Windows clients can support multiple printers on one port using the clientname#printername naming convention for printer mapping. DOS clients must use the clientname#portname naming convention and can assign only one printer to any given port.

Mapping Client COM Ports, Clipboard, and Audio

Mapping client COM ports, clipboard, and audio contributes to creating a seamless environment for users. As mentioned earlier in this chapter, Citrix's seamless environment model is designed so that users can do their work just as if they were computing on standalone PCs. Clients are not required to remember which resources are local and which are on the network. Network administrators can use drive, printer, COM port, clipboard, and audio mapping so that users feel like all of these network resources are running locally.

As with printer mapping, COM port, clipboard, and audio mapping is enabled by default for all network protocols. You can establish mappings for any of the individual protocols by using the CCC utility.

Seamless access to network resources is a major feature of MetaFrame 1.8. It allows users to access network resources (e.g., applications, network printers, server-based clipboard, COM ports, and audio) as easily as they access their workstation resources. This minimizes both employee training and user problems.

Client COM Port Mapping

Client COM port mapping enables Windows or DOS ICA clients to redirect traffic going to the server's COM port to their local COM port. When the mapping is enabled, applications that run on the server automatically redirect the traffic to client-side peripheral devices.

You can set client COM port mappings manually using the following procedure:

➤ From a command prompt on the client's workstation, type: "net use comx: \\client\comy" (where x is the server serial port number and y is the client serial port number).

➤ You can use the **net use** command to see if the mapping was accomplished.

Client Clipboard Mapping

Another feature that is part of seamless desktop integration is client clipboard mapping. This type of mapping allows clients to use Microsoft Explorer to copy, cut, and paste text and graphics between applications running on the server and applications running on the client hard drive. Clipboard mapping is only supported on Windows and Unix clients; DOS and Macintosh ICA clients cannot utilize this feature.

Client Audio Mapping

Client audio mapping allows users to hear server-based audio broadcasts and .wav files on their local workstation speakers. This capability is supported only for DOS and Windows clients, and all workstations must be equipped with a Sound Blaster-compatible sound card. Because audio can consume a great deal of network bandwidth, Citrix provides three different audio quality options that you can select based on the available bandwidth:

➤ *High (1.3Mbps)*—This level delivers very high audio quality but it also uses the most network bandwidth.

➤ *Medium (64Kbps)*—This is the default setting. It compresses the data stream to 64Kbps and represents the best choice for most networks.

➤ *Low (16Kbps)*—A compressed data stream of 16Kbps is the logical choice for dial-up connections.

Local clients can set the audio quality level in two ways:

➤ For published applications in an application set, go to the Tools/Settings menu.

➤ For published applications in custom ICA connections, access the File/Properties menu.

 For the CCA exam, make sure you understand the parameters used in audio and printer mapping.

Practice Questions

Question 1

> Which ICA clients can utilize Program Neighborhood without having to also use any other MetaFrame utilities?
>
> ○ a. Win32 ICA clients
>
> ○ b. DOS clients
>
> ○ c. Macintosh ICA clients
>
> ○ d. Web ICA clients

Answer a is correct as Program Neighborhood was designed to be used by the Win32 ICA clients. DOS, Macintosh, and Web clients require you to use another MetaFrame utility (i.e., ICA PassThrough) to be able to use Program Neighborhood.

Question 2

> Your organization's staffers wish to be able to check voice messages stored on a network server at headquarters. The employees wish to access the server from remote offices and from home via a 56K dial-up connection. What audio quality level would be configured for these dial-up connections?
>
> ○ a. 16Kbps
>
> ○ b. 28Kbps
>
> ○ c. 56Kbps
>
> ○ d. 128Kbps

Answer a is correct. Dial-up connections should be configured to MetaFrame's Low audio setting of 16Kbps. Answers b, c and d are incorrect as they are not available MetaFrame audio quality levels.

Question 3

> You are network administrator for a bank with branches throughout the United States. What encryption level would you configure for your SecureICA clients for maximum security?
>
> ○ a. 56 bit
>
> ○ b. 128 bit
>
> ○ c. 256 bit
>
> ○ d. 512 bit

Answer b is correct as 128 bit is the highest encryption level available with SecureICA. Answer a is incorrect as 56-bit encryption is less secure than 128-bit. Answers c and d are incorrect as these encryption levels are not available with SecureICA.

Question 4

> Some of your DOS ICA clients want to use Program Neighborhood for seamless access to server applications. What MetaFrame tool can you use to accommodate the DOS clients?
>
> ○ a. Server Administration
>
> ○ b. CCC utility
>
> ○ c. ICA DOS Client Wizard
>
> ○ d. ICA PassThrough

Answer d is correct as it is the technology used to allow non-Win32 ICA clients to utilize Program Neighborhood. You use the Server Administration tool to manage servers. Therefore, answer a is incorrect. You use the CCC utility to manage ICA connections and to enable drive and printer mapping. Therefore, answer b is incorrect. The DOS Client Wizard does not exist. Therefore, answer c is incorrect.

Question 5

> Which two methods can you use to install DOS ICA clients? [Check all correct answers]
>
> ❑ a. Network share
>
> ❑ b. MetaFrame CD-ROM
>
> ❑ c. Program Neighborhood
>
> ❑ d. Client Resources utility

Answers a and b are correct since the DOS clients can be installed from a network share or by using the MetaFrame CD-ROM. You use Program Neighborhood to manage published applications on ICA Win32 clients. Therefore, answer c is incorrect. The Client Resources utility does not exist. Therefore, answer d is incorrect.

Question 6

> You wish to install Win16 and Win32 ICA clients on your network workstations. Which two methods can you employ?
>
> ❑ a. ICA Client Installation CD-ROM
>
> ❑ b. MetaFrame CD-ROM
>
> ❑ c. ICA Client Creator-produced installation diskettes
>
> ❑ d. DirectICA tool

Answers b and c are correct as both types of Windows clients can be installed using either the MetaFrame CD-ROM or the installation diskettes. There is no separate ICA Client Installation CD-ROM. Therefore, answer a is incorrect. DirectICA provides high-speed server connections for graphics-intensive applications. Therefore, answer d is incorrect.

Question 7

> To configure an ICA asynchronous connection on a MetaFrame server, you must:
>
> ○ a. Use an ISDN or higher-speed connection
>
> ○ b. Use a port that has not been configured for RAS
>
> ○ c. Select Asynchronous Connection in the Remote Access utility
>
> ○ d. Use the connection for Windows and DOS clients only

Answer b is correct since ICA asynchronous connections cannot use RAS ports. MetaFrame asynchronous connections do not require high-speed connectivity. Therefore, answer a is incorrect. There is no Remote Access utility. Therefore, answer c is incorrect. All ICA clients can use Direct Asynchronous connections. Therefore, answer d is incorrect.

Question 8

> Which network protocol is supported by the Macintosh ICA clients?
>
> ○ a. TCP/IP
>
> ○ b. NetBIOS
>
> ○ c. IPX/SPX
>
> ○ d. ATM

Answer a is correct as TCP/IP is the only protocol that can be used by Macintosh ICA clients. Macintosh ICA clients do not support the NetBIOS or IPX/SPX protocols. Therefore, answers b and c are incorrect. ATM is not a network protocol. Therefore, answer d is incorrect.

Question 9

You are the network administrator for the Acme Explosives Corporation. You work in the headquarters office in New York, but the company also has branch offices in Toronto and Tokyo. There are separate NT 4 networks at each site. New York's MetaFrame 1.8 servers support 90 local Win32 ICA clients. The Toronto and Tokyo offices have smaller user populations that run a mix of Win32 and Mac clients.

Required Results:
Run and maintain all company applications on the New York MetaFrame servers, which have SecureICA installed.

Allow all remote Windows and Macintosh clients to access the company's hosted applications.

Optional Desired Results:
Provide secure LAN and WAN traffic.

Allow remote clients to use PN so they can work in a seamless environment.

Proposed Solution:
Install 128-bit SecureICA client software on all remote clients.

Configure PN for all remote clients.

Which result does the proposed solution produce?

○ a. The solution meets all required and optional desired results.

○ b. The solution meets all required results but meets only one optional desired result.

○ c. The solution meets all the required results.

○ d. The solution does not meet the required results.

Answer d is correct. There are two problems with the proposed solution. First, although the New York and Toronto offices can use the 128-bit North American version of the SecureICA client, the Tokyo office cannot (this has been changed by the U.S. government, but it still holds true for the CCA certification exam). Tokyo users would be legally permitted to use only the international SecureICA client with 40-bit encryption. Thus, you cannot meet the required result to provide access for all remote clients using 128-bit SecureICA. Even after you resolved the SecureICA encryption-level issue, you still could not deploy Program Neighborhood for the remote Macintosh clients. (Unless you first install another Citrix technology (i.e., ICA PassThrough), PN supports only Win32 ICA clients.)

Question 10

> You work as a network administrator for ABC Corp. Your CIO has decided to combine the three company networks into a single Windows NT/MetaFrame 1.8 network. There are 75 Win32 ICA clients in the main office, but the engineering and warehouse clients use a mixture of Windows, Unix, and DOS clients.
>
> Required Result:
> Allow DOS and Unix users to access Windows applications on the MetaFrame servers.
>
> Optional Desired Results:
> Deliver medium-quality audio feeds to all clients.
>
> Provide three of your engineers with high-speed access to the server to run their heavy-on-graphics design applications.
>
> Proposed Solution:
> Install Windows, DOS, and Unix ICA clients on the appropriate workstations.
>
> Enable audio on all clients. Install a DirectICA solution for high-speed connections for the three engineers.
>
> Which result does the proposed solution produce?
>
> ○ a. The solution meets all required and optional desired results.
>
> ○ b. The solution meets the required result but meets only one optional desired result.
>
> ○ c. The solution meets the required result.
>
> ○ d. The solution does not meet the required result.

Answer b is correct. Installing the Windows, DOS, and Unix clients on the appropriate workstations allows all clients to attach to and run Windows applications from the MetaFrame server. However, the Unix clients cannot receive audio signals from the server. You can achieve the optional result of allowing the three engineers to access the server at high speed by installing the Citrix DirectICA solution.

Need to Know More?

 Kaplan, Steve and Marc Mangus. *Citrix: MetaFrame for Windows Terminal Services: The Official Guide.* Osborne/McGraw-Hill, Berkeley, CA, 2000. ISBN 0-07-212443-1. Chapter 6 briefly discusses ICA and RDP. Chapter 17 covers printing.

 Mathers, Todd and Shawn Genoway. *Windows NT Thin Client Solutions: Implementing Terminal Server and Citrix MetaFrame.* Macmillan Technical Publishing, Indianapolis, IN, 1999. ISBN 1-57870-065-5. Chapter 14 offers a good introduction to ICA client installation/configuration as well as to seamless windows.

 www.citrix.com/support/ has a great deal of information in the Solution Knowledge Base (KB). From the KB, select Additional Knowledge Base Resources, then Product Documentation, and then MetaFrame 1.8 for Windows NT Terminal Server. This large .pdf manual offers in-depth coverage of all aspects of MetaFrame. For an excellent ICA overview, search the KB for Citrix ICA and Server-Based Computing. This smaller .pdf file presents a good overview of ICA.

MetaFrame Administration

. . . .

Terms you'll need to understand:

✓ Citrix server farm
✓ Independent Computing Architecture (ICA) gateway
✓ Connection
✓ Listener port
✓ Idle session
✓ Citrix license pooling
✓ Server console session

Techniques you'll need to master:

✓ Knowing which tasks the Citrix Server Administration utility performs
✓ Understanding the difference between the NT domains management scope and the Citrix server farm management scope
✓ Knowing which tasks the Citrix Connection Configuration (CCC) utility performs

Citrix's CCA exam places heavy emphasis on the MetaFrame administration tools, especially Citrix Server Administration, Citrix Connection Configuration (CCC), and Published Application Manager (PAM). When studying for the CCA exam, keep in mind that MetaFrame loads on top of and enhances the underlying Windows NT Terminal Server functions. The exam will focus on Citrix, not on Windows NT, utilities. A solid knowledge of how to use the utilities is critical to success on the exam. Be sure to understand the specific tasks performed by each of the Citrix tools.

This chapter begins with an overview of the Citrix administrative tools and the relationship between the Citrix and NT tools. Then, we will discuss Citrix's definition of a server farm. This is important because Citrix's server farm architecture makes it possible to manage large numbers of servers from a single MetaFrame server console. We then cover the Independent Computing Architecture (ICA) Administrator toolbar. The remainder of the chapter focuses on the Citrix utilities that you use to manage MetaFrame servers and server farms: Citrix Server Administration, Load Balancing Administration, PAM, CCC, the Session Shadowing tools, Citrix Licensing Activation Wizard, ICA Client Update, ICA Client Creator, and ICA Client Printer Configuration tool.

MetaFrame Administrative Tools Overview

You use the MetaFrame administrative tools to manage Terminal Server- and Citrix MetaFrame-enhanced services. In a Terminal Server/MetaFrame environment, you perform management tasks using Microsoft's and Citrix's graphical tools and wizards. Like Windows NT's standard utilities, Citrix's utilities are intuitive, point-and-click-type windows and dialog boxes. You use the MetaFrame utilities to manage and monitor the Citrix-specific enhancements, like Citrix Load Balancing, ICA protocol support, published applications, Program Neighborhood (PN), and Web connectivity. You can use Citrix utilities to administer a single MetaFrame server or a group of servers located in a server farm from the console of any MetaFrame server in the server farm. You can modify application settings, along with Citrix ICA browser and Load Balancing settings, centrally.

 It is important to understand the functions and options of the MetaFrame utilities before taking the CCA exam. The Server Administration, PAM, and CCC utilities receive the most attention on the certification exam.

You manage general user configuration and network security at the Windows NT Primary Domain Controller (PDC) or Backup Domain Controller (BDC), not at a MetaFrame server. You create and manage groups on an NT PDC or

BDC using NT's User Manager for Domains utility. Terminal Server-specific services (like printer configurations and Terminal Server user profile information) are managed at the Terminal Server Edition (TSE) server. As discussed in Chapter 6, you can configure printer configurations for ICA and Remote Desktop Protocol (RDP) clients with the User Manager for Domains utility on a TSE machine, but not on a standard NT 4 server. In the User Properties area, the TSE machine has a Config button where you modify the printer mapping and other Terminal Server-specific settings.

Server Farms

As mentioned in Chapter 2, server-based computing relies on the concept of the server farm. A *server farm* is a group of Citrix servers treated as a single system that allows centralized administration of the entire network. In most cases, the farm will be located in a single domain and subnet. Citrix originally used the term to describe a group of load-balanced WinFrame servers. With the release of MetaFrame 1.8, Citrix modified its original definition of a server farm. Instead of describing a simple group of servers, a server farm is now defined as a centralized management group (sometimes referred to as a *virtual group*). The Citrix utilities—like Citrix Server Administration, Citrix Load Balancing, and PAM, discussed later in this chapter—allow enterprise-wide centralized administration from a single location. With Citrix Load Balancing Services installed on the MetaFrame servers in a server farm, you can balance user load among the servers, increasing application availability and performance. From an administrative standpoint, a server farm is a group of Terminal Servers running MetaFrame 1.8 that you can manage from a single MetaFrame console. From a user's perspective, a published application appears to be hosted from a single MetaFrame server, although the application may be load balanced among multiple servers in one or more server farms in completely different locations.

The individual servers in a server farm can be located in the same domain, in multiple domains, on different subnets, or in completely different locations. By definition, even a single server in a workgroup is considered a server farm. A server farm can be a single server in a workgroup or domain, multiple servers in a single domain, or multiple servers in multiple domains. If the servers are in different locations (e.g., New York and Los Angeles), they must be connected by a wide area network (WAN) or asynchronous connection. For users to access hosted applications, you must establish the appropriate trust relationships between the resource and account domains. If the servers in a server farm are located in different domains, the ICA client that accesses services belongs to the trusted account domain, and the MetaFrame servers are in the resource, or trusting, domain.

By default, MetaFrame servers do not become members of a server farm. A server farm is created on a single MetaFrame server, and additional servers then join the existing farm using PAM (discussed later in this chapter). A server cannot be a member of multiple server farms. Once a server joins a farm, it cannot then become a non-server farm machine, although it could change membership to a different server farm.

Note: The use of Citrix Load Balancing is not a requirement for creating a server farm, although it does increase application availability and performance.

Server Farm Configurations

A MetaFrame server farm can contain a single standalone server or hundreds of servers. The following is a list of the various server farm configurations:

➤ A standalone server in a Windows NT domain

➤ A standalone server in a Windows NT workgroup

➤ Multiple servers in a single Windows NT domain

➤ Multiple servers in multiple Windows NT domains

You can configure Citrix servers in different geographical locations to join a server farm located in a different subnet, providing the subnets are connected by an ICA gateway. You must install ICA gateways at each remote site as well as at the server farm.

Generally, a corporation implements a single server farm instead of having multiple server farms. As mentioned earlier, a server farm is considered a centralized management group. Therefore, adding multiple server farms within a single network adds more complexity and administration, with no additional performance gains. MetaFrame servers located on different subnets and domains can still be members of the same server farm, provided that the following conditions are met:

➤ For users to access published applications, the appropriate trust relationships between the resource and account domains must be established; the users that access published applications belong to the trusted account domain, and the MetaFrame servers are in the resource domain.

➤ In a situation with multiple NT domains, there must be a trust relationship in which the resource domain trusts the account domains.

To manage a server farm, the person(s) responsible for administering the MetaFrame servers must have administrative rights on all servers in the farm. This is an NT issue because you manage the administrative rights via User Manager for Domains on the PDC or BDC, or with the User Manager utility on member or standalone servers. If administrators do not have administrative rights on all servers in the farm, they cannot manage the servers on which they do not have administrative rights. Some servers in a farm are dedicated to running certain applications. This may call for more smaller servers as opposed to fewer larger servers.

An important characteristic of the server-based model is scalability. Networks can be scaled horizontally or vertically. Horizontal scaling requires adding or removing client workstations, which may impact performance. Vertical scaling means upgrading to a larger and faster server. Scalability is a major consideration in a TSE server farm, where applications run 100 percent on the servers. The scalability of a Terminal Server-based server farm depends on the user load, the type of applications running on the server, the server configuration, and the network bandwidth. When one or more servers in the server farm is running out of resources, simply add a server (or servers) to the farm to scale up to meet the demand.

Setting up a Server Farm

If you group your servers in one physical location in the same domain and subnet, you can simplify the management of the server farm, although all the servers in a server farm do not have to be physically or logically grouped together. When both the server farm and the users are within the same domain and subnet, less configuration is required compared to multi-domain farms.

By using Citrix's ICA gateway feature, you can configure servers in different subnets and domains to join a server farm. An ICA gateway must be established on the primary MetaFrame server (which is referred to as the *master ICA browser*) on each subnet so that the MetaFrame servers can communicate. Without an ICA gateway, no communication between logically or physically remote MetaFrame servers can occur. Along with the ICA gateway, the account and resource domains must have the appropriate trust relationships. When the MetaFrame server farm is located in the resource domain and the users are in the account domain, the server farm is the trusting domain and the account domain is the trusted domain.

It is important to remember that Load Balancing is not a mandatory component of a server farm. A MetaFrame 1.8 server farm does not automatically offer Citrix's Load Balancing Services. Load Balancing Services is sold separately, and you must install the license before you can use the service. With Citrix Load Balancing, users are redirected to the least busy server when the user requests services from the server farm. This improves both application availability and performance. Load Balancing is *not* considered a fault-tolerant solution; if a server crashes, the user is disconnected. However, it does offer some redundancy because disconnected users are routed to one of the other servers when they log back on to the network.

ICA Administrator Toolbar

This chapter focuses on the MetaFrame administrative tools, so a quick description of the ICA Administrator toolbar is useful. The ICA Administrator toolbar offers you a way to access the MetaFrame administrative tools by simply clicking on the console's toolbar icons. By default, the ICA Administrator toolbar is docked on the right side of a MetaFrame server's desktop and contains a default set of tool icons. You can publish the toolbar, allowing approved users to access the MetaFrame administrative tools from PN or from a Web page. To access the default toolbar file, icabar.exe, look in the Winnt\System32 directory. Figure 7.1 shows an image of an undocked ICA Administrator Toolbar. If the Citrix tools are accessed from the Start menu, administrators have the option of disabling the Server Console toolbar.

The ICA Administrator toolbar will be a familiar utility if you are a Microsoft Office user. Microsoft and Citrix have an agreement whereby Citrix was able to modify the Microsoft Office toolbar for MetaFrame. The MetaFrame installation process places the toolbar on the server desktop with a default set of tool icons. Right-clicking on an open portion of the toolbar brings up a menu that allows an administrator to add, delete, rename, or rearrange the toolbar icons (and their associated tools). The menu also has options for Autohide, Always On Top, Customize, and Exit.

If you select the Customize option, shown in Figure 7.2, various tools are included in the Administrator toolbar after the MetaFrame installation. Most of the following tools are covered in more detail later in this chapter:

➤ *Citrix Connection Configuration*—Use the CCC tool, first introduced in Chapter 6, to add, change, or delete client-to-server connections and to manage connection security.

➤ *Citrix Licensing*—After obtaining a license activation code from Citrix, use this tool to manage licenses for WinFrame or MetaFrame or for the optional Citrix products.

Figure 7.1   The ICA Administrator toolbar.

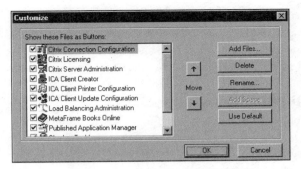

Figure 7.2 The Administrator toolbar Customize window.

➤ *Citrix Server Administration*—Use this tool to manage users and user sessions; to find out information about domains, servers, and sessions; to configure ICA browsers and gateways; and to manage the connections that the CCC tool creates.

➤ *ICA Client Creator*—Use this tool to create ICA client installation diskettes (you can also install clients onto client workstations using the MetaFrame CD-ROM or from a network share).

➤ *ICA Client Printer Configuration*—Users can employ this tool to create and connect to ICA client printers. You can also use it to set up print queues for ICA clients that do not have their own print queues (e.g., ICA DOS clients). You can use this utility only within an ICA session.

➤ *ICA Client Update Configuration*—Use this tool to add the latest versions of the various ICA clients to the client update database and to configure the automatic client download process.

➤ *Load Balancing Administration*—Use this tool to configure the Load Balancing settings on Citrix servers. By default, the User Load parameter determines how much of the network traffic is routed to the server.

➤ *MetaFrame Books Online*—This tool offers online help information for MetaFrame administrators.

➤ *Published Application Manager*—Use PAM to publish and manage applications on MetaFrame servers, and to manage server farms.

➤ *Shadow Taskbar*—Use this tool to shadow one or several user sessions. It allows administrators to view and control a user's workstation. It is also useful for troubleshooting and for user training. As with the Printer Configuration tool, the Shadow taskbar can be used only from within an ICA session.

As mentioned earlier in this chapter, administrators can right-click on an open area in the Administrator toolbar to display a menu. The Customize option allows you to add other icons to provide access to additional tools and files. By adding configured icons to the Administrator toolbar, you can access even non-MetaFrame files.

Citrix Server Administration Utility

The Server Administration tool displays the domain, server, and user session information of all servers in a server farm. You can also use it to configure ICA browsers and gateways and to manage client-to-server connections. Just as the CCC utility (covered later in this chapter) enhances the native Terminal Server Connection utility, the Citrix Server Administration tool extends the functionality of the Terminal Server Administration utility. These Citrix enhancements were designed to provide centralized management of users, user sessions, processes, and published applications on multiple servers or server farms. The Citrix Server Administration utility is an important and versatile tool. It is one of the enterprise-wide utilities that allow you to centrally administer MetaFrame and Terminal Server servers in a server farm. It allows an administrator to monitor ICA and RDP session information, published applications, active users, and running processes within the server farm.

The Citrix Server Administrator utility allows administrators to display detailed information from all MetaFrame and Terminal Servers in the network from a single console. This offers centralized management within a server farm and allows an administrator to manage all the servers in an enterprise from a single console of any MetaFrame server within the farm. You can use the Server Administration tool to monitor session status or to connect/disconnect sessions. It can also be employed to log off or reset user sessions, to send messages to users, to shadow user sessions, or to terminate network processes. Finally, this tool allows you to manage ICA browsers and ICA gateways.

The layout of the Server Administration screen is similar to that of Microsoft's Windows Explorer. The left pane presents a hierarchical ordering of servers, domains, sessions, and published applications. The left side also has three tabs located on the bottom of the pane that allow the administrator to view details about servers, published applications, and video servers (the Video Servers tab is used for VideoFrame, a Citrix product that is not covered on the CCA exam). The right pane displays detailed information about the items highlighted in the left pane, along with detailed information available from the six tabs (Users, Sessions, Processes, Licenses, ICA Browser, and Information), located across the top section of the right pane. As with Windows Explorer, right-clicking on an item within a window displays a menu of options. Figure 7.3 shows the Server Administration screen with the Servers tab selected on the bottom of the left pane and the ICA Browser tab selected in the right pane.

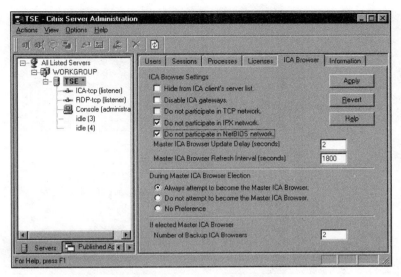

Figure 7.3   The Server Administration screen with the Servers and ICA Browser tabs selected.

When you first start the Citrix Server Administration utility, the current MetaFrame or Terminal server is highlighted (selected) in the left pane by default. The left pane displays the connection status of the server, whereas the right pane's tabs present more detailed server information. An additional tab—ICA Gateway—is available when the All Listed Servers object is highlighted in the left pane; use this tab to configure ICA gateways between servers in different networks. Excluding the currently highlighted server, all other MetaFrame and Terminal servers, domains, and published applications on the network appear as grayed-out icons. To display a list of all servers, domains, and sessions within the left pane of the Server Administration window, click on Expand All from the View menu.

Note: To administer a MetaFrame server using the Server Administrator utility, you must have a user account with administrative rights on the server.

To manage a non-selected MetaFrame or Terminal server within the network, click on the grayed-out server name to access the server and display detailed server information. If the server you wish to manage is in a different domain, double-click on the domain in the left pane to receive a list of available MetaFrame and Terminal servers. To view the status of a published application, click on the published application name in the left pane. Figure 7.4 shows the Server Administration screen with the All Listed Servers object selected in the left pane and the ICA Gateways tab selected in the right pane.

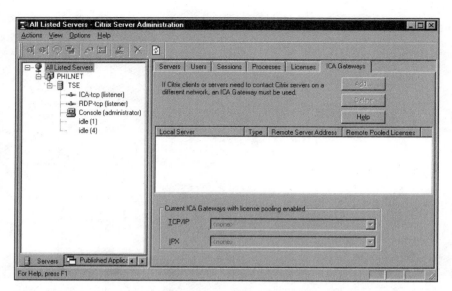

Figure 7.4 The Server Administration screen with the ICA Gateways tab selected.

 The ICA Gateways tab is available only when All Listed Servers is highlighted in the left pane.

Load Balancing Administration Tool

One of the tools available from the ICA Administration toolbar is the Load Balancing Administration utility. Although we will examine Load Balancing in detail in Chapter 8, this section briefly introduces you to Citrix Load Balancing and the use of the associated Administration tool.

Citrix's optional Load Balancing allows an administrator to load balance published applications that are installed on the servers in a Citrix server farm. When an ICA client requests an application, the ICA master browser examines current server loads—this information is gathered from the other Citrix servers. The master browser then calculates the server loads and routes the client to the least busy server. Because user load scales linearly in a MetaFrame environment, it is easy to compute the server resources needed for however many users there are. If 1 server supports 20 typical users, 3 identical servers will support 60 users. So, IT staffs know that they can combine Load Balancing with a set number of servers to enable high availability to hosted applications.

When you install the Load Balancing license, the Load Balancing utility is enabled and made available. The utility comes preconfigured, although it does offer additional configuration options. Like the Citrix Server Administration utility, the Load Balancing tool provides enterprise-wide management that allows an administrator to view and fine-tune the Load Balancing settings on each server in a server farm. These settings allow you to adjust how Load Balancing calculates the server load for each server. Staying with the default settings means that the user load is the only relevant factor utilized when the Load Balancing service routes an ICA connection to the least busy server. Also, keep in mind that all of the settings are independent variables; changing the value of one setting does not affect the importance of any other setting.

After starting the Load Balancing Administration tool, select the desired load-balanced server from the left panel of the displayed window. The right panel then displays the Basic tab of the tool. Figure 7.5 shows the default settings of the Basic tab in the Load Balancing tool. The right-side panel allows you to adjust the Basic setting, which is based on User Load. The User Load Is 100% At setting determines the ratio of the current number of logged-on users to the maximum number of users. The default maximum number of users is 10000. We recommend reducing this setting to the maximum number of users that will actually access the server. To accept User Load as the criterion for determining server usage, make sure the slider bar is set to Very Important. To choose another factor to determine the server load, click on the Advanced tab in the right panel, shown in Figure 7.6.

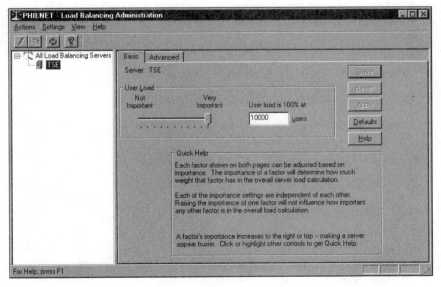

Figure 7.5   The Load Balancing window showing the default settings.

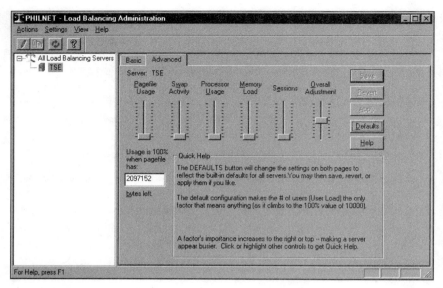

Figure 7.6   The Load Balancing window showing the Advanced tab.

As you can see in the Advanced tab, six adjustable settings are available:

➤ *Pagefile Usage*—Is the current pagefile size as related to the allowed minimum free space in the pagefile. You use the Bytes Left field to set the minimum number of pagefile bytes that will be kept available even when the server indicates 100 percent utilization.

➤ *Swap Activity*—Sets how frequently the pagefile can be accessed.

➤ *Processor Usage*—Is computed as the percentage of time that the processor is busy.

➤ *Memory Load*—Is the ratio of total RAM to available memory.

➤ *Sessions*—Is the ratio of the total number of configured ICA connections to the number of free ICA connections.

➤ *Overall Adjustment*—Adjusts the overall calculated load of a server. Unlike the other settings, the default setting for this slide bar is in the middle (i.e., 0). Moving the slider bar down to −10 assigns the least importance to this setting, whereas a +10 setting assigns a maximum importance.

All but the Overall Adjustment setting have sliders that you can adjust from a value of 0 (no adjustment) to a value of +10 (maximum importance assigned to the parameter).

PAM

Just as the Citrix Server Administration tool enhances the native Terminal Server functions, the PAM utility extends the functionality of Terminal Server. PAM is an important and versatile tool used both to publish and manage applications (making the applications available to domain users via the Web and ICA 32-bit Windows clients) and to centrally manage multiple servers in a server farm. Applications and desktops that are published on a standalone MetaFrame server or on multiple servers within a farm are automatically available to Win32 ICA clients via PN. The applications are grouped together in PN and presented as application sets.

PAM allows enterprise-wide management of individual or load-balanced applications; i.e., it lets an administrator monitor the status and modify the setup parameters of all an organization's published applications. PAM is also the utility used to produce ICA and HTML files for Web enabling published applications (this topic is covered in detail in Chapter 9).

 For the CCA exam, you need to know that PAM is the primary tool used to Web enable applications, even though NFuse is currently the preferred approach (the CCA exam does not cover NFuse).

As mentioned in the "Server Farms" section earlier in this chapter, a MetaFrame server can be a member of only one server farm at a time. You can use PAM's Change Server Farm Wizard to move a server from one farm to another.

Win32 ICA clients can access published applications available from Citrix server farms via a Web page or application set. These clients can access published applications without knowing details about the application's directory or executable name, or from which server that application is running. Once an application is published and the appropriate permissions are assigned via PAM, users can view and access the available application sets that contain the published applications. The non-Win32 ICA clients (i.e., Win16, DOS, Unix, and Macintosh) that do not support PN can use the legacy Remote Application Manager (RAM) utility to access the published applications.

Publishing Applications and Managing Applications

You view, manage, and create published applications within either a server farm or an NT domains scope. Applications published in the server farm management scope are automatically added to application sets, which are then immediately available to ICA Win32 clients via PN. Clients that are using PN while an application is being published can access the newly published application by refreshing the PN window or logging off and then back on. The user does not have to do any additional configuration to access the new application.

The NT domains management scope provides backward compatibility for existing WinFrame 1.7 and MetaFrame 1 servers that host published applications. Unlike the applications published in the server farm scope, applications published in the domains scope are not added to an application set and are published as individual applications. Employing the domains scope results in applications that are not automatically configured for PN clients. The NT domains scope provides backward compatibility for ICA clients that do not support PN. These legacy clients must utilize the RAM to access published applications.

Note: You can identify the scope of a published application by the icons that appear in the PAM utility.

You can migrate applications published on WinFrame 1.6 and 1.7, on MetaFrame 1, or in the NT domains management scope to a server farm management scope using the Application/Migrate menu option in PAM. Migrating an application into a server farm makes the published application available to PN clients.

Use the following procedure to publish applications from within the PAM utility:

1. Select the desired management scope by accessing PAM's View menu and clicking on the Select Scope option. To publish an application in the NT domains management scope, click on the Using Only NT Domains radio button and then select the server's domain from the domain list. To publish an application in the server farm management scope, click on the Within A Citrix Server Farm radio button and then select the server farm where the server is located.

2. Make sure you are viewing the server on which you wish to publish the application. As mentioned earlier in this chapter, PAM is a global utility from which you can manage any server in the farm, so be sure that you are configuring the correct server. You can verify this by accessing the View menu and then clicking on Select Server. From the Select Server dialog box, choose the server from the list and click on OK. If the desired server does not appear in the list, click on Refresh Server List to display a current list of servers.

3. Once you have selected the proper management scope, go to the Application menu (top left) and click on New to start the New Application Wizard. You are then presented with 10 windows that you must configure to publish an application. On each of the windows is a Help button that offers an explanation of the various configuration entries. The New Application Wizard windows are:

   ➤ Enter Application Name.

   ➤ Choose Application Type.

➤ Define The Application.

➤ Specify Window Properties.

➤ Specify Program Neighborhood Client Settings.

➤ Specify Neighborhood Administration Features.

➤ Select Domain Or Citrix Server.

➤ Configure Accounts.

➤ Add The Application To The Citrix Servers.

➤ Finish Adding The Application.

When you click on the Finish button from this window, the application is then officially published and available to Win32 clients.

Note: You do not have to memorize the New Application Wizard windows list. It is included here to give you a better understanding of PAM's functionality.

As mentioned in Chapter 4, it is important to understand why the anonymous user accounts were created during the MetaFrame installation and how PAM employs these accounts. Anonymous user accounts are local user accounts that belong to the MetaFrame server's Guest and Anonymous Users Groups. Anonymous users are allowed network access without an explicit logon (an explicit logon requires both a username and password).

If a MetaFrame server is set up as a PDC or BDC, you cannot create anonymous user accounts and the server cannot publish anonymous applications. This is due to the Windows NT authentication process (covered in Chapter 5), whereby a PDC or BDC must authenticate all clients to log on to a domain.

When MetaFrame is installed on a member server, anonymous users log on using a local guest account rather than an NT domain account. Although these local guest accounts are less secure than authenticated domain accounts, they are very useful for enabling Internet access. Anonymous accounts are local, non-authenticated accounts, not global domain accounts.

Table 7.1 explains the various parameters you use to configure a published application. You do not need to memorize them; the table is included to give you a better understanding of the properties and workings of the important PAM utility.

Before you can modify application settings, you must determine which server hosts the desired published application; in a server farm, the desired application could be on any of the servers. Once you locate the application using PAM, click on View/Select Server, and pick the server that has the application to be edited. Once you have chosen the server, its published applications are displayed. If the

Table 7.1	Parameters used to configure published applications.
Parameter	**Explanation**
Citrix Server	The name of the server that hosts the application.
Enter Application Name	The application name that will be used in PN.
Detailed Description	An optional application description.
Choose Application Type	The application type. Choose explicit or anonymous logon. Applications published for explicit logon are published for an explicit user/group. Clients that access this type of application have to supply a valid Windows NT username, domain name, and password. Applications published for anonymous logon are published for the Citrix Anonymous user group. Anonymous users can access this type of application without providing a username, domain name, and password. For security reasons, applications are generally published using the explicit application type.
Command Line	The path to the application's executable file; i.e., C:\Program Files\Microsoft Office\office\winword.exe. Use the Browse button to locate the application's executable file. If this field is left blank, the server's desktop is published.
Working Directory	The path to the application file's directory. Using the Browse button to locate the application's executable file automatically enters the path to the application's Working Directory.
Window Properties	Select whether a title bar will appear at the top of the published application and if the application window will be maximized on the ICA client workstation.
Client Settings	Specify the sound, video, encryption, window size, and window color settings. This option is not available in the NT domains management scope.
Specify Neighborhood Administration Features	Add shortcuts (Start menu or desktop) to the client workstation for the published application or application set. Also, you can create a PN folder to store groups of applications. By default, applications are presented in the root directory of PN, not in a folder. This option is not available in the NT domains management scope.
Groups And Users	An administrator can grant access to published applications to domain groups and users.
Servers	An administrator can specify which server(s) will run the application. In a load-balanced environment, you can select multiple servers.

server farm has multiple servers with different applications and settings, use the Filter Servers option. This allows filtering by server capabilities, operating system type, and encryption levels. For example, the Load Balancing filter displays applications installed on the server farm's load-balanced servers.

CCC Utility

As explained in Chapter 6, you can use the CCC tool to add, change, or delete network and asynchronous connections; to administer client device mapping, including drive, printer, COM port, clipboard, and audio mapping; and to configure and test TAPI-compliant modems. The mapping options support Citrix's seamless desktop integration, whereby users can access network applications, printers, and other resources as if they were located on their workstations. This seamless user environment, centralized network administration, and application load balancing are the primary enhancements that MetaFrame 1.8 adds to Microsoft's Terminal Server.

Before we look at how to configure connections with CCC, it is important to understand what constitutes a Citrix connection. To begin with, MetaFrame connections are virtual sessions, not hardware links (Citrix characterizes these virtual links as logical ports). Note that in a MetaFrame environment there are two types of connections:

➤ Network local area network (LAN) or WAN connections configured for Transmission Control Protocol/Internet Protocol (TCP/IP), Internetwork Packet Exchange (IPX), Sequence Packet Exchange (SPX), or NetBIOS

➤ Serial connections using TAPI-compliant modems or direct cables

On a MetaFrame server, each installed network protocol has a corresponding listener port that monitors network traffic for any clients asking to connect to the server. The protocol-specific listener port passes the connection request to one of the server's two idle sessions (you can view the listener ports and idle sessions by using the Citrix Server Administrator utility). The idle session then creates the client-to-server connection. Once the connection is established, a new idle session is created. This strategy means that only two idle sessions exist on each server. Each idle session uses 1MB of RAM, so the two sessions require only 2MB of memory. Each server has one listener port for each installed protocol but only two idle sessions to service all client connection requests.

 A MetaFrame server can have multiple listener ports (one listener port for each protocol) but only two 1MB idle sessions.

You can use the CCC tool to add, administer, or delete listener ports on MetaFrame servers. Adding or deleting one of the protocol-specific listener ports adds or deletes the associated MetaFrame connection. When installing MetaFrame, you can enable any or all of the supported protocols (i.e., TCP/IP, IPX, SPX, or

NetBIOS) plus one asynchronous connection for each TAPI-compliant modem. After the MetaFrame installation, you can add other protocols and their associated listener ports using the CCC utility only.

The CCC tool is an extension of the Terminal Server Connection Configuration utility. The major difference between the two is that CCC allows you to manage the Citrix enhancements, unlike the native Terminal Server utility. Both the Citrix Server Administration and CCC tools were designed to support Citrix's centralized administration model. An administrator can manage or modify all sessions, users, processes, and ICA connections from one location. Large organizations with multiple server farms typically use the MetaFrame management tools in combination with Citrix's license pooling and the optional Load Balancing software (license pooling is discussed in the "License Pooling" section later in this chapter. This approach allows you to manage all users, printers, data, and other network resources from a single server console.

Connection Settings

You can launch the CCC tool from Start|Programs|MetaFrame Tools or from the desktop ICA Administrator toolbar. To access the connection settings, highlight the connection in the CCC window. Next, choose Edit from the Connection menu then click on the Client Settings button to display the Client Settings dialog box (shown in Figure 7.7). From here, an administrator can control both the ICA connection's printer and drive settings as well as the client device mapping options.

The connection settings on the left side of the Client Settings screen determine if the client drives and printers will be automatically connected when a user logs on to the ICA connection. The five connection checkboxes are:

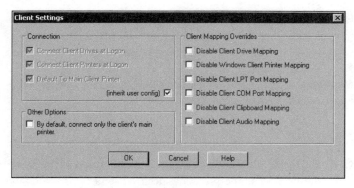

Figure 7.7   CCC's Client Settings dialog box.

➤ *Connect Client Drives At Logon*—Checked by default. Connects the client drives to the ICA connection when a user logs on.

➤ *Connect Client Printers At Logon*—Also checked by default. Connects the client's mapped printers during logon.

➤ *Default To Main Client Printer*—Another default option. If clients are working at a Windows workstation, their local default printer is available after logon (this option works by using the Windows Print Manager service).

➤ *By Default, Connect Only The Client's Main Printer*—Connects the client's default printer at logon. Many MetaFrame administrators find that this printer option causes the least user confusion (and therefore the fewest Help Desk inquiries).

➤ *Inherit User Config*—As discussed in Chapter 6, checking this box means that the user or group settings in Terminal Server's User Manager for Domains will override the ICA drive and printer connection settings.

Client Mapping Overrides

The right side of the Client Settings dialog box (refer back to Figure 7.7) allows the administrator to disable the default client device mappings. Remember that Citrix ICA connections are protocol specific; i.e., a connection is enabled for each installed network protocol. The client mappings are enabled by default for all installed protocols. Thus, administrators check the Client Mapping Override checkboxes only if they wish to disable one of the automatic client mappings.

Note: In a MetaFrame network, all client device mappings are disabled whenever a user logs off a connection. When the user logs back on, the mappings are automatically enabled (unless one or more of the Client Mapping Override boxes has been checked).

Six Mapping Override options are available on the right side of the Client Settings dialog box:

➤ *Disable Client Drive Mapping*—If unchecked, this option makes the client's drives available at logon. If this is checked, users can use the Terminal Server's mappings (if the Inherit User Config box is checked) or manually connect to their drives after logon. To change the assigned drive letters, you must use the Disk Administrator tool.

➤ *Disable Windows Client Printer Mapping*—If this is unchecked, Windows clients can print to their local printers while running server-based applications. As with drive mapping, if the Inherit User Config box is checked, the session will use the printers mapped in Terminal Server. Note that you must set up print shares on the print server to allow the network clients to access network printers.

➤ *Disable Client LPT Port Mapping*—If this is unchecked, users can print to their local LPT ports.

➤ *Disable Client COM Port Mapping*—If this is unchecked, users can redirect traffic from the server's COM port to their local COM port.

➤ *Disable Client Clipboard Mapping*—If this is unchecked, ICA clients can copy, cut, or paste data from server-to-client-based applications (or vice-versa). Similarly, clients can use Windows Explorer to copy, cut, and paste files and folders among client and server applications.

➤ *Disable Client Audio Mapping*—As mentioned in Chapter 6, Windows and DOS workstations with Sound Blaster-compatible sound cards can listen to .wav files or audio broadcasts playing on a MetaFrame server. The three available audio quality options are High, 1.3Mbps; Medium, 64Kbps compressed setting (the default setting); and Low, 16Kbps compressed setting (for dial-up or other low-bandwidth connections). Note that only the client can adjust the volume level of the audio feed.

 When the audio level is set differently for an application and for the application's ICA connection, the most restrictive level is utilized.

Session Shadowing

Chapter 6 provided an overview of MetaFrame's user shadowing tools, but a more detailed examination of shadowing is required when you are preparing for the CCA exam. The ability to shadow user sessions is very useful in medium-sized to large networks. Instead of visiting client workstations, administrators can sit at their desks and monitor one or several user sessions. Administrators can use this one-to-one, one-to-many, or many-to-one shadowing for troubleshooting and for training users on new software or upgrades.

 You should know the capabilities and restrictions of shadowing for both network administration and the CCA exam.

One of the important restrictions of shadowing is that it must take place within an ICA session rather than from a console session. A console session occurs when you are working directly at the server console or when accessing the server through a direct serial connection (i.e., a DirectICA link). All LAN or WAN connections are ICA connections that access the server across the network (you cannot shadow

RDP sessions). If you attempt to shadow a user and the ICA client is not installed on the server, the ICA Client Software Wizard displays. Once the client is installed, user shadowing is enabled.

 You can shadow sessions only from within an ICA client session. On a related theme, note that all remote connections are ICA—not console—connections.

As mentioned in Chapter 6, you initially configure session shadowing in the CCC tool. However, you actually do the shadowing from within the Server Administration utility.

When shadowing is first enabled, the default settings allow administrators to take over the user's keyboard and mouse while viewing the user session. Also, by default, the user is notified and given the option to refuse the session shadowing. You can initiate shadowing from either the Shadow button in the Citrix Server Administration tool or from the Shadow taskbar, located on the ICA Administrator toolbar. The Shadow button is available if you are working within an ICA session and if a user's ICA session is selected in the left panel of the Server Administration utility. Although the Shadow taskbar allows one or several users to be shadowed at the same time, only one user can be shadowed using the Shadow button.

The restrictions/limitations of session shadowing are:

➤ The window size and number of colors of the client session must be equal to or less than those of the shadower's session.

➤ Only an administrator (or a user who has been assigned Special Access permission in the CCC utility) can initiate or end a shadowing session.

➤ Shadowing must be done from within an ICA session. A MetaFrame/WinFrame console can neither shadow nor be shadowed.

➤ Audio is not available when you are shadowing.

➤ Administrators can shadow users only within the domain they are logged onto (but shadowing can be used across MetaFrame and WinFrame servers).

Shadowing One User or Multiple Users with the Shadow Taskbar

Although the Shadow button permits you to shadow only one user session at a time, the Shadow taskbar allows an administrator to shadow one or multiple users. Icons that represent the user session(s) allow administrators to access the user sessions from their workstation taskbar. Also, you can right-click on the session icons to display a menu that allows the shadowing to be terminated. Right-clicking on an empty portion of the taskbar brings up a menu that allows the administrator to select the following options:

➤ *Help Topics*—Provides detailed information on Citrix Shadowing

➤ *Always On Top*—Makes the Shadow taskbar visible at all times

➤ *Cascade Shadowed Sessions*—Cascades the shadowed session windows on the desktop for easy access to any session

➤ *Stop All Shadowed Sessions*—Terminates all open shadow sessions, just as Stop Shadow ends an individual session

➤ *Logging Options*—Allows you to log the shadow sessions

➤ *Exit*—Closes the Shadowing tool

Using MetaFrame's Shadow taskbar is straightforward. Follow these steps:

1. First make sure that you are working from within an ICA session. If you have administrative rights (or an administrator has assigned you Special Permission to shadow), you can then access the Shadowing icon from the MetaFrame toolbar or from MetaFrame tools in the Start menu.

2. Once the Shadow taskbar is started, a Connection Information dialog box is displayed. Enter a valid administrator's username and password to access the taskbar, and then click on the Shadow button to display a list of users.

3. Highlight the user(s) to be shadowed and click on the Add button.

4. Click on the OK button to start the shadow session. If multiple user sessions were added to the shadow list, multiple icons will be available on the taskbar.

5. Right-click on a session and select Stop to end the shadow session.

Shadowing a single user session with the Shadow button is as simple as using the Shadow taskbar. Follow these steps:

1. Log on to an ICA session with Administrative or Special Access rights, and access the Server Administration utility.

2. Select a single user session to shadow from the left pane of the utility.

3. Click on the Shadow button on the toolbar or choose Shadow from the Action menu. You are prompted to accept or change the hotkey combination used to end the shadowing session.

4. Click on OK and the selected user's screen displays on your desktop. Use the hotkey combination mentioned in Step 3 to end the shadowing session.

Citrix Licensing Tool and Licensing Procedures

MetaFrame and the optional add-on products must be licensed separately from Microsoft Terminal Server. Citrix offers two types of licenses for MetaFrame or WinFrame:

➤ *Base License*—You can think of this as a server license. When activated, it provides Citrix's multiuser functionality. This license includes 15 client licenses.

➤ *Server Extension Licenses*—To expand a MetaFrame or WinFrame network beyond the 15 users included with the Base License, you must also purchase Server Extension Licenses. These client add-on license bundles are called *bump packs*. In addition to the MetaFrame/WinFrame client bump packs, licenses are available for Citrix's optional products (e.g., Load Balancing).

As discussed in Chapter 4, all Citrix licenses must be activated after the products are installed. While installing Citrix software, you are prompted to type in the product serial number, located on the CD-ROM case. The serial number is a 21-character string that starts with 3 letters. After you enter the serial number, an eight-character machine code is generated. This unique combination number is required before Citrix will issue an activation code for the software. The software will function for 30 days without an activation code; after this time, it will shut down until you obtain and enter the activation code (actually, Citrix allows 35 days for the activation, but remember 30 days for the exam).

License Pooling

MetaFrame and WinFrame allow you to pool licenses across servers on the same subnet (for the CCA exam, remember that you cannot pool licenses across an ICA gateway). If a network contains 2 MetaFrame servers and each server has 30 client licenses installed and activated, up to 60 users could access resources on either server. When first installed, all licenses are added to the license pool by default. Because one server could use up all of the licensed connections through pooling, users might not be able to access any of the other network servers. To prevent this from happening, an administrator can use the Licensing utility to remove from the license pool some of the licenses on each server.

Citrix License Activation

All licensed Citrix products require an activation code to function beyond the grace period. During the MetaFrame installation, you must enter the product serial number. Entering the serial number generates an eight-character machine code unique to the server. The combination of the serial number and the eight-character machine code is then used to obtain an activation code from Citrix. You can get the activation code from Citrix in three ways:

➤ *Citrix Activation Wizard*—This tool uses Internet or dial-up telephone access to Citrix to obtain the code.

➤ *By telephone*—The product documentation contains telephone numbers that you can call to obtain the code.

➤ *By fax*—The documentation also contains fax numbers you can use to obtain the activation code.

To activate a license using the Citrix Licensing utility, follow these steps:

1. Obtain the license activation code from Citrix.

2. Next, open the Licensing utility, select the license to activate, and then choose the Activate License option from the License menu.

3. Enter the activation code in the space provided, and then click on OK. To remove a license, highlight the license and then select Remove from the License menu.

ICA Client Update Configuration Tool

Citrix's Client Update feature enables ICA clients to be automatically updated when they log on to a MetaFrame server or server farm. When MetaFrame is first installed, a database is created to store DOS, Win16, and Win32 ICA client installation files. You use the Client Update tool to configure and manage the database as well as the client files. The Update tool is also used to add new versions of ICA clients to the database. After the updated clients are added, clients connecting to the MetaFrame server can have the appropriate client automatically downloaded to their local workstations. The server offers to upgrade the client if it detects that the client has an earlier version than the version in the server's client database. Administrators can also keep the older versions of the ICA clients in the client database. If there are any problems with updated clients, you can use the Update Configuration tool to enable an earlier (and less problematic) version of the ICA client.

By default, a client database is installed on each Citrix server. In server farms, a better alternative is to override the default choice and install the database to a network share. This approach is easier for the administrator, plus the updated clients are immediately available to all users. The client database is in the *%systemroot%*\ICA\ClientDB directory.

The Client Update tool contains the New Client Wizard, which you use to install new clients to the client database.

The Update tool can update clients only to newer versions of the same client; e.g., it cannot update an ICA Win16 client to the Win32 client.

During the client installation, the administrator is presented with several options. Users can be allowed to refuse the new client download. Users can also be forced to log off after the client download (this is required to complete the new client install). Finally, the administrator can set a limit on the maximum number of simultaneous client downloads.

Before installing a new ICA client to the client database, make sure you have downloaded and extracted files for the latest version of the desired client from the Citrix Web site. Although only DOS and Windows ICA clients are placed in the client database during the MetaFrame installation, administrators can subsequently install the other available ICA clients. Follow these steps to install a new ICA client to the client database:

1. Start the Client Update utility from the ICA Administrator toolbar on the MetaFrame server.

2. Select New from the Client menu and then click on Next.

3. Type the path to the previously downloaded and extracted client files, or use the Browse button to locate the files. Then, click on Next.

4. The New Client Wizard displays the client name and version number. Click on Next.

5. The Update Options window appears. It presents the following choices:

   ➤ *Client Download Mode options*—You can set the client files to download automatically and transparently; users can be notified before the files are downloaded, or users can be asked if they wish to refuse the download.

   ➤ *Version Checking options*—The choices here are to update only older client versions or to update any client version. The latter choice is useful if there were problems with the current installed clients and you wanted all users to use an earlier version of the client.

   ➤ *Force Disconnection*—This forces users to log off after the client download. The logoff (and subsequent logon) allows MetaFrame to complete the client update.

   ➤ *Allow Background Download*—This allows the client files to be downloaded in the background while users continue to work.

6. Clicking on Next on the Update Options screen brings up the Event Logging dialog box. The available options are to Log Downloaded Clients and Log Errors During Download. Click on Next to summon the Enable Client screen.

7. Check the Enabled option to activate the client. When you click on the Finish button, the client files are downloaded into the client update database.

ICA Client Creator Tool

You can access the Client Creator from the server console's ICA Administration toolbar or from Start|Programs|MetaFrame Tools. The Client Creator creates the ICA client diskette(s) used to install ICA clients on user workstations. To create the client install diskettes, click on the ICA Client Creator icon on the Administration toolbar, highlight the desired client in the dialog box, and click on OK to transfer the client files to the diskette(s). There is also a checkbox option for formatting the diskettes.

You can also copy the client installation files from the MetaFrame CD-ROM or from the *systemroot*\System32\Clients\ICA directory.

ICA Client Printer Configuration Tool

You use the Client Printer Configuration utility to view, connect, or disconnect any printers that were created on the MetaFrame server. As with session shadowing, you access the printer utility from within an ICA session rather than from the server console. (To open an ICA session from the server console, open PN and create a custom ICA connection. Then, click on the icon for the newly created ICA connection to start the ICA session).

You access the Printer Configuration tool from the Administrator toolbar or from Start|Programs|MetaFrame Tools. After the utility launches, it displays a dialog box that contains the available printers, along with their assigned ports. You can individually connect or disconnect the displayed printers using the dialog box's Printer menu or via the right-click pop-up menu.

Windows ICA clients can easily connect to client printers because the Windows Print Manager provides MetaFrame with the local printer information. Also, Windows clients use the *clientname#printername* naming convention, which allows multiple printers (with different printer names) to share a printer port. DOS and other non-Windows ICA clients must manually configure printers and print queues. You must specify a printer name and LPT or COM port and install the printer driver. Finally, non-Windows ICA clients use the *clientname#portname* naming convention, which means that only one printer can be assigned to a printer port.

Practice Questions

Question 1

> Which of the following statements best describes an ICA connection?
>
> ○ a. It requires use of the TCP/IP transport protocol.
>
> ○ b. It allows ICA asynchronous clients to access Remote Access Service (RAS) sessions.
>
> ○ c. It allows a connection to a Citrix server using one of four available idle sessions.
>
> ○ d. It is a virtual connection.

Answer d is correct. ICA connections are virtual, not physical connections. ICA connections can be configured for all standard network protocols, not just TCP/IP. Therefore, answer a is incorrect. ICA asynchronous connections cannot access RAS ports. Therefore, answer b is incorrect. There are only two idle sessions on a MetaFrame server. Therefore, answer c is incorrect.

Question 2

> How many listener ports are available on a MetaFrame server for each installed protocol?
>
> ○ a. One
>
> ○ b. Two
>
> ○ c. Four
>
> ○ d. Six

Answer a is correct. Each server has only two idle sessions to handle all connection requests, but there is one listener port for each installed protocol.

Question 3

> How much total memory is used by the available idle sessions on a MetaFrame server?
>
> ○ a. It depends on the number of installed network transport protocols.
>
> ○ b. It depends on whether non-Windows clients attach to the server.
>
> ○ c. 2MB.
>
> ○ d. It depends on the total user load on the network.

Answer c is correct. All client connection requests are passed from a protocol-specific listener port to one of the two idle sessions (when an idle session is used, another is created, so there are always two available idle sessions). Each of the two available idle sessions uses 1MB of memory. Answers a, b, and d are incorrect because the number of installed protocols, the existence of non-Windows clients, and the network user load are all unrelated to the amount of memory used by the idle sessions.

Question 4

> ICA connections can be created, managed, or reset using the Citrix Server Administration tool.
>
> ○ a. True
>
> ○ b. False

Answer b is correct. The Server Administration tool can be used to manage or reset ICA connections, but these connections can be created using the CCC utility only.

Question 5

> Citrix's Base License for WinFrame or MetaFrame includes how many client licenses?
>
> ○ a. 0
>
> ○ b. 5
>
> ○ c. 15
>
> ○ d. 25

Answer c is correct. The MetaFrame Base License includes 15 client licenses. Thus answers a, b, and d are incorrect (Note: Although the Base License automatically includes the 15 client licenses, buyers do have the option of buying more client licenses when they initially purchase the Base License).

Question 6

Which MetaFrame utility is used to add a Citrix server to a server farm?

○ a. CCC

○ b. Citrix Server Administration

○ c. PAM

○ d. PN

Answer c is correct. PAM is the tool used to join Citrix servers to Citrix server farms. You use CCC to create ICA connections. Therefore, answer a is incorrect. You use Server Administration to manage users, sessions, and connections. Therefore, answer b is incorrect. PN is a client-side tool used to provide clients with access to published applications. Therefore, answer d is incorrect.

Question 7

Which two statements are true about a MetaFrame server farm?

❏ a. After a server becomes a member of a server farm, it cannot be reconfigured as a non-server farm member.

❏ b. To set up a Citrix server farm, you must install the Load Balancing Option Pack.

❏ c. A server can be a member of only one server farm at a time.

❏ d. Servers configured as part of a workgroup can join a domain.

Answers a and c are correct. Answer a is correct because a Citrix server cannot be converted back to non-farm status. Answer c is correct because a Citrix server can only belong to one farm at a time. Load Balancing is not required to set up a server farm. Therefore, answer b is incorrect. There can be no trust relationship between a workgroup and a domain. Therefore, answer d is incorrect.

Question 8

> Most commonly, companies set up a separate server farm for each department.
>
> ○ a. True
>
> ○ b. False

Answer b is correct. Although separate server farms can be used, most companies prefer to use a single server farm to centralize and simplify network administration.

Question 9

> ZoomCo Inc. has two corporate locations, one in San Diego and the other in Houston. The two locations are separate domains, named SD and HU. The two networks are not connected, and employees have to share information by using email attachments or UPS Next Day service. The owners of ZoomCo Inc. have agreed that they need to share information and network resources, so they have established a WAN link between the San Diego and Houston offices. The goal is to allow all of the employees to share information from the company databases and other network resources. The San Diego office has 500 users, 1 PDC, 4 BDCs, 1 MetaFrame server farm, 6 print servers, and 1 SQL database. The Houston office has 400 users, 1 PDC, 3 BDCs, 1 MetaFrame server farm, 2 SQL databases, 4 print servers, 1 Exchange server, and 5 Web servers.
>
> Required result:
> Allow users in San Diego and Houston access to the hosted applications from both the San Diego and Houston server farms.
>
> Optional desired results:
> Load balance the hosted applications from both server farms.
>
> Allow users to be able to share data between the two networks.
>
> Proposed solution:
> Establish a two-way trust, where both domains trust each other.
>
> Which result does the proposed solution produce?
>
> ○ a. The solution meets all required and optional desired results.
>
> ○ b. The solution meets the required result but meets only one optional desired result.
>
> ○ c. The solution meets only the required result.
>
> ○ d. The solution does not meet the required result.

Answer d is correct. Without an ICA gateway established on each network, the server farms will not communicate and users in the two networks/domains will not be able to access the hosted applications in the remote domains. Since the solution does not meet the desired result, answers a, b, and c are incorrect.

Question 10

Darla, the network administrator for the non-profit Save the Marsupials Fund, wants to train four users on a new marketing application recently installed on the Save the Marsupials Fund's LAN. Darla would like to demonstrate the features of the new software but does not want to visit each user's workstation for the training. The Fund currently has a MetaFrame 1.8 server farm for its Marketing domain plus a smaller farm for its Accounting and Sales domain.

Required Result
Train the four users in the Marketing domain in the use of the new marketing application as quickly and efficiently as possible.

Optional Desired Result
While training the Marketing domain users, also train two users in the Accounting and Sales domain on the new program.

Use MetaFrame's audio feature to talk with the users during the training session.

Proposed Solution
Darla decides to use MetaFrame's session shadowing feature to help train the users. She plans to access the server's Shadow taskbar after starting an ICA session on the server. She also intends to activate the medium (64K) audio bandwidth option for the client connections.

Which results does the proposed solution produce?

- ○ a. The solution meets all required and optional desired results.
- ○ b. The solution meets the required result but meets only one optional desired result.
- ○ c. The solution meets only the required result.
- ○ d. The solution does not meet the required result.

Answer c is correct. Using the Shadow taskbar from within an ICA session allows Darla to shadow multiple sessions or to be shadowed by multiple sessions in a MetaFrame 1.8 environment. However, the optional result of training the users in the Accounting and Sales domain is not possible because sessions that run in different domains cannot be simultaneously shadowed. The optional result of using audio to communicate during the shadowing session is also not possible because audio cannot be used during a Citrix shadowing session.

Need to Know More?

 Search **www.thethin.net** for MetaFrame or CCA. This is a very good source for links to Citrix issues—including the CCA exam. Try the **http://thethin.net/links.cfm** link and look under the Training and Certification section.

 www.ccaheaven.com contains good Citrix- and CCA-related articles and links. It even has a short but useful CCA cram session.

 www.thinplanet.com is a good Web site for articles on Citrix and other thin-client vendors. This is one of the major Web sites for server-based and thin-client industry news.

 www.citrix.com/support/ has a great deal of information in the Solution Knowledge Base (KB). From the KB, select Additional KB Resources|Product Documentation|MetaFrame 1.8 for Windows NT Terminal Server. You are presented with the online MetaFrame 1.8 Administration Manual. Chapter 4 covers MetaFrame administration and the MetaFrame utilities.

Citrix Load Balancing

Terms you'll need to understand:

✓ Citrix Independent Computing Architecture (ICA) browser

✓ User Datagram Protocol (UDP) port 1604

✓ Browser election

✓ ICA gateway

✓ Transmission Control Protocol (TCP) port 1494

✓ Firewall

✓ Network Address Translation (NAT) services

✓ Public and private addresses

✓ Alternate Internet Protocol (IP) addresses

Techniques you'll need to master:

✓ Knowing the tabs used to configure load-balanced servers

✓ Understanding the ICA browser and the ICA browser election process

✓ Understanding the steps needed to configure an ICA gateway

✓ Knowing how to configure Citrix servers behind a firewall

This chapter explains Citrix Load Balancing in detail. As mentioned in Chapter 2, the Citrix Certified Administrator (CCA) exam has 10 unequally weighted sections, and because Load Balancing is one of Citrix's major enhancements to Terminal Server, this section of the exam has great importance. To succeed in the Citrix Load Balancing section, you need to know how to configure and manage a load-balanced server in a server farm. This requires a solid understanding of server farms and how to configure load-balanced servers within a farm, including the mechanics involved in Citrix Load Balancing. To completely understand Load Balancing, it is necessary to know the relationship among the different components that allow Citrix Load Balancing to operate. These components are the server farm, Independent Computing Architecture (ICA) browsers, and ICA gateways. This chapter is broken down into four sections. We begin with a detailed introduction to Citrix Load Balancing configuration and management. Then, we examine the Citrix ICA browser service, Citrix ICA gateways, and the use of load-balanced servers behind a firewall.

Load Balancing Overview

Load Balancing enhances MetaFrame manageability, scalability, and Web publishing capabilities. Along with Load Balancing, Citrix offers SecureICA, Resource Management Services (RMS), Installation Management Services (IMS), and NFuse. You use these optional products in large networks that contain multiple servers in server farms with hundreds or thousands of users. Load Balancing is an optional system service that requires licensing on a per-server basis and that automatically routes ICA clients to the least-busy server. You install the license using the Citrix Licensing utility; as with other Citrix licenses, you must activate it.

Citrix Load Balancing allows multiple WinFrame and MetaFrame servers to participate in a server farm's Load Balancing. Citrix Load Balancing is *not* considered a fault-tolerant solution. When a server crashes, it disconnects any connected users, and the users are not automatically reconnected. However, it is considered a high-availability solution because when users log back on to the network, they are routed to the least-busy server, which could be any server in the server farm. Load Balancing promotes network scalability because you can add additional servers whenever user demand increases. The following list highlights the main features of Citrix Load Balancing:

➤ Using the Published Application Manager (PAM) utility, you can publish applications across multiple servers in a server farm.

➤ You can take down a server in a load-balanced farm for routine maintenance and the published applications will still be available from a different load-balanced server.

➤ Citrix Load Balancing allows you to centrally manage load-balanced servers from one console.

➤ The Citrix Load Balancing service promotes high application availability. However, it is not considered a fault-tolerant solution.

➤ You can load balance WinFrame and MetaFrame servers across a local area network (LAN) or a wide area network (WAN).

It is important to mention that Load Balancing is not the same as a server farm. MetaFrame 1.8 server farms do not automatically offer Citrix load-balancing services unless there is an activated Load Balancing license on each server. Citrix's Load Balancing Services is sold separately from MetaFrame, and the license must be installed before the service is enabled. Also, keep in mind that Load Balancing works only with published applications; clients must select non-published applications using the Remote Application Manager (RAM). Here are the requirements to load balance applications:

➤ Each server in the server farm that will load balance hosted applications must have a Load Balancing Management licensed installed. You install this license using the Citrix Licensing utility, and you must activate the license.

➤ The application that will be load balanced must be installed on each server using the PAM. In a load-balanced server farm, you can select multiple servers within PAM via the Add The Application To Citrix Servers window (provided that the Load Balancing licenses are installed). The Edit Configuration button from the Add The Application To Citrix Servers window is where you specify the location of the application's executable file and working directory. Verify that the path to the executable file is entered correctly for each server (be especially careful if the server drives have been remapped to different drive letters).

The Load Balancing Process

Once the servers are licensed and the applications published, the master ICA browser collects the list of available servers as well as the information about the license and published applications from the member browsers (ICA browsers are explained in detail later in this chapter). A client can then request to access an application using Program Neighborhood (PN), RAM, or a hyperlink on a Web page. The client request causes the master ICA browser to calculate the load information that the member servers provide. This calculation determines which server is least busy and redirects the user to that server.

Before Citrix introduced Load Balancing, administrators had to manually balance server loads and users had to configure the connections to different servers by the name or Internet Protocol (IP) address of the server hosting the desired application.

Basic and Advanced Load Balancing Configurations

The Load Balancing utility comes preconfigured and is optimized for simple load-balanced server farms. Citrix recommends using the default settings and allowing the system to optimize itself. In most circumstances, the default configuration is adequate, especially for small networks with only a few Citrix servers. But as a server farm grows larger, the Load Balancing settings could require adjustment. You set the Load Balancing parameters on an individual server-by-server basis using the Load Balancing Administration tool, which you can access from the console of any load-balanced server in a server farm.

The Load Balancing Administration tool allows an administrator to view and fine-tune the Load Balancing settings on each server in the farm, providing the administrator has administrative rights on each load-balanced server. The settings allow you to adjust the various load calculations on the servers. The tool offers two configuration modes: Basic and Advanced. Both modes allow you to adjust the Load Balancing calculations to suit any network environment. You calculate the basic Load Balancing configuration using the User Load parameter, located on the Basic tab. You should use the Advanced tab settings in a network with Remote Desktop Protocol (RDP) clients because such clients are not included when you compute the number of concurrent connections on a server (the Basic tab's User Load parameter only measures the impact of the network's ICA clients).

Basic Tab

Once the Load Balancing Administration tool is running, select one of the load-balanced servers from the left panel of the display window. The right panel displays the tool's Basic tab, which you use to adjust the basic settings. Use the Quick Help feature for a detailed explanation of any Load Balancing parameter.

Note: To access the Quick Help feature, click on any of the parameters from the Basic or Advanced tab to receive an explanation of the selected Load Balancing parameter.

Using the default settings means that the User Load is the only relevant factor utilized when an ICA connection is routed to the least-busy server. To accept User Load as the criterion for determining server usage, move the slider bar to Very Important and click on apply. The User Load Is 100% At setting determines the ratio of the current number of logged-on users to the maximum number of users. The default setting for the maximum number of users is 10,000. User Load is the simplest method to configure load-balanced servers; try adjusting the User Load Is 100% At parameter to adjust the balance between your servers before turning to the Advanced tab.

The default User Load option is recommended for use in most small to medium-sized Citrix server farms. However, in more complex networks, you can configure the advanced Load Balancing parameters. Also, networks containing RDP clients should adjust server loads via the advanced settings.

Suppose you have two servers, A and B. You would like to direct more users to server B because it has more memory and dual processors. You can do this by adjusting the maximum number of users on server A to 11,000, whereas server B retains the factory setting of 10,000 maximum users. This configuration places a greater user load on server A, by approximately 10 percent. This makes server A appear as if it is busier than server B, redirecting more users to server B during the logon process. In general, Citrix recommends reducing the maximum number of users from the default 10,000 setting to the maximum number of users that will access the server. Figure 8.1 shows a screenshot of the default settings on the Basic tab.

Advanced Tab

The Advanced parameters allow you to take a more granular approach to administering Citrix Load Balancing. As discussed in Chapter 7, Advanced Load Balancing tab, shown in Figure 8.2, has six settings:

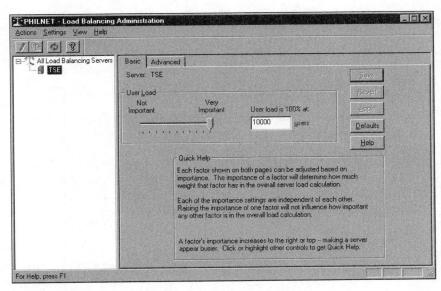

Figure 8.1   The Load Balancing window showing the default settings.

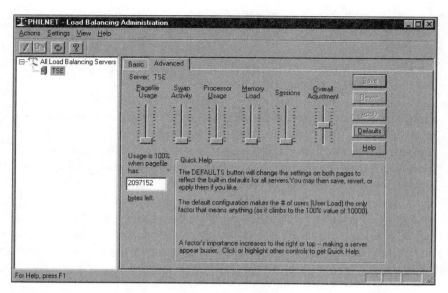

Figure 8.2   The Advanced tab of the Load Balancing utility window.

➤ *Pagefile Usage*—Is the current pagefile size as related to the allowed minimum free space in the pagefile. You use the Bytes Left field to set the minimum number of pagefile bytes that will be kept available even when the server indicates 100 percent utilization.

➤ *Swap Activity*—Sets how frequently the pagefile can be accessed.

➤ *Processor Usage*—Is computed as the percentage of time the processor is busy.

➤ *Memory Load*—Is the ratio of total RAM to available memory.

➤ *Sessions*—Is the ratio of the total number of configured ICA connections to the number of free ICA connections.

➤ *Overall Adjustment*—Adjusts the overall calculated load of a server. Unlike the other settings, the default setting for this slide bar is in the middle (i.e., 0). Lowering the slider bar below the default 0 setting causes the server to appear less busy. Raising the bar above 0 makes the server appear busier. If a server appears busier to the network master browser, network traffic is routed to a less-busy server.

To configure a server to not participate in Load Balancing, adjust Pagefile Usage, Swap Activity, Processor Usage, and Memory Load to 0. Set the Overall Adjustment setting to –10 on the server.

An explanation of the complex Advanced parameters is beyond the scope of this book. For the CCA exam, it is not necessary to understand these settings in detail. It is sufficient to be able to identify them.

Before you adjust the Advanced Load Balancing parameters, you must change the User Load setting on the Basic tab from the default Very Important setting to Not Important. All of the parameters on the Advanced tab are ignored when the User Load setting is at the default Very Important value. Also, keep in mind that each of the six Advanced tab settings are independent variables, and changing the value of one of the settings does not affect the others.

ICA Browser Service

Citrix's ICA Browser Service is an integral component of MetaFrame and WinFrame in any network. Every MetaFrame server runs the ICA Browser Service and is itself an ICA browser. The master ICA browser houses a database that contains information about the network servers, their applications, license information, and each server's Load Balancing settings. Without the ICA Browser Service, Citrix servers could not communicate information to other Citrix servers or ICA clients. The ICA Browser Service consists of a single master browser for each network protocol, backup ICA browsers (if there is more than one Citrix server), and the ICA clients. By default, all MetaFrame and WinFrame servers are member browsers that automatically update the master browser's database by sending server, application, and Load Balancing information to the master browser. The network ICA clients query the master browser for the connection information needed to access their applications.

Each network or subnet has one master browser for each installed protocol. An ICA client wishing to access a published application sends packets via User Datagram Protocol (UDP) port 1604 to the master browser to find out which Citrix servers are available. As clients query the master browser, the master browser examines its database and then directs the clients to the least-busy server. This routing of clients to the least-busy server is the core function of Citrix's Load Balancing services.

To determine which server will be the master browser for a given network protocol, Citrix uses an election process similar to the one used by the Windows NT's domain master election. An election is triggered in three ways:

➤ When an ICA client or a Citrix server does not receive a response after a query to the master browser, the client or server forces an election among all of the Citrix servers in the network to select a new master browser.

➤ If two master browsers exist on the same network/subnet, an election results.

➤ If any network Citrix server is either started or shut down, an election is triggered.

After failing to get a response from the master browser, an ICA client or browser broadcasts an election packet across the local network to start the election process. An ICA browser receiving the packet examines it to see if the browser that broadcast the packet has a higher ranking based on the master browser election criteria than the recipient browser. Here is the ranking order of the election criteria, where the first listed criterion is ranked the highest:

1. The ICA browser with the newest browser version number.

2. The ICA browser configured as the master browser in the Server Administration utility.

3. The ICA browser that is located on a domain controller.

4. The ICA browser that has been running for the longest time.

5. The ICA browser whose name ranks lowest in terms of alphabetical order.

Note: On a local network/subnet, there is a master browser for each available network protocol. Therefore, an election can be triggered for each active protocol.

During a browser election, if the recipient browser has a lower ranking than the broadcasting browser, it passes the election packet along to another server. If the browser receiving the packet has a higher ranking, it then broadcasts its own election packet. If no other network browser answers with higher election criteria, the browser is promoted to master browser. Conversely, if another browser answers with a higher ranking, it broadcasts an election packet to try to become the master browser.

Once a new master ICA browser is selected, all ICA browsers send update information about their applications and Load Balancing parameters to the new master browser. The latter then confirms receipt of the information. However, if an ICA browser does not receive a confirmation from the master browser, it forces another election. Conversely, when a browser stops responding to requests for updated information, the master browser drops the browser from its network browse list. This makes the browser unavailable to network clients and to the other browsers.

The qserver Command

To identify the master browser on a MetaFrame network, use the **qserver** command (short for **query server**; either form of the command can be used) from the command prompt. This command also provides the license and connection information of the network's Citrix servers. The command has several switches available for gathering information about the different network protocol connections, ICA gateways, installed licenses, and server farms. Table 8.1 lists the switches used with the **qserver** (or **query server**) command.

ICA Browser Tab

Unless an administrator chooses to manually tweak the Windows Registry settings, you configure ICA browsers using the ICA Browser tab in Citrix's Server Administration utility. The tab offers several configuration options, including Always Attempt To Become The Master ICA Browser, Do Not Attempt To Become The Master ICA Browser, and the No Preference options. Another available selection is the Master ICA Browser Refresh Interval, which controls how often the browser updates the master browser on its application and Load Balancing status. Shorter Refresh Intervals are recommended for load-balanced environments; for non-load-balanced networks, increase the delay time to save on processor overhead and reduce network congestion.

Table 8.1 The qserver command switches.	
Switch	**Function**
/TCP	Shows TCP/IP information
/IPX	Shows Internetwork Packet Exchange (IPX) information
/NETBIOS	Shows NetBIOS information
/TCPSERVER:x	Shows the TCP/IP default server address
/IPXSERVER:x	Shows the IPX default server address
/NETBIOSSERVER:x	Shows the NetBIOS default server address
/LICENSE	Shows user license information
/APP	Shows the names of the application and the server load
/GATEWAY	Shows gateway addresses
/SERIAL	Shows the serial numbers of the licenses
/DISC	Shows information about disconnected sessions
/SERVERFARM	Shows the names of the server farm and server load
/PING	Shows the ping-specified server
/COUNT:n	Specifies the number of times to ping (default: 5)
/SIZE:n	Specifies the size of ping buffers (default: 256 bytes)
/STATS	Shows the browser information of the specified server
/RESET	Resets the browser statistics of the specified server
/LOAD	Shows information about the load data of the specified server
/ADDR	Shows the address data of the specified server
/CONTINUE	Does not stop after each page of output

The ICA Browser tab also includes checkboxes that allow you to disable any of the installed network protocols (i.e., TCP/IP, IPX, and NetBIOS) on the server. After a protocol is disabled, network clients cannot connect to the server's applications using that protocol. The Hide From ICA Client's Server List checkbox allows network clients to view the server's applications but not the server itself. The Disable gateways checkbox allows ICA gateways to be disabled (ICA gateways are discussed later in this chapter). Figure 8.3 is a screenshot of the ICA Browser tab.

ICA Member Browsers

By definition, all Citrix servers are considered member ICA browsers, and each server is capable of being the master or backup ICA browser. Even a Citrix server with the Do Not Attempt To Become The Master ICA Browser option selected can become a master browser or backup ICA browser. Essentially, the function of member browsers is to send updated load and licensing information to the master browser.

The member browser's application information list describes which of its applications are managed and which are not (managed applications are published from a Citrix server farm scope; non-managed applications are published from an NT domain scope). Also, the server's Load Balancing settings are transmitted to the master browser. In addition to their current User Load status, the member browsers transmit their Pagefile Usage, Swap Activity, Processor Usage, Memory Load, Number Of Sessions, and Overall Adjustment settings. This information is then

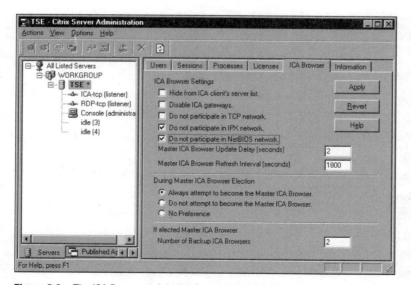

Figure 8.3 The ICA Browser tab in the Server Administration tool.

used by the master browser to generate a numeric index rating for all network browsers. The index is used to route ICA client connection requests to the least-busy network server.

Dedicated ICA Browsers

Citrix recommends using a dedicated master browser and dedicated backup browser(s). The use of dedicated browsers in larger server farms can substantially reduce network congestion caused by the ICA browser election process. In real-world environments, even relatively small networks can benefit by using a dedicated ICA master browser. An additional benefit of deploying a dedicated master browser is the reduction of the Citrix license management burden. You can pool and manage all client license Bump Packs on the master browser. Normally, when a Citrix server dies, you must reinstall the client Bump Packs on the replacement server. Also, if the dead server is offline for more than 48 hours, its client licenses will no longer be available until the server is repaired and the client licenses reinstalled. You can avoid these problems by installing the client license Bump Packs on the dedicated master browser.

After a MetaFrame server crashes, its pooled client licenses remain available to the network clients for only 48 hours.

Finally, configure the dedicated browsers to allow only administrators to access them. You can achieve this by setting the login permissions using the Citrix Connection Configuration (CCC) utility.

To set up a dedicated master ICA browser, follow these steps:

1. From the Server Administration utility, highlight the MetaFrame server that will be the network master ICA browser.

2. Access the ICA Browser tab and select the Always Attempt To Become The Master Browser option, and then exit the Server Administration tool.

3. From the command prompt, type, "qserver /election" to initiate an election to choose a new master browser.

4. From the command prompt, type, "qserver". Confirm that the server listing includes the letter M, which indicates that the server is now the master browser.

5. From the command prompt, type "qserver /update" to force the master browser to update its database.

6. The final step is to relaunch the Server Administration tool and configure it to prevent the other network servers from becoming the master browser. First, select a server in the left panel, and then click on the ICA Browser tab in the right panel of the Administration utility. Then, click on the Do Not Attempt To Become The Master ICA Browser button.

Repeat the procedure for the other Citrix servers in the local network.

ICA Gateways

As mentioned in Chapter 7, a server farm is a centralized management group that in most cases is located in a single domain. Grouping the servers in one physical location simplifies the management of the servers. When this is not the case, administrators can use Citrix's ICA gateway feature to allow ICA clients and servers in one network to be configured to communicate with servers located in a different network.

An ICA gateway uses a routable protocol (e.g., TCP/IP or IPX) to get a list of available servers, license information, and published applications from the master browsers of each network segment. As mentioned in the "ICA Browser Service" section earlier in this chapter, all Citrix servers are considered ICA browsers. The license and published applications information that is exchanged between the master ICA browser and the other Citrix servers is transmitted over the network using directed packets. To enable the master ICA browser to ICA browser communications, the master ICA browser must know the network address of every participating Citrix server. To have communication between separate networks, an ICA gateway must be established on the master browser located on each subnet or network. Without the ICA gateway, there is no communication among the MetaFrame servers located on different networks. Along with the need for an ICA gateway, the account and resource domains must have the appropriate trust relationship to allow the users to access the resources.

To establish an ICA gateway, a Citrix server on *each* network must have a configured ICA gateway. Once the gateway is established, the master ICA browsers on the separate networks can communicate and distribute ICA browser information across the configured gateway. Providing the proper trusts are configured and the proper routable protocols used, ICA clients on each network can access published applications across the gateway.

Citrix servers support allocating user count licenses either locally or from a license pool. As far as the CCA exam is concerned, MetaFrame licenses cannot be pooled across a gateway. Licenses from all servers within one subnet can be pooled, regardless of domain or server farm membership.

Here are some ICA gateway considerations:

➤ Licenses cannot be pooled across an ICA gateway. (This is true only for the test. MetaFrame servers that have a HotFix, Service Pack, or FR1 installed can pool licenses across gateways. The CCA exam is based on an out-of-the-box configured server without HotFixes or Service Packs, unless otherwise stated.)

➤ On a TCP/IP network, an ICA gateway uses the UDP protocol to send ICA browser information to other networks. This requires that routers or firewalls be configured to allow UDP traffic over port 1604.

➤ An ICA gateway increases network traffic. This is due to the communication between the ICA browsers over the LAN or WAN link.

➤ To send ICA browser traffic across an ICA gateway via the IPX protocol, a router must be configured to pass raw IPX packets. For networks using the TCP/IP protocol, routers must open UDP port 1604.

Once an ICA gateway is established, client-to-server communications take place over TCP port 1494 and UDP port 1604.

Creating an ICA Gateway

You create an ICA gateway using the Citrix Server Administration utility. If you want to access the ICA Gateways tab, the All Listed Servers object must be selected on the left pane. Select Add from the ICA Gateways tab and select a Citrix server from the local subnet. Then, select the type of gateway (TCP/IP or IPX) and enter the address of the server on the remote network. Because all Citrix servers are ICA browsers, any server on a network can be configured as an ICA gateway. Figure 8.4 shows the ICA Gateways tab.

When the CCA exam was created, ICA gateways were not bi-directional (this feature is available in the more recent MetaFrame upgrades). With a one-way gateway, if networks A and B wanted to communicate, each network would have to have a configured ICA gateway. Suppose that network A had a configured ICA gateway with network B, but network B did not have a gateway established with network A. In this case, users from network A would be able to access hosted application on network B, but network B users could not access hosted applications on network A.

To configure an ICA gateway, highlight the All Listed Servers option in the left pane of Citrix Server Administration utility, and then select the ICA Gateways tab in the right pane.

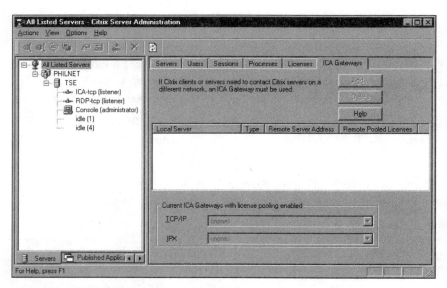

Figure 8.4 The ICA Gateways tab.

Accessing Citrix Servers behind a Firewall

A *firewall* is a router, computer, or other dedicated hardware or software solution that filters access to a network. All network traffic entering or leaving the corporate network must pass through the firewall. The firewall scrutinizes each message and blocks those that are not allowed. Along with filtering message blocks, a firewall normally provides Network Address Translation (NAT) services, which separate the outside or public network from the inside or private network (NAT is explained later in this chapter).Usually, a firewall's purpose is to keep unwanted hackers and disgruntled ex-employees out of the corporate network while still allowing employees network and Internet access. Firewalls can also be used as internal access control devices by allowing only approved employees within the organization to access the Internet. Many firewalls now contain features to control, authenticate, and secure users who want to access a company's internal data and hosted applications over the Internet.

To allow access to hosted applications on a Citrix server located behind a firewall, you must configure the firewall to pass ICA browser packets over UDP port 1604 and TCP packets over port 1494. ICA clients use UDP port 1604 to browse a Citrix network for available Citrix servers and published applications. The ICA client then uses TCP port 1494 to establish a connection to the Citrix server once the desired server or application has been found.

When an ICA client sends a connection request via TCP port 1494 to a Citrix server, the server returns the internal IP address of the master ICA browser to the client. At this point, the ICA client contacts the ICA master browser and receives a browse list or the IP address of an available Citrix server. Then, the client can connect to the desired server or application over the TCP port.

When you add a firewall to the network, you must configure the Citrix servers to send the external—not the internal—IP address of the Citrix server to ICA clients located outside the firewall. This is due to the NAT service, which separates the public IP addresses from the private IP addresses. By default, a Citrix server returns the internal IP address of a Citrix server to the ICA client. But, if the client tries to access the server using its internal IP address, the firewall ignores the request.

NAT Explained

To understand how ICA clients communicate with Citrix servers located behind firewalls, it necessary to have a general understanding of how NAT works (if you are familiar with NAT, you can skip to the next section). NAT is a method of connecting multiple computers to the Internet or any other IP network using one IP address. For any computer or Internet device to communicate with other devices on the Internet, it must be assigned a minimum of one TCP/IP network address. For example, when a user dials up an Internet Service Provider (ISP), the ISP assigns an IP number to the user's machine. Every time users dial their ISP, their machines are assigned a different IP address. The public servers on the Internet, along with routers and firewalls, are generally assigned static or fixed IP addresses.

NAT serves two main purposes:

➤ It provides security by hiding internal IP addresses.

➤ It allows an organization to use a large number of internal private IP addresses. Because the addresses are used internally only, there are no conflicts with IP addresses used by other companies and organizations.

In its simplest form, NAT is a service that runs on a router that connects two networks. NAT works by converting a range of IP addresses to a different IP address. The IP addresses to be converted are those assigned to the individual machines on an organization's internal network. As an ICA client tries to communicate with a Citrix server inside the network, NAT translates the public IP address to the private addresses. It does the opposite with traffic from the inside that travels out to the public network, translating the inside IP addresses to the fixed external IP address. This allows communication through the firewall. NAT is essentially a specialized type of IP routing. Table 8.2 lists some NAT terms you should be familiar with.

Table 8.2 NAT terms.	
Term	Explanation
Private address	The internal IP address that will be translated into the fixed IP address of the firewall. This is the IP address that was assigned to a client on the internal network.
Public address	The external IP address. This address is normally a valid Internet address.
Simple translation	A translation entry that maps one IP address to another.

Configuring Alternate IP Addresses on Citrix Servers

When a firewall is placed between the ICA client and the Citrix servers, you must configure the Citrix servers to send the external—not the internal—IP address of the Citrix server to ICA clients located on the public side of the firewall. When an ICA client sends a connection request via TCP port 1494 to a Citrix server, by default, the Citrix server returns the internal IP address (private address) of the master ICA browser to the client. When the client then tries to connect to the master browser using the internal address, the connection attempt fails. An alternate address is assigned to a Citrix server using the **ALTADDR** command from the command prompt. From the command prompt of the server that lies inside the firewall, type "altaddr /set *xx.xx.xx.x*". The *xx.xx.xx.x* should be the external or public address of your firewall.

With the proper alternate address configured on the Citrix server, the external ICA client can gain access to the Citrix servers via the assigned alternate address. The firewall translates the alternate address request from the ICA client into the internal IP address of the Citrix server.

Practice Questions

Question 1

> From the command prompt on a Citrix server, which is the correct command to set an alternate IP address?
>
> ○ a. **ALTADD /alt x.x.x.x**
>
> ○ b. **ALTADDR /set xx.xx.xx.x**
>
> ○ c. **NEWADD /set x.x.x.x**
>
> ○ d. **ADDADD /new x.x.x.x**

Answer b is correct. An alternate address is assigned to a Citrix server using the **ALTADDR** command from the command prompt. From the command prompt, type "altaddr /set *xx.xx.xx.x*". The *xx.xx.xx.x* should be the external or public address of your firewall. Answers a, c, and d are fictitious commands.

Question 2

> What two components are required on each Citrix server to use Citrix Load Balancing? [Check all correct answers]
>
> ❑ a. Published applications
>
> ❑ b. Citrix Load Balancing license
>
> ❑ c. Firewall
>
> ❑ d. ICA gateway
>
> ❑ e. Same applications

Answers b and e are correct. Each server in the server farm that will load balance hosted applications must have a Load Balancing Management licensed installed. The license is installed using the Citrix Licensing utility and must be activated. In addition, each server involved in Load Balancing should host the same applications. Thus, answer a is incorrect because it does not specify that the applications must be identical. Answers c and d are incorrect since firewalls and ICA gateways have nothing to do with load balancing.

Question 3

What are the Advanced Load Balancing parameters? [Check all correct answers]

❏ a. Processor Usage

❏ b. Sessions

❏ c. Pagefile Usage

❏ d. Memory Load

❏ e. Swap Activity

❏ f. Overall Adjustment

❏ g. All of the above

Answer g is correct. The Advanced Load Balancing tab has six settings that allow you to configure the Pagefile Usage, Swap Activity, Processor Usage, Memory Load, Sessions, and Overall Adjustment parameters.

Question 4

When an ICA client requests a connection to a Citrix server via TCP port 1494, by default, the Citrix server returns the external IP address of the master ICA browser to the client.

○ a. True

○ b. False

Answer b is correct. When an ICA client sends a connection request via TCP port 1494 to a Citrix server, by default, the Citrix server returns the internal IP address (private address) of the master ICA browser to the client. The external IP address can be mapped to multiple internal IP addresses by the NAT service located on a router.

Question 5

> Which port does an ICA client use to browse for Citrix services?
>
> ○ a. 1494
>
> ○ b. 1404
>
> ○ c. 1694
>
> ○ d. 1604

Answer d is correct. ICA clients use UDP port 1604 to browse a Citrix network for available Citrix servers and published applications. Answer a, 1494, is incorrect because it lists the TCP port used by the ICA client to establish a connection to the Citrix server that hosts the desired application (or other network resources). Answers b and c are incorrect because they are not related to the Citrix browser service.

Question 6

> Which Citrix utility is used to configure an ICA gateway?
>
> ○ a. CCC
>
> ○ b. Citrix Server Administration
>
> ○ c. PAM
>
> ○ d. Citrix Licensing Activation Wizard
>
> ○ e. ICA Gateway Manager

Answer b is correct. To access the ICA Gateway tab, you must select the All Listed Servers object on the left pane of the Server Administration utility. You use CCC to add, change, or delete client to server connections and manage connection security. Therefore, answer a is incorrect. You use PAM to publish and manage applications on MetaFrame servers. Therefore, answer c is incorrect. You use the Citrix Licensing Activation Wizard to activate Citrix licenses. Therefore, answer d is incorrect. The ICA Gateway Manager is not a Citrix tool. Therefore, answer e is incorrect.

Question 7

> Applications can be published across multiple servers in a load-balanced server farm using which utility?
>
> ○ a. CCC
>
> ○ b. Citrix Server Administration
>
> ○ c. PAM
>
> ○ d. PN

Answer c is correct. PAM is used to publish applications to server farms. You use the CCC utility to create or modify ICA connections and to configure connection security. Therefore, answer a is incorrect. You use the Server Administration tool to manage users, sessions, and connections. Therefore, answer b is incorrect. PN is a client-side tool used to provide clients with access to published applications. Therefore, answer d is incorrect.

Question 8

Which of the following correctly ranks the master browser election criteria?

○ a. The ICA browser with the newest browser version number.
The ICA browser configured as the master browser in the Server Administration utility.
The ICA browser that is located on a domain controller.
The ICA browser that has been running for the longest time.
The ICA browser whose server name ranks lowest in terms of alphabetical order.

○ b. The ICA browser configured as the master browser in the Server Administration utility.
The ICA browser with the newest browser version number.
The ICA browser that is located on a domain controller.
The ICA browser that has been running for the longest time.
The ICA browser whose server name ranks lowest in terms of alphabetical order.

○ c. The ICA browser that is located on a domain controller.
The ICA browser whose server name ranks lowest in terms of alphabetical order.
The ICA browser with the newest browser version number.
The ICA browser configured as the master browser in the Server Administration utility.
The ICA browser that has been running for the longest time.

○ d. The ICA browser that has been running for the longest time.
The ICA browser whose server name ranks lowest in terms of alphabetical order. The ICA browser with the newest browser version number.
The ICA browser configured as the master browser in the Server Administration utility.
The ICA browser that is located on a domain controller.

○ e. The ICA browser that is located on a domain controller.
The ICA browser that has been running for the longest time.
The ICA browser whose server name ranks lowest in terms of alphabetical order.
The ICA browser with the newest browser version number.
The ICA browser configured as the master browser in the Server Administration utility.

Answer a is correct as it correctly ranks the master browser election criteria. Answers b through e are incorrect as they list the election criteria in the wrong order.

Question 9

Your company, Allied Affiliates International, is in the process of acquiring a large competitor, which has a MetaFrame 1.8 network installed. Allied has four MetaFrame and two WinFrame servers. The company to be acquired has six MetaFrame servers and a dedicated SQL database server. Your boss has ordered you to do some research and find a product or strategy to minimize the problems involved in consolidating the two networks. All servers will be housed in one location and will be connected to Allied Affiliates' TCP/IP network. This scenario assumes that all of the usual Windows NT configuration issues are taken into account (i.e., join the new servers to the existing domain and add the new users to existing user groups).

Required Results:
Combine the two networks so that administration can be performed from one location (i.e., cut administrative overhead).

Provide application access to a larger user base while minimizing both user access problems and licensing costs.

Optional Desired Results:
Pool ICA client licenses across the network.

Provide fault tolerance.

Proposed Solution:
Install the optional Citrix Load Balancing product on the MetaFrame servers. Use the PAM utility to migrate the acquired company's MetaFrame servers to the Allied Affiliates server farm.

Which results does the proposed solution produce?

O a. The solution meets all required and optional desired results.

O b. The solution meets all required results but meets only one optional desired result.

O c. The solution meets only the required results.

O d. The solution does not meet the required results.

Answer b is correct. Citrix Load Balancing allows applications to be installed on multiple Citrix servers and made available to all network users. The applications can then be administered from one location. The first optional result of client license pooling is provided for in the proposed solution. However, the second optional result of providing fault tolerance is not available with Citrix MetaFrame. MetaFrame offers high availability but not fault tolerance (i.e., in the event of a server crash, users are routed to other servers but session data from the crashed sessions will be lost). The PAM tool does allow MetaFrame servers to be migrated from one Citrix server farm to another. However, re-member that once a Citrix server becomes a member of a server farm, you cannot convert it back to a standalone or member server.

Question 10

You are the network administrator for the Megahard Corporation. The com-pany has a MetaFrame network with 5 load-balanced servers, 1 specialized imaging server, and 100 32-bit Windows users. The MetaFrame 1.8 servers are a mix of old, slow computers and modern, dual Xenon units.

Required Result:
Direct more of the network traffic to your Citrix network's newer, faster servers.

Optional Desired Results:
Allow Citrix's license pooling to more efficiently dole out the existing client licenses.

Provide high-speed access to the imaging server for all users.

Proposed Solution:
Access the Load Balancing Administration tool's Basic tab. On the slower servers, lower the Overall Adjustment slider from the default 0 setting to a minus setting (e.g., –4 or –5). Configure high-speed user access to the imaging server in the Server Administration utility.

Which results does the proposed solution produce?

- ○   a. The solution meets all required and optional desired results.
- ○   b. The solution meets the required result but meets only one optional desired result.
- ○   c. The solution meets only the required result.
- ○   d. The solution does not meet the required result.

Answer b is correct. You can use the Load Balancing utility to adjust the apparent load on a Citrix server. For example, if you lower the Overall Adjustment slider to a negative number on the slower servers, the ICA master browser assigns them fewer user connections.

The first optional result is achieved since Citrix license pooling is enabled by de-fault (an administrator has to actively configure license pooling only if she wishes to withhold some of a server's client licenses from the network license pool).

You cannot achieve the second optional desired result of providing the ICA cli-ents high-speed access to the imaging server by using the Server Administration utility. You can provide high-speed access by using Citrix's VideoFrame software or via a DirectICA cable connection to the server.

Need to Know More?

Harwood, Ted. *Windows NT Terminal Server and Citrix MetaFrame.* New Riders Press, Indianapolis, IN, 1999. ISBN 1-56205-944-0. Chapter 20 briefly examines Citrix Load Balancing and application publishing.

Kaplan, Steve and Mark Mangus. *Citrix MetaFrame for Windows Terminal Services: The Official Guide.* Osborne/McGraw-Hill, Berkeley, CA, 2000. ISBN 0-07-212443-1. Chapter 15 discusses Citrix Load Balancing topics, including ICA browsers and ICA gateways.

www.citrix.com/products/lb/default.htm is a good site for reviewing the features of Citrix Load Balancing. Click on the License Pooling White Paper link for a good explanation of license pooling features and management. There is also a brief but informative discussion of ICA browsers and browser elections.

www.citrix.com/support is a good site to search for several types of Citrix technical support. Go to the Solution Knowledge Base, select MetaFrame 1.8 for Windows NT Terminal Server, and then select the MetaFrame 1.8 for Windows NT Terminal Server Administrator's Guide. Chapter 6, Advanced Topics, offers a good overview of Citrix Load Balancing. You can also click on the Solution Knowledge Base tab, type Load Balancing in the search box, and then click the Go button. Select the link for the article titled Load Balancing and ICA Gateways on MetaFrame 1.8 Explained. Other articles displayed on the same page cover related topics such as dedicated ICA master browsers and dedicated ICA backup browsers.

Configuring Web Connectivity

Terms you'll need to understand:

✓ Application Launching and Embedding (ALE)

✓ Launched application

✓ Embedded application

✓ Intranet

✓ Extranet

✓ Multipurpose Internet Mail Extensions (MIME) types

✓ ALE Wizard

✓ Independent Computing Architecture (ICA) file

✓ Hypertext Markup Language (HTML)

✓ HTML Wizard

Techniques you'll need to master:

✓ Understanding the difference between a launched and embedded application

✓ Knowing the Web computing components

✓ Understanding the steps needed to configure an ICA or HTML file

✓ Knowing the various Web clients and their installation methods

This chapter will prepare you for the "Configuring Web Connectivity" section of the Citrix Certified Administrator (CCA) exam. We begin with an overview of Citrix Web computing that includes an introduction to Citrix's Application Launching and Embedding (ALE) technology and to intranets and extranets. Next, we focus on the components of Citrix Web computing, including a brief explanation of Multipurpose Internet Mail Extensions (MIME) types, the creation and modification of Independent Computing Architecture (ICA) and Hypertext Markup Language (HTML) files, and an in-depth examination of Citrix's Web clients. Even though NFuse is now the preferred utility to allow access to published applications over the Internet, the CCA exam focuses 100 percent on the deployment of applications using the Published Application Manager (PAM), not NFuse.

Today, Citrix allows Application Service Providers (ASPs) and corporations to provide clients with a secure, single logon to applications hosted on MetaFrame servers. The applications can be accessed via a Web page on the Internet or private intranet. Before Citrix developed NFuse, PAM was the utility used to Web enable applications using Citrix's ALE technology. MetaFrame supports Web features that allow applications to be published and managed via PAM within a server farm from a single console. This provides corporations with a way to offer network services to employees or customers via the Internet or from a private corporate intranet. With PAM's ALE Wizard, an administrator can publish an application and then generate ICA and HTML files, which allow applications to be accessed via a hyperlink on a Web page. Once the ICA and HTML files are created and placed on a Web server, ICA Web clients can use a Web browser to access hosted applications that are embedded within a Web page or launched in a separate browser window.

ALE

Citrix's ALE technology is the foundation of Citrix Web computing. ALE allows you to access published applications on a MetaFrame server via an intranet/extranet/Internet Web page link; clicking on the link starts an ICA session with the MetaFrame server. The Citrix ICA Web clients support application launching (where the application runs in a separate window) with any Web browsers that support configurable MIME types (e.g., Internet Explorer (IE) and Netscape Navigator). If the application is published as an explicit rather than an anonymous application, the user receives a logon window. After a successful authentication, the user receives the requested application, just as with Program Neighborhood (PN).

ALE has provided corporations and the ASP industry with a way to provide local area network (LAN) services to their clients over an intranet, an extranet, or the

Internet. This allows any authorized user a way to access published applications and corporate data from a Web page. To gain access to applications and data, a user needs only an Internet connection, a Web browser, and the appropriate ICA Web client. Citrix offers three ICA Web clients: an ActiveX control, a Netscape plug-in, and a Java applet supported by either of the two Web browsers; these are discussed later in this chapter. Additional benefits of Citrix Web computing are the ability to offer services from custom and legacy corporate applications, rapid distribution of applications, and virtual LAN access for remote offices and employees.

Virtually any Windows-based Web browser that supports configurable MIME types—discussed later in this chapter—can launch applications via ALE. Microsoft's IE and Netscape's Navigator support the use of launched or embedded applications.

Launched vs. Embedded Applications

MetaFrame and WinFrame application servers allow published applications to be launched from, or embedded into, a Web page. Citrix's ALE enables standard Windows- and Java-based applications to be opened from an HTML Web page that users can access with a Web browser using an ICA Web client. Publishing applications using Citrix's ALE allows you to publish an off-the-shelf application without rewriting any of the application's source code. To the client, the published application looks and feels like it is running locally, even though it could be running on a MetaFrame server located at an ASP on the other side of the globe.

Launched Applications

When a user clicks on a hyperlink that is associated with a launched application, the application runs in a separate window on the client's local desktop (provided an ICA Web client is installed). The application can then be used as if it were running locally. You can maximize, minimize, and resize it just as you can a local application. If you want to close the Web browser window, the published application is not automatically closed and continues to run independent of the browser. You can even have multiple published applications running while browsing the Internet.

Application launching is an ideal way of offering applications remotely over the Internet. The ASP industry, along with most corporations, prefers application launching over application embedding because it allows you to run multiple applications from a single Web page. If you want to access a launched application, you must install an ICA Web client; the ICA client is not automatically installed by clicking on a hyperlink.

Embedded Applications

Unlike launched applications that run in separate windows, embedded applications run from within the Web page. Moreover, closing the Web browser window that contains an embedded application also closes the application. If a user chooses to load another Web page while using an embedded application, the user's connection to the ICA server and the embedded application is terminated. Also, the application is embedded in the browser window, so when you scroll or resize the browser window, the application moves along with it.

 With embedded applications, closing the Web browser window closes the application. By contrast, launched applications continue to run even if the browser is shut down.

Intranets and Extranets

Using ALE allows you to access published applications via a hyperlink from a Web page. The Web page can be located on the Internet or on a private intranet or extranet. It is important to understand the distinction between Internet, intranet, and extranet networks because ALE allows applications to be published over all three types. You can access intranet or extranet data using published applications, so administrators must understand the security risks involved with this form of application publishing.

Like the Internet, intranets are used to share information. An *intranet* is a private network protected behind a firewall that is based on Transmission Control Protocol/Internet Protocol (TCP/IP). An intranet site can look like any Internet Web site, but it is accessed from within a private corporate network. Corporations use intranets as a platform to share sensitive corporate data and to save time spent on routine communication tasks. For example, companies spend a great deal of time simply explaining company benefits to individual employees. Placing employee benefit information on an intranet site can greatly reduce the workload of the Human Resources department. The department can securely provide employees with forms and questionnaires via the intranet site (confidential data is protected by the intranet firewall). This type of network can rely on MetaFrame to supply the applications that allow access to the data.

When a private intranet is connected to the Internet, you get an *extranet*. A corporation can utilize an extranet as a business-to-business network based on the TCP/IP protocol. An extranet is created when two or more private intranets are connected together over the Internet. Once you establish an extranet, you can use it to share data and published applications among business partners.

Citrix, along with most security professionals, recommends that you not connect extranet sites to a production network. Networks accessible from the Internet risk unwanted intrusions. Therefore, it is advisable to keep the Web server on a separate network outside of the company firewall.

Citrix Web Computing Components

Citrix's ALE technology consists of four components: the Web server, the Citrix server, ICA and HTML files, and an ICA Web client. You must properly configure each of the four elements to offer published applications on the Internet or intranet.

The Citrix Web Computing Model differs from the Common Gateway Interface (CGI) or Microsoft Active Server Pages (ASP) approach, which requires that the Web server execute the CGI or ASP scripts on the server. The Citrix Model does not require the Web server to execute any scripts or run any additional software. With ALE, the Web server contains the ICA and HTML files that are downloaded to the Web browser to be processed by the ICA Web client. Except for the firewall configuration, Citrix Web Computing employs the same user configurations and security measures as those used by the standard published applications.

Note: The acronym ASP was originally used to describe Microsoft's Active Server Pages. Today, there is still occasional confusion between the Microsoft and the Application Service Provider definitions of the acronym.

Before we discuss the four Web computing components, let's briefly discuss MIME types.

MIME Types Explained

MIME is a specification for formatting non-ASCII (text) messages so they can be transported over the Internet. Each Web page on a Web server has a predefined content type that describes the type of data that is being sent to the Web browser. Web browsers use the predefined content type to interpret the file and then present it in the proper format (like HTML, GIF, JPG, and BMP) or as a Real Audio streaming video. These different MIME types have all become Internet standards. A MIME type is a pair of elements separated by a slash ("/"). The first element describes the *type* of data, the second element describes the file extension. Here are some examples of MIME types:

➤ application/x-ica

➤ text/html

➤ text/plain

➤ image/gif

➤ image/jpeg

➤ video/mpeg

➤ application/zip

➤ application/x-tar

➤ audio/basic

➤ audio/x-wav

➤ video/quicktime

With Citrix Web computing, both the Web server and the client's Web browser must support configurable MIME types. This enables the browser to display or output files that are not in the native HTML format. The Citrix ICA Web clients support application launching using any Web browser that allows configurable MIME types (e.g., IE and Netscape Navigator). ICA is a MIME type that you must register before the ICA file can function. If you use a file or MIME type that has not been configured, it will not be displayed.

Web Servers

You can configure a Web server to run on a Terminal Server Edition (TSE)/ MetaFrame server or on a dedicated standalone machine. The Web server is where the ICA and HTML files are stored and presented to the users. If you want to offer published applications from a Web server, the Web server software must support application MIME types. It is necessary to register ICA as an application MIME type to allow the ICA file to function. ICA files, described in more detail later in this chapter, are plain-text files that contain connection parameters needed to establish an ICA connection between the ICA client and a Citrix server. The ICA files are downloaded from the Web server to the client's Web browser. The ICA client then processes the ICA files, and a connection can be established. As mentioned earlier in this chapter, you create an ICA file using the ALE Wizard within PAM. The ICA files and the associated HTML files must be located together on the Web server.

Citrix Servers

The Citrix server runs the published applications that are presented via hyperlinks on a Web page. To a Citrix server, there is no difference between an ICA connection activated by a hyperlink or a connection established by the more traditional Citrix methods (e.g., PN). To publish applications over the Internet, you employ the same guidelines as those you use within a private network (e.g., applications can be published as explicit or anonymous). Unlike explicit authentications, anonymous logons do not require a user name and password. User accounts that require explicit authentication must be created with User Manager for Domains on a Primary Domain Controller (PDC) or Backup Domain Controller (BDC).

ICA and HTML Files

Both ICA and HTML files must be present on the Web server to establish an ICA session: The ICA and HTML files should be placed in the same directory on the Web server.

ICA Files

ICA files are plain-text files that you can create with the ALE Wizard in the PAM utility. They contain connection files containing a series of command tags needed to establish an ICA connection. The connection parameters in an ICA file include color depth, encryption level (provided you select anything other than Basic encryption), the IP address or NetBIOS name of the MetaFrame server, application information, the transport protocol, and the name of the published application. The ICA files are downloaded from the Web server to the client's Web browser. Then, the ICA client processes the ICA file, and a connection between the ICA client and the Citrix server is established. You can create ICA files using any text editor. However, for non-programmers, using PAM to create ICA files is the preferred method.

HTML Files

HTML is the major authoring language of the World Wide Web. Using HTML allows you to present text, pictures, sounds, and links on Web pages. HTML files are plain-text files that you can edit with virtually any text editor on any type of computer. The links on a Web page can point to ICA files, which define the ICA connection parameters. Once a Webmaster creates the default HTML file using PAM's ALE Wizard, he or she can edit the page, move the links, and edit the text and graphics. The ICA files, along with the associated HTML files, must be located together on the Web server.

The HTML Wizard offers two options for creating HTML files: simple or verbose. The simple page contains only the necessary HTML tags and the desired ICA link. In a verbose page, the text provides helpful hints about how you can customize the HTML file to suit your needs. You can modify the HTML files to include text and graphics along with additional ICA links. Later in this chapter, we will include some code listings to illustrate the differences.

Creating ICA and HTML Files Using PAM

The PAM is an important and versatile tool used mainly to publish and manage applications. But you can also use PAM to produce ICA and HTML files by using its ICA and HTML wizards. Once an application is published, you can use the wizards to create the ICA and HTML files. You access the wizards by highlighting the desired application and then accessing the Application menu, or by clicking on the ICA or HTML buttons from the toolbar and right-clicking on a published application. When the wizard is started, you are presented with the Choose Your Path window, shown in Figure 9.1. It asks you to how much assistance you require; you can select A Lot or Not Much Assistance. The difference is that the Not Much option has two windows and very little text, whereas the A Lot option has additional text and windows. In the following paragraphs, we describe a complete ICA file build using the A Lot option.

PAM is used to create the ICA and HTML files that allow Web clients to connect to a Citrix server.

The next window is the ICA File Window Size And Colors window, shown in Figure 9.2. This is where you select the window size (in pixels or percent of the application or desktop) and the color depth (ranging from 16 through 256 colors).

Note: The High Color and True Color options are available only on MetaFrame servers with Feature Release 1 (FR1) installed and licensed. FR1 is not covered in the CCA exam, so High Color and True Color are not valid options.

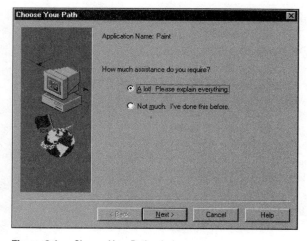

Figure 9.1 Choose Your Path window.

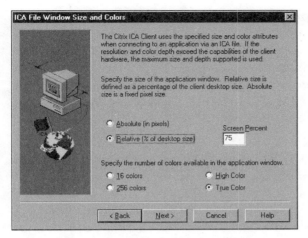

Figure 9.2   The ICA File Window Size And Colors window.

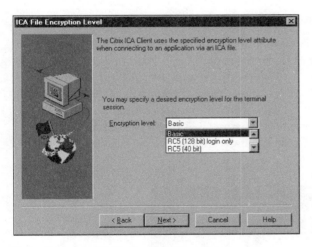

Figure 9.3   The ICA File Encryption Level window.

We next examine the ICA File Encryption Level window, shown in Figure 9.3. It allows you to choose between the Basic, RC5 128-bit login only, RC5 40-bit, RC5 56-bit, and RC5 128-bit encryption levels. The standard ICA client uses what Citrix calls Basic encryption. If you select any option other than Basic, you must install and license the SecureICA services on the MetaFrame server, and you must install an unlicensed component on the client workstations. With SecureICA, client-to-server connections cannot be established unless both the server- and client-side components are present. Clients must have encryption levels equal to or greater than that on the server connection the client accesses. If the server connection encryption is set to 56 bit, for instance, all clients must have 56-bit or higher encryption installed on the workstations. However, if a client has a higher encryption level configured than the server connection, the resulting connection supports the higher encryption level. As explained in Chapter 6, the SecureICA client is an optional upgrade that secures the traffic between a client and the Citrix server by using RC5 encryption. SecureICA is available in a North American version, which offers 40-, 56-, and 128-bit encryption levels, and in an international version, which offers 40-bit encryption.

The next window is the ICA File TCP/IP+HTTP Server Location window, shown in Figure 9.4. This is where you configure the location and port of your Citrix server. Most corporations and small businesses use firewalls that restrict broadcast and User Datagram Protocol (UDP) packet traffic across routers and gateways. When a firewall or router is present, you must configure TCP/IP+HTTP Server Location to be able to pass server and published application information across the firewall or router. In the TCP/IP+HTTP Server Location and port fields, you can enter the NetBIOS name or IP address of the Citrix server and the desired port number (the default is port 80).

Next is the ICA File Name window, shown in Figure 9.5. This is where you specify the path and file name for the new ICA file. You should include the .ica file extension after the file name. By default, the ICA files are saved in *%SystemRoot%*\System32. You can save the ICA file in the default folder or in any other desired location. Citrix suggests using file allocation table (FAT) file names of eight characters or fewer to name ICA files. You use FAT file names to accommodate legacy Web browsers and servers that do not handle long file names or file names with special characters and blanks.

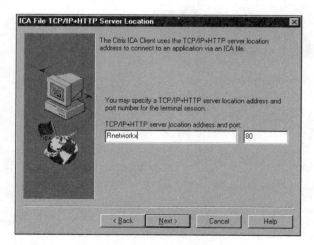

Figure 9.4   The ICA File TCP/IP+HTTP Server Location window.

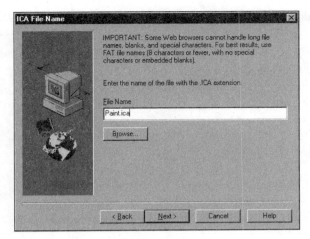

Figure 9.5　The ICA File Name window.

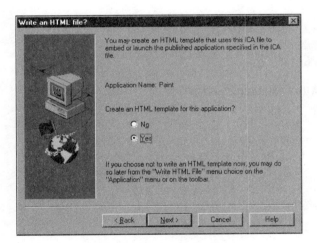

Figure 9.6　The Write an HTML file? window.

The final window is the Write An HTML File window, shown in Figure 9.6. If you wish to make an HTML file (you can also do this later), start the Write An HTML File Wizard and run through the entire process. Click on Finish to save the ICA file.

If you did not use the HTML Wizard in the Write An HTML File? window remember to run the HTML File Wizard later to create the HTML file that is needed to work with the ICA file. The wizard allows you to create HTML files for launched or embedded ICA sessions. Listing 9.1 shows the code created by the process of generating a typical ICA file.

Listing 9.1   ICA File code example.

```
[WFClient]
Version=2
HttpBrowserAddress=Rnetworkx
TcpBrowserAddress=10.65.1.0

[ApplicationServers]
Paint=

[Paint]
Address=Paint
InitialProgram=#Paint
DesiredHRES=640
DesiredVRES=480
DesiredColor=8
TransportDriver=TCP/IP
WinStationDriver=ICA 3.0
```

The ICA file shown in Listing 9.2 differs from the example shown in Listing 9.1 because it includes lines that specify 128-bit encryption. Note the addition of the encryption information including the SecureICA driver information.

Listing 9.2   ICA code with 128-bit encryption.

```
[WFClient]
Version=2
HttpBrowserAddress=Rnetworkx
TcpBrowserAddress=10.65.1.0

[ApplicationServers]
Paint=

[Paint]
Address=Paint
InitialProgram=#Paint
DesiredHRES=640
DesiredVRES=480
DesiredColor=2
TransportDriver=TCP/IP
WinStationDriver=ICA 3.0
EncryptionLevelSession=EncRC5-128

[EncRC5-128]
DriverNameWin32=PDC128N.DLL
DriverNameWin16=PDC128W.DLL
```

```
[Compress]
DriverName=PDCOMP.DLL
DriverNameWin16=PDCOMPW.DLL
DriverNameWin32=PDCOMPN.DLL
```

Listing 9.3 shows the HTML file that was created to be used in conjunction with the above ICA file with Basic encryption (a verbose page). Note the included ICA hyperlink, **<a href="Paint.ICA">Paint.ICA</a>**.

Listing 9.3   Sample HTML file.

```
<!DOCTYPE HTML PUBLIC "-//IETF//DTD HTML//EN">
<html>
<head>
<meta http-equiv="Content-Type" content="text/html;
 charset=iso-8859-1">
<meta name="METAMARKER" content="null">
<title>Demo Application Page</title>
</head>

<body bgcolor=#FFFFFF link=#CC0000 vlink=#660099
topmargin=0 leftmargin=0>
<table border=0 cellpadding=4 cellspacing=0>
<tr>
<td bgcolor="#FF9900" width=110> </td>
<!-- Delete this line to remove the orange band!! -->
<td valign=top bgcolor=#FFFFFF>


<a href="Paint.ICA">Paint.ICA</a></td>
</tr>
</table>
</td>
</tr>
</table>
</body>
</html>
```

The HTML file shown in Listing 9.4 is an example of a simple HTML file.

Listing 9.4   A sample of a simple HTML file.

```
<!DOCTYPE HTML PUBLIC "-//IETF//DTD HTML//EN">
<html>
<head>
<meta http-equiv="Content-Type" content="text/html;
 charset=iso-8859-1">
<meta name="METAMARKER" content="null">
<title>Demo Application Page</title>
```

```
</head>

<body>
<p><p>

<a href="paint.ica">paint.ica</a>

</body>
</html>
```

Web Clients

Citrix ICA Web clients support application launching with any Web browsers that support configurable MIME types, like IE and Netscape Navigator. Citrix has developed three ICA Web clients, which Microsoft's IE and Netscape's Communicator and Navigator browsers support:

➤ *ActiveX control*—Designed for Microsoft's IE versions 3.01 and later.

➤ *Netscape plug-in*—Designed for Netscape's Communicator and Navigator versions 3.0 and later.

➤ *Java applet*—A small program that is intended not to be run on its own, but rather to be embedded inside another application, in this case, a web browser.

Note: The Web clients support only TCP/IP connections.

Here are the minimum hardware requirements for Citrix ICA Web clients:

➤ 486 or higher processor CPU

➤ 8MB of RAM

➤ 2.5MB of free disk space

➤ Video VGA or SVGA adapter

➤ Network card or modem

➤ Mouse and keyboard

➤ An operating system that supports a Web browser

Both the IE and Netscape browsers display ICA sessions that are embedded in Web pages, but to use application launching, you must install the full client, wfica32.exe, on the client's workstation. The wfica32.exe client supports application launching with any Web browsers that support configurable MIME types. Both IE and Netscape support embedded applications in Web pages. When a user clicks on a hyperlink that contains the ICA connection information, the wfplug32.exe or wfplug16.exe runs on the client and processes the three files needed to run a published application: wfica32.exe, wfica.ocx, and wfica.inf. The wfica.ocx file is the ActiveX control file that will reside on the client workstation. Table 9.1 shows the Web browsers supported by the ICA Web clients.

Web servers pass the requested ICA file to wfica.ocx on IE clients or to npicax.dll on Navigator clients. The ICA file is then passed to the client's wficax.exe file to process. The wficax.exe file launches the application that the ICA file defines. When a user clicks on a hyperlink that is associated with an ICA file or loads an HTML page that contains an embedded application, the ICA files are downloaded to the Web browser and processed by the ICA Web client. Once the ICA session is established, only the keystrokes, mouse clicks, and updated screen images pass between the server and the client workstation.

In contrast to Citrix's 32-bit WindowsICA client (wfica32.exe), sometimes referred to as the *full client* or *PN client*, Web clients do not offer full functionality. Unlike full clients, Web clients do not support seamless windows or client LPT-port and COM-port mapping. LPT-port and COM-port mapping are available only within a session using the Win32 client.

 Citrix's Web clients do not support true seamless windows or client-side LPT and COM port mapping.

There are two Java clients that run in completely different modes: Application Mode and Applet Mode. For the Java client to run in Application Mode, the Java Virtual Machine (JVM) 1.1 or higher must be installed on the client device. As with the full ICA client, the Java Application Mode client is installed on (and remains on) the client machine. When running in Applet Mode, the client and the application execute completely on the server. The Java Applet Mode client is downloaded from the Web server each time an application is run. If you want to run in either of the Java modes, the Web browser must be Java Development Kit

Table 9.1	The supported ActiveX control and Netscape plug-in Web browsers.
Client	**Browser Versions**
ActiveX control	Microsoft IE 3.x, 4.x, and 5.x for Windows 9x, NT 4, and 2000
Netscape plug-in	Netscape Navigator 2.02, 3.x, 4.x, and 5.x for Windows 3.1, 9x, NT 4, and 2000, and for Macintosh; Netscape Communicator 4.x for Windows 3.1, 9x, NT 4, and 2000 and for Macintosh

(JDK) 1.1 compliant. Three Java class archive files are provided during the client installation. Without these files the Java client will not function. They are:

➤ jicaengm.cab

➤ jicaengj.jar

➤ jicaengn.jar

Installing ICA Windows Web Clients

You can install the ICA Windows Web clients either by remote installation or by diskette. Remote installation allows users with Internet or network connectivity to automatically download and install the ActiveX control Web client from a Web page on the Internet or an intranet. When a Web page with an embedded application is accessed, the Windows ActiveX Web client is automatically installed on the client machine (unlike with the Netscape plug-in, which you must install manually). Only Web browsers with configurable MIME types support remote installations.

A diskette installation allows users to use a preconfigured diskette to install the ICA Web client. The only requirements are that the client device have a floppy drive and that the Web browser support configurable MIME types. You must download and manually install the Netscape plug-in because no automatic installation is available.

Microsoft's IE ActiveX control is automatically installed when a Web page with an embedded application is accessed. However, the Netscape plug-in must be manually installed.

You install the ICA Java Web client running in Application Mode by running the setup.class executable on the client workstation. Unlike the other Web clients, the ICA Java Web client in Applet Mode is installed by running the setup.class executable on the JVM on the server rather than on the client.

The Java Web client that runs in Applet Mode is the only client that is not installed on the client machine.

Practice Questions

Question 1

What is the encryption level in the ICA file shown below?

```
[WFClient]
Version=2
HttpBrowserAddress=jerry
TcpBrowserAddress=10.65.1.0

[ApplicationServers]
NotePad=

[NotePad]
Address=NotePad
InitialProgram=#NotePad
DesiredHRES=640
DesiredVRES=480
DesiredColor=2
TransportDriver=TCP/IP
WinStationDriver=ICA 3.0
EncryptionLevelSession=EncRC5-0

[EncRC5-0]
DriverNameWin32=PDCON.DLL
DriverNameWin16=PDCOW.DLL

[Compress]
DriverName=PDCOMP.DLL
DriverNameWin16=PDCOMPW.DLL
DriverNameWin32=PDCOMPN.DLL
```

○ a. 40 bit

○ b. 56 bit

○ c. 128 bit

○ d. 128 bit logon only

○ e. Basic

Answer d is correct. The line of code **EncryptionLevelSession=EncRC5-0** indicates that the encryption level is set at 128-bit logon only. This encrypts the login with 128-bit encryption but will not use 128-bit encryption for the session data. The different code entries that specify the encryption levels are: **EncryptionLevelSession=EncRC5-40** (40 bit), **EncryptionLevelSession =EncRC5-56** (56 bit), and **EncryptionLevelSession=EncRC5-128** (128 bit). Therefore answers a, b, and c are incorrect. An ICA file with Basic encryption will not contain the **EncryptionLevelSession=EncRC5-0** line of code. Therefore, answer e is incorrect. Remember that when using any encryption level other than Basic, you must install and license the SecureICA services on the MetaFrame server. Also, you must install an unlicensed component on the client workstations.

Question 2

What is the main similarity between application launching and application embedding?

○ a. All Web browsers support them.

○ b. Applications are not available to Macintosh users.

○ c. They are supported only on a LAN network.

○ d. They allow ICA Web clients to access applications on the Internet or an intranet.

Answer d is correct. ICA Web clients can connect to Citrix servers via the Internet or an intranet. Only Web browsers that support configurable MIME types allow ALE. Therefore, answer a is incorrect. Macintosh Web clients do support ALE. Therefore, answer b is incorrect. ICA Web clients support both LAN and wide area network (WAN) connections. Therefore, answer c is incorrect.

Question 3

Which clients can access published applications via a hyperlink on a Web page? [Check all correct answers]

❑ a. ActiveX control

❑ b. Netscape plug-in

❑ c. Java applet

❑ d. wfica32.exe

❑ e. All of the above

Answer e is correct. Citrix offers three ICA Web clients: an ActiveX control, a Netscape plug-in, and a Java applet. The wfica32.exe client is the PN client and is capable of accessing published applications if you click on a hyperlink on a Web page.

Question 4

Which Web client can be installed automatically? [Check all correct answers]

❏ a. ActiveX control

❏ b. Netscape plug-in

❏ c. Java applet

❏ d. wfica32.exe

❏ e. All of the above

Answer a is correct. ActiveX controls are downloaded and installed on a client machine from a Web page on the Internet or an intranet without user intervention. When a Web page with an embedded application is accessed, the Windows ActiveX control Web client is automatically installed on the client machine. Only Web browsers with configurable MIME types support remote installations. Answers b, c, and d are incorrect as these clients must be installed manually. Answer e is incorrect because only one of the listed clients can be installed without user intervention.

Question 5

Jim has accessed an embedded application over the Internet. He is using the application to write his resume. On the Web site, along with the embedded application, are links to other helpful resume Web sites. Jim has not saved his work but would like to visit one of other resume sites for additional information. He wants to visit the other sites and then return to complete and save his resume. If Jim clicks on one of the links on the Web page containing the embedded application, will the ICA session to the application be terminated?

○ a. Yes, the session will be terminated.

○ b. No, he can return to the published application by using the Back button and resume his work.

○ c. No, as long as he returns to the published application promptly, the ICA session will still be available.

○ d. None of the above.

Answer a is correct. Unlike launched applications that run independently in separate windows, embedded applications run within a Web page. Also, unlike launched applications, embedded applications are terminated when the Web browser is shut down. Further, if a user chooses to load another Web page while running an embedded application, the user's connection to the ICA server (along with the embedded application) is terminated. Therefore, answers b and c are incorrect since the embedded application is terminated when the browser is closed. Answer d is wrong because answer a is correct.

Question 6

For a Web browser to support ALE, what must be configurable on the browser?

- ○ a. ALE
- ○ b. ASP
- ○ c. MCP
- ○ d. MIME
- ○ e. None of the above

Answer d is correct. With Citrix Web computing, both the Web server and the client's Web browser must support configurable MIME types. ALE is not configurable on a Web browser. Therefore, answer a is incorrect. ASP is not related to ALE browser support. Therefore, answer b is incorrect. MCP (Microsoft Certified Provider) is a Microsoft certification type and is thus not applicable to ALE and Web browsers. Therefore, answer c is incorrect.

Question 7

A launched application is characterized by which features? [Check all correct answers]

❑ a. Clicking on a link in a Web page opens a rectangular box that connects to a server.

❑ b. Clicking on a hyperlink launches a new, separate window that connects to a Citrix server.

❑ c. The published application is not a part of the Web page and runs in its own separate window.

❑ d. Closing the Web page does not affect the application.

❑ e. If the user scrolls the Web page, the application also scrolls.

❑ f. The application running in the separate window is closed when the Web page is closed.

Answers b, c, and d are correct. When a user clicks on a hyperlink that is associated with a launched application, the application runs in a separate window. If the user closes the Web browser window, the published application is not automatically closed and continues to run independent of the browser. Answers a, e, and f describe embedded applications that run within a Web page and are therefore incorrect. Unlike the behavior of a launched application, closing the Web browser window that contains an embedded application shuts down the application. Also, if a user chooses to load another Web page while using an embedded application, the connection is terminated. Finally, when the user scrolls the Web page it also scrolls the application.

Question 8

What two files are required on the Web server for a Citrix ICA Web client to make a connection with a Citrix server? [Check all correct answers]

❑ a. ICA file

❑ b. Java class file

❑ c. HTML file

❑ d. wfica.exe

Answers a and c are correct. Both ICA and HTML files are required to establish an ICA session. The ICA file is a plain-text file that can be created with the ALE Wizard in PAM. It is used to specify the ICA connection parameters. The ICA file contains connection parameters that contain a series of command tags needed to establish an ICA connection. HTML files are plain-text files that may contain the links that point to ICA files.

Question 9

The two HTML files shown below contain a hyperlink to the same ICA file.

```
<!DOCTYPE HTML PUBLIC "-//IETF//DTD HTML//EN">
<html>
<head>
<meta http-equiv="Content-Type" content="text/html;
 charset=iso-8859-1">
<meta name="METAMARKER" content="null">
<title>Demo Application Page</title>


</head>

<body bgcolor=#FFFFFF link=#CC0000 vlink=#660099
topmargin=0 leftmargin=0>
<table border=0 cellpadding=4 cellspacing=0>
<tr>
<td bgcolor="#FF9900" width=110> </td> <!
Delete this line to remove the orange band!! -->

<td valign=top bgcolor=#FFFFFF>
Click on the link below for the application you
specified to appear in its own window. You can
easily use this template for other applications.
The source for this page is well documented and
easily customizable.<p>

<a href="Paint.ICA">Paint.ICA</a></td>
     </tr>
   </table>
   </td>
 </tr>
```

(continued)

Question 9 *(continued)*

```
</table>
</body>
</html>
```

The HTML Wizard offers two options for creating HTML files: simple or verbose. The HTML file above is a verbose page, less 80 percent of the text. The text provides helpful hints about how you can customize the HTML file to suit your needs. The HTML file below is an example of a simple HTML file.

```
<!DOCTYPE HTML PUBLIC "-//IETF//DTD HTML//EN">
<html>
<head>
<meta http-equiv="Content-Type" content="text/html;
    charset=iso-8859-1">
<meta name="METAMARKER" content="null">
<title>Demo Application Page</title>


</head>

<body>
<p><p>

<a href="paint.ica"paint.ica</a>

</body>
</html>
```

○ a. True
○ b. False

Answer a is correct. Both HTML files contain the ICA hyperlink
<a href="paint.ica">paint.ica</a>.

Question 10

> You are the network administrator for XYZ Corporation. You work in the head-quarters office in New York, but the company also has branch offices in Toronto and Tokyo. There are separate NT 4 networks at each site. New York's MetaFrame 1.8 server farm currently supports 350 local Win32 ICA clients, although testing revealed that the server farm in New York could handle close to 600 concurrent users. Toronto and Tokyo have smaller user populations that run a mix of Win32 and Macintosh clients.
>
> Required Results:
> Run and maintain all applications on the New York MetaFrame server farm.
>
> Allow all users from each corporate location to access corporate data and applications over the Internet and work at LAN speed.
>
> Optional Desired Result:
> Allow remote clients to access applications via a Web page, on the Internet.
>
> Proposed Solution:
> Using User Manager for Domains at the New York network, create two glo-bal groups named Toronto and Tokyo and populate them with the Toronto and Tokyo users. Create ICA and HTML files using PAM and locate them on a Web server in the same directory.
>
> Which results does the proposed solution produce?
>
> ○ a. The solution meets all required and optional desired results.
>
> ○ b. The solution meets only the required result.
>
> ○ c. The solution does not meet the required result.

Answer a is correct. From the User Manager for Domains utility at the New York office, create two global groups named Toronto and Tokyo and populate them with the Toronto and Tokyo users to fulfill the required results. Creating the ICA and HTML files using PAM and locating them on a Web server in the same directory fulfills the optional desired result.

Need to Know More?

 Mathers, Todd. *Windows NT/2000 Thin Client Solutions: Implementing Terminal Services and Citrix MetaFrame.* New Riders Publishing, Indianapolis, IN, 2000. ISBN 1-57870-239-9. This is an excellent all-around thin-client reference. See Chapter 15, which discusses Web computing with MetaFrame.

 www.citrix.com/products/nfuse/default.asp is the main Citrix NFuse page. Although not covered on the CCA exam, NFuse is replacing Citrix's legacy ALE technology for publishing applications on intranets and the Internet. NFuse certification is now available, and Citrix has announced that prospective Citrix Certified Enterprise Administrator (CCEA) candidates can select NFuse as one of the four exams required for the CCEA certification.

 www.citrix.com/support is a good site to search for several types of Citrix technical support. Click on the Solution Knowledge Base tab. Next, type "Web client" in the search box and then click on Go. This displays approximately 10 pages of links covering all aspects of the Citrix Web clients, including installation, configuration, and troubleshooting.

 www.win2000mag.com is a good site for Citrix web connectivity issues. Search for ALE. The displayed May 1999 article, titled "ALE Distributes Applications," is an excellent piece that discusses application publishing (including the associated ICA and HTML files), Citrix Web clients, and Web server requirements.

Sample Test

Question 1

How would a MetaFrame administrator initiate the shadowing of three user sessions?

- ○ a. By clicking on the Shadow button in the CCC utility
- ○ b. By clicking on the Shadow button in the Server Administration tool
- ○ c. By clicking on the Shadow icon on the desktop taskbar/toolbar
- ○ d. By clicking on the Shadow icon in PN

Question 2

Which MetaFrame add-on improves network resource availability?

- ○ a. SecureICA
- ○ b. RMS
- ○ c. IMS
- ○ d. Load Balancing

Question 3

What are the correct minimum hardware requirements for a TSE server? [Check all correct answers]

- ❏ a. 32-bit *x*86 microprocessor (such as Intel Pentium or higher).
- ❏ b. Memory: 32MB of RAM, plus 4MB to 8MB for each typical connected user (8MB to 12MB for each power user).
- ❏ c. VGA or higher-resolution monitor with a maximum of 256 colors.
- ❏ d. 3.5-inch floppy.
- ❏ e. CD-ROM drive.
- ❏ f. NIC: an NT-compatible, 100MB network adapter is recommended.
- ❏ g. A network protocol, preferably TCP/IP.
- ❏ h. One or more hard disks, with a minimum of 128MB free hard disk space on the partition that will contain the Terminal Server system files. This is the absolute minimum space needed according to Microsoft, but a minimum of 300MB is recommended.

Question 4

What are two benefits of deploying Citrix's Load Balancing option in a MetaFrame network? [Check all correct answers]

- ❏ a. Promotes network scalability
- ❏ b. Provides fault tolerance
- ❏ c. Provides redundancy
- ❏ d. Improves network bandwidth

Question 5

Which is a component of the optional RMS?

- ○ a. Data Source
- ○ b. Disk Administrator
- ○ c. PAM
- ○ d. Client Resources Manager

Question 6

What are the three components that Citrix RMS provides for in-depth application and system management for WinFrame, MetaFrame, and TSE on Windows NT networks? [Check all correct answers]

❏ a. Data Collection Agent

❏ b. Data Analysis Tools

❏ c. ODBC database

❏ d. Data Collection Terminal

❏ e. Data storage device

Question 7

Which MetaFrame tools can you use to place published application icons on user desktops?

○ a. PAM

○ b. PN

○ c. Citrix Server Administration

○ d. ICA Client Update Configuration

Question 8

Seamless desktop integration means that the MetaFrame ICA client can do what? [Check all correct answers]

❏ a. Access local and network applications from desktop icons or from the Start menu

❏ b. Access local and network printers from the local File|Print menu

❏ c. Access the Internet and the company intranet without having to configure any network protocols or connections

❏ d. Access internal and external email from the desktop

Question 9

What is the maximum session encryption level of the international version of SecureICA?

○ a. 28 bit

○ b. 40 bit

○ c. 56 bit

○ d. 128 bit

Question 10

What NOS is included in WinFrame?

○ a. Sun Solaris

○ b. OS/2

○ c. Windows NT 4

○ d. Windows NT 3.51

Question 11

Citrix's add-on IMS product consists of three components. Which is not a component of IMS?

○ a. IMS Packager

○ b. IMS Application Publishing Enhancements

○ c. IMS Installer

○ d. IMS Synchronization Services

Question 12

Citrix's optional RMS works with which type of database software?

○ a. LDAP-compliant databases

○ b. ODBC-compliant databases

○ c. RMON-compliant databases

○ d. SNA-compliant databases

Question 13

With which database is Citrix's RMS not compatible?

○ a. Microsoft Access

○ b. Microsoft Excel

○ c. Microsoft SQL

○ d. Microsoft Exchange

Question 14

Which hardware component is not usually found on a network computer?

○ a. CPU

○ b. RAM

○ c. NIC

○ d. Video card

○ e. Hard drive

Question 15

Which network model is considered the least bandwidth intensive?

○ a. Traditional Network Model

○ b. Client/Server Computing Model

○ c. Network Computing Model

○ d. Server-Based Computing Model

Question 16

Which network model could be described as a mainframe model with a Windows interface?

○ a. Traditional Network Model

○ b. Client/Server Network Model

○ c. Network Computing Model

○ d. Server-Based Computing Model

Question 17

What is the minimum hard disk space needed for both a Terminal Server and MetaFrame installation?

❍ a. TSE requires 300MB; MetaFrame requires 32MB.

❍ b. TSE requires 300MB; MetaFrame requires 128MB.

❍ c. TSE requires 128MB; MetaFrame requires 128MB.

❍ d. TSE requires 128MB; MetaFrame requires 32MB.

Question 18

What must an anonymous user who wishes to log on to a MetaFrame server do?

❍ a. Use an explicit logon

❍ b. Have membership in a global domain

❍ c. Enter a username but not a password

❍ d. Log on to a non-PDC or BDC server

Question 19

Which utility is used to view the available system resources in a TSE/MetaFrame network?

❍ a. Citrix Server Administration

❍ b. CCC utility

❍ c. PN

❍ d. Windows NT Performance Monitor

Question 20

Which two license codes must be supplied to Citrix to activate the MetaFrame server license? [Check all correct answers]

❏ a. An 18-character serial number taken from the MetaFrame CD-ROM

❏ b. A 21-character serial number taken from the MetaFrame CD-ROM

❏ c. An 8-character machine code generated by the MetaFrame installation process

❏ d. An 11-character machine code generated by the MetaFrame installation process

Question 21

If the server drives are remapped during the MetaFrame installation, what is the default drive letter displayed for the first server drive?

○ a. C:

○ b. D:

○ c. M:

○ d. X:

Question 22

If the server drives are not remapped during the MetaFrame installation, what two drive letters will be assigned to the client's drives? [Check all correct answers]

❏ a. E:

❏ b. F:

❏ c. U:

❏ d. V:

Question 23

If Terminal Server is installed over an existing Windows 3.51; Windows NT 4; or WinFrame 1.6, 1.7, or 1.8 installation, what will be preserved?

○ a. All Windows 32-bit applications

○ b. All Windows 16-bit applications

○ c. All DOS applications

○ d. Local user database

Question 24

When you are installing Terminal Server, what size hard drive partition should you configure?

○ a. At least 1GB

○ b. 2GB or less

○ c. 4GB or less

○ d. At least 4GB

Question 25

During the Terminal Server installation, which option should you select for assigning an IP address to the server?

○ a. Allow the TSE connection utility to assign the IP address after the installation.

○ b. Allow the DHCP utility to assign the IP address after the installation.

○ c. Assign a static IP address after the installation.

○ d. Have the TSE Server Administration utility assign the IP address after the installation.

Question 26

Because of drive mapping issues, when should applications be installed on the MetaFrame server?

- ○ a. During the Terminal Server installation
- ○ b. Before the MetaFrame installation
- ○ c. During the MetaFrame installation
- ○ d. After the MetaFrame installation

Question 27

What types of modems are supported by MetaFrame?

- ○ a. MAPI
- ○ b. V.90
- ○ c. 56Flex
- ○ d. TAPI

Question 28

How many anonymous user accounts are automatically created during the MetaFrame installation?

- ○ a. 10
- ○ b. 15
- ○ c. 25
- ○ d. 30

Question 29

Which RAID level is recommended for a TSE/MetaFrame server's hard drives?

- ○ a. RAID 0
- ○ b. RAID 1
- ○ c. RAID 5

Question 30

Which two Terminal Server client licenses are required for a network with Windows 9x clients? [Check all correct answers]

❑ a. Windows NT CALs

❑ b. Windows NT Server Connection licenses

❑ c. Windows TSE CALs

❑ d. Windows NT Client Packs

Question 31

The Per Server client licensing option is recommended for TSE/MetaFrame servers.

○ a. True

○ b. False

Question 32

Which two NOSs does MetaFrame 1.8 support? [Check all correct answers]

❑ a. Windows NT 3.51

❑ b. Windows NT 4

❑ c. Sun Solaris

❑ d. Linux

Question 33

What is the normal grace period before you must activate your Citrix licenses?

○ a. 15 days

○ b. 30 days

○ c. 35 days

○ d. 45 days

Question 34

In a Windows NT network, what is an account domain?

- ○ a. A domain containing file and print servers
- ○ b. A domain containing users and groups
- ○ c. A domain dedicated to NT client licenses
- ○ d. A domain containing the Performance Monitor

Question 35

In a Windows NT trust relationship between two NT domains, what is the trusted domain?

- ○ a. The domain containing the PDC for the two domains
- ○ b. The domain containing the users and groups
- ○ c. The domain containing the file and print servers
- ○ d. The member domain that does not have a domain controller

Question 36

In a trust relationship between two Windows NT domains, which is the trusting domain?

- ○ a. The remote domain
- ○ b. The local domain
- ○ c. The domain containing authorized users
- ○ d. The domain containing network file servers

Question 37

MalCo Inc. has two corporate locations—San Jose and New York—each with separate domains and networks. The two domains are named SJ and NY. The two locations share corporate data by sending email attachments. Currently, users from each of the networks can access only local network resources. The need to share corporate data and hosted applications between the two offices has been recognized and the network administrators have been asked to join the two networks. A high-speed WAN link between the San Jose and New York offices is established, but the administrators still need to make the proper configurations on each side of the WAN link. The San Jose office has 952 users, 1 PDC, 4 BDCs, 1 MetaFrame server farm, 6 print servers, 3 Exchange servers, and 2 SQL database servers. The New York office has 670 users, 1 PDC, 3 BDCs, 1 MetaFrame server farm, 2 SQL database servers, 4 print servers, 1 Exchange server, and 5 Web servers.

Required Result
Allow the users in the San Jose and New York offices to access hosted applications from either server farm.

Optional Desired Results
Load balance the hosted applications.
Allow administrators to shadow sessions in both locations.

Proposed Solution
Establish a two-way trust, whereby both domains trust each other. Establish an ICA gateway at the SJ and NY server farms. Use the PAM utility to enable application access for all approved MalCo Inc. groups and individual users in each domain. Install the Load Balancing licenses on the servers with the desired load-balanced applications.

Which results does the proposed solution produce?

- ○ a. The solution meets all required and optional desired results.
- ○ b. The solution meets the required result but meets only one optional desired result.
- ○ c. The solution meets only the required result.
- ○ d. The solution does not meet the required result.

Question 38

Based on a user request, a Windows NT administrator changes a desktop setting in the user's profile. The user complains that the setting has not changed. What is the most likely source of the problem?

○ a. The administrator forgot to also change the user setting in the SAM database.

○ b. The user's access permissions were not adjusted to reflect the change.

○ c. The user's workstation has inadequate resources to implement the change.

○ d. The user did not log off the network.

Question 39

When a user logs on to a Windows NT domain, which of the following occurs first?

○ a. The user application set is launched.

○ b. The user activity log is launched.

○ c. The user profile is loaded.

○ d. The user policy is activated.

Question 40

After you log on to a Windows NT network, which of the following procedures is handled last?

○ a. The user profile is processed.

○ b. The user policy is processed.

○ c. The computer policy is processed.

○ d. The user log is updated.

Question 41

Which of the following is not included in a Windows NT domain?

○ a. Centralized administration of network resources

○ b. Single logon access to all domain resources

○ c. A database with user and group account information

○ d. Anonymous user accounts

Question 42

What can you use ICA PassThrough for?

○ a. Enable users to access servers on different networks or subnets

○ b. Allow Win16 clients to access published applications

○ c. Allow Macintosh clients to use the features available in PN

○ d. Allow DOS clients to access network printers

Question 43

When you are configuring a client audio connection for a remote client using a dialup connection, what level of bandwidth compression should be mapped?

○ a. 12Kbps

○ b. 16Kbps

○ c. 20Kbps

○ d. 25Kbps

Question 44

One of the users on your company's 100Mbps LAN needs to play high-quality music demos for clients. Assuming bandwidth consumption is not an issue, what bandwidth level would you map for the client's workstation?

○ a. 784Kbps

○ b. 1.1Mbps

○ c. 1.3Mbps

○ d. 1.5Mbps

Question 45

Your company CEO wants to deliver audio stock market updates to all LAN clients. As network administrator, you need to deliver voice-quality audio to all users, but you cannot afford to overburden the network. What quality of audio should you configure for the clients?

○ a. 28Kbps

○ b. 64Kbps

○ c. 128Kbps

○ d. 256Kbps

Question 46

Which procedure will allow network clients to utilize SecureICA when logging on to the server?

○ a. Install the SecureICA software on an available network share on the MetaFrame server(s).

○ b. Install the SecureICA software on the MetaFrame server and install the ICA client on all workstations.

○ c. Install the licensed SecureICA software pack on the MetaFrame server and install SecureICA on the client workstations.

○ d. Install SecureICA on all non-Windows ICA clients.

Question 47

You are the network administrator for XYZ Corporation. You work in the head-quarters office in New York, but the company also has branch offices in Toronto and Tokyo. There are separate NT 4 networks at each site. New York's MetaFrame 1.8 server farm currently supports 350 local Windows32 ICA clients, although testing revealed that the NY server farm could handle up to 600 concurrent users. Toronto and Tokyo have smaller user popula-tions running a mix of Win32 and Macintosh clients.

Required Results
Run and maintain all applications on the New York MetaFrame server farm. Allow all users from each corporate location to access corporate data and appli-cations over the Internet and work at LAN speed. Provide 128-bit security for the logon and session traffic between the ICA clients and MetaFrame servers.

Optional Desired Result
Allow remote clients to access applications via a Web page on the Internet.

Proposed Solution
Use User Manager for Domains at the NY network to create two global groups (named Toronto and Tokyo) and to populate the groups with the Toronto and Tokyo users. Install 128-bit SecureICA client software on all remote clients and configure the servers to allow 128-bit encryption. Cre-ate the ICA and HTML files using PAM and locate them on a Web server in the same directory.

Which results does the proposed solution produce?

○ a. The solution meets all required and optional desired results.

○ b. The solution meets only the required results.

○ c. The solution does not meet the required results.

Question 48

Your company has not yet purchased the SecureICA client pack to protect your network traffic. What level of encryption is used for the client-to-server connections?

○ a. 16 bit

○ b. 32 bit

○ c. 64 bit

○ d. Basic

Question 49

Which of the following methods can be used to install Win32 ICA clients?

○ a. CCC utility

○ b. From a network share

○ c. Citrix Server Administration utility

○ d. ICA Client Resources utility

Question 50

As network administrator, you need to install Win16 ICA clients on all work-stations. Which installation method would you use?

○ a. Install diskettes created by the ICA Client Creator utility.

○ b. Use the Win16/DOS Client Installation utility.

○ c. Use the Client Installation tool in the Server Administration utility.

○ d. Use the MetaFrame installation diskettes.

Question 51

When you are setting up a custom ICA connection, which of the following properties must be configured?

○ a. Description

○ b. Password

○ c. Bandwidth compression level

○ d. Client drive mappings

Question 52

You want to set up a custom ICA connection to run Win16 applications. Which property must you include to successfully create the connection?

○ a. User name

○ b. Amount of network bandwidth to allocate

○ c. Network protocol

○ d. Password

Question 53

You wish to configure some Unix ICA clients to access your MetaFrame server. Which network protocol can you use?

○ a. TCP/IP

○ b. ISDN

○ c. NetBIOS

○ d. IPX/SPX

Question 54

Which network protocols are supported when you are using DOS clients? [Check all correct answers]

❑ a. TCP/IP

❑ b. IPX/SPX

❑ c. NetBIOS

❑ d. DLL

Question 55

Microsoft's RDP client for Terminal Server works with which network protocol?

○ a. TCP/IP

○ b. NetBIOS

○ c. IPX/SPX

○ d. SNA

Question 56

Which hardware component is recommended for DirectICA environments?

○ a. High-speed DSL or T1 phone connection

○ b. Modem pool

○ c. MultiVGA adapter

○ d. Gigabit Ethernet cabling

Question 57

How many idle sessions are available on a MetaFrame server?

○ a. One

○ b. Two

○ c. Three

○ d. Four

Question 58

Which Citrix tool is used to manage ICA gateways?

○ a. CCC utility

○ b. Citrix Load Balancing Administration

○ c. PN

○ d. Citrix Router Configuration

○ e. None of the above

Question 59

Which Citrix tool can you use to manage ICA browsers?

○ a. Citrix Server Administration

○ b. CCC utility

○ c. PAM

○ d. PN

Question 60

Which task can be done using the Citrix Server Administration tool?

○ a. Set permissions on ICA connections

○ b. Connect/disconnect a user session

○ c. Set audio levels on user connections

○ d. Publish an application

Question 61

Which task can be done using the Citrix Server Administration tool?

○ a. Set up and configure session shadowing

○ b. Activate a MetaFrame server license

○ c. Publish custom applications

○ d. Display sessions and listener ports

Question 62

Which management task can be performed using the Citrix Server Administration tool?

○ a. Display domain information

○ b. Set up client clipboard mapping

○ c. Set audio quality on an ICA connection

○ d. Set user permissions

Question 63

Which does Citrix session shadowing support? [Check all correct answers]

❑ a. One administrator can shadow one user.

❑ b. One administrator can shadow multiple users.

❑ c. Multiple administrators can shadow one user.

Question 64

Which client cannot be shadowed on a Citrix network?

○ a. Win32 ICA

○ b. Win16 ICA

○ c. DOS ICA

○ d. Win32 RDP

Question 65

In which two ways can administrators shadow users? [Check all correct answers]

- ❏ a. Only in the domain they are currently logged onto
- ❏ b. Across domains
- ❏ c. Across domains and across subnets
- ❏ d. On both WinFrame and MetaFrame servers

Question 66

Which two statements are true about session shadowing in a MetaFrame network? [Check all correct answers]

- ❏ a. In the Citrix Server Administration utility, the Shadow button can be used to shadow one or multiple user sessions.
- ❏ b. Administrators can shadow only ICA and RDP clients.
- ❏ c. Audio is not available when you are shadowing user sessions.
- ❏ d. The server console cannot be used to shadow user sessions.

Question 67

In a MetaFrame network, which two people can start and end a shadowing session? [Check all correct answers]

- ❏ a. An authenticated network user
- ❏ b. A network administrator
- ❏ c. A user who has been assigned Special Access permission in the CCC utility
- ❏ d. A user who has been assigned Special Access permission in Terminal Server's User Manager for Domains utility

Question 68

Which statement is true about Citrix session shadowing?

- ○ a. The screen resolution and color settings of the shadowed session must be equal to or less than those of the session doing the shadowing.
- ○ b. The shadow button in Server Administration can be used to shadow one or multiple users.
- ○ c. Audio is available when you are shadowing.
- ○ d. Shadowing can be done from a console session or from an ICA session.

Question 69

Which of the following is a client cache setting?

- ○ a. Auto bandwidth
- ○ b. Inherit user config
- ○ c. Maximum size bitmap cache
- ○ d. Minimum size bitmap cache

Question 70

What is client clipboard mapping used for?

- ○ a. To copy documents between ICA clients
- ○ b. To enable the client clipboard
- ○ c. To allow ICA clients to copy local clipboard data to a printer
- ○ d. To allow ICA clients to copy data between the server and local applications

Question 71

What two actions must you take to allow MetaFrame users on different Citrix networks to share resources? [Check all correct answers]

❏ a. Set up an ICA gateway on each network.

❏ b. Set up ICA PassThrough on each network.

❏ c. Enable license pooling on the two networks.

❏ d. Set up the appropriate trust relationship between the two network domains.

Question 72

How many ICA master browsers are there in a WinFrame or MetaFrame network?

○ a. One

○ b. Two

○ c. One for each configured network protocol

○ d. Two for each configured network protocol

Question 73

In a MetaFrame network running TCP/IP, IPX, NetBIOS, and Citrix Load Balancing, how many ICA master browsers are available?

○ a. One

○ b. Two

○ c. Three

○ d. Four

Question 74

If a company network is split into two subnets, how many ICA master browsers are needed?

○ a. One

○ b. Two

○ c. One for each network protocol

○ d. One for each network protocol on each subnet

Question 75

What triggers a master browser election?

○ a. When there are no more client licenses available on the subnet

○ b. When a new Win32 ICA client is installed

○ c. When a MetaFrame server is restarted

○ d. When a Win32 ICA client is restarted

Question 76

Which two events cause a new ICA master browser to be elected? [Check all correct answers]

❏ a. There is no response when an ICA client queries the master browser.

❏ b. There is no response when a Citrix server queries the master browser.

❏ c. There is a different master browser on each network subnet.

❏ d. An ICA workstation crashes without logging off the network.

Question 77

What will happen if two ICA master browsers are detected in a subnet?

○ a. The master browser with the older version number will shut down.

○ b. The longest running master browser will shut down.

○ c. The master browser not running on a domain controller will shut down.

○ d. A master browser election occurs.

Question 78

If an ICA client or MetaFrame server forces an ICA master browser election, which of the following ICA browsers will become the new master browser?

○ a. The browser with the most recent version number

○ b. The browser that has been running the longest

○ c. The browser with the most resources

○ d. The browser most recently restarted

Question 79

What are the two functions of the ICA master browser? [Check all correct answers]

❏ a. Keep track of ICA servers

❏ b. Monitor ICA clients

❏ c. Track ICA server Load Balancing information

❏ d. Monitor ICA client bandwidth

Question 80

When a MetaFrame server crashes, what happens to its pooled client licenses?

○ a. The licenses are unavailable to the network until the server is brought back online.

○ b. The licenses are unavailable until the server is brought back online and the licenses are reactivated.

○ c. The licenses are still available for 48 hours after the server crashes.

○ d. The licenses are still available without restriction.

Question 81

A Citrix ICA gateway can work over which two network protocols? [Check all correct answers]

❏ a. TCP/IP

❏ b. IPX

❏ c. NetBIOS/NetBEUI

❏ d. 10bt

Question 82

Citrix ICA gateways are used to enable ICA clients to access resources on different networks/subnets. If two subnets with configured gateways each have 25 pooled client licenses available, how many licenses are available to each subnet?

○ a. 15

○ b. 25

○ c. 50

○ d. 75

Question 83

What does the Citrix Load Balancing option actually do?

○ a. Routes ICA clients to the least busy load-balanced server during logon only

○ b. Re-routes ICA clients to the least busy load-balanced server during the ICA session

○ c. Dynamically routes ICA and RDP clients to available servers after logon

○ d. Routes ICA and RDP clients to the least busy server based on the default User Load parameter

Question 84

Which statement describes the process that takes place within a load-balanced server farm when an ICA client connects with a published application?

○ a. An ICA client connects to an ICA browser, which then creates a numeric index from information provided from the ICA master browser. The ICA master browser then responds with the list of published applications. Once an application is requested, the ICA browser provides the client with the address of the least busy Citrix server. The ICA client then makes a connection with the proper Citrix server.

○ b. An ICA client sends a packet to the ICA master browser asking which applications are published. The ICA master browser then responds with the list of published applications and addresses of available Citrix servers. The client then connects with an available server.

○ c. The ICA master browser requests the numeric load and licensing data from the ICA member browsers. Then, an ICA client sends a packet to the ICA master browser asking which applications are published. The ICA master browser responds to the client's request and sends the address of the Citrix server to connect with. The ICA client then makes a connection with the proper Citrix server.

○ d. An ICA client sends a packet to the ICA master browser asking which applications are published. The ICA master browser creates a numeric index from information provided from the ICA member browsers, which allows the master browser to calculate which Citrix server is least busy. Once an application is requested, the ICA master browser provides the client with the address of the Citrix server to connect with. The ICA client then makes a connection with the proper Citrix server.

○ e. All of the above.

○ f. None of the above.

Question 85

Jim has accessed a launched application on a Web site over the Internet. He is using the application to write his résumé. On the page with the link to the application are additional links to other helpful résumé Web sites. Jim has not saved his work but would like to visit one of the other résumé Web sites for additional information and then return to complete and save his résumé. If Jim clicks on one of the links on the Web page with the ICA hyperlink, will the application session be terminated?

○ a. Yes, the session will be terminated.

○ b. No, he can return to the published application and resume his work by using the Back button.

○ c. No, as long as he returns to the published application promptly, the ICA session will still be available.

○ d. None of the above.

Question 86

Citrix offers products that enhance MetaFrame's manageability. These products are Load Balancing, IMS, SecureICA, and RMS. Which description is correct?

○ a. Load Balancing is a system service that routes ICA clients to the Citrix server that is least busy. It allows the Load Balancing of multiple WinFrame and MetaFrame servers into a single server farm. Load Balancing is not considered a fault tolerant solution because a server crash will disconnect any connected users.

○ b. IMS allows an administrator to install an application simultaneously onto servers in a load-balanced server farm. This tool is composed of three elements: the IMS Packager, which readies the application files for installation; the Application Publishing Enhancements, which load the prepared files onto the servers; and the Installer, which executes the installed files and represents the only licensed component. The IMS Packager component must be installed onto a dedicated computer; this is where the packages are created and distributed to a network file server.

○ c. SecureICA provides a high level of security for all traffic between the servers and clients. SecureICA services must be installed and licensed on the MetaFrame server, and an unlicensed component must be installed on the client workstation. SecureICA services use the RC5 encryption algorithm developed by RSA to encrypt the ICA session data.

(continued)

Question 86 *(continued)*

○ d. Citrix RMS provides in-depth application and system management for WinFrame, MetaFrame, and TSE on Windows NT networks. RMS is composed of three components: Data Collection Agent, Data Source, and Analysis Tools. The Data Collection Agent is installed on each monitored MetaFrame server and collects information on user access and application usage (note that Excel and text files are not compatible with RMS). The Data Collection Agent is the only component of RMS that must be licensed. The Data Source is any ODBC-compliant database. It can be a client/server database or a desktop database like Access. The Analysis Tools display the collected data to the user.

○ e. All of the above.

○ f. None of the above.

Question 87

Where are ICA gateways configured?

○ a. From the ICA Gateway tab in the PAM utility

○ b. From the ICA Gateway tab in the CCC utility

○ c. From the ICA Gateway tab in the Server Administration utility

○ d. From the ICA Gateway tab in the Load Balancing Administration utility

Question 88

Two Citrix servers on the same subnet pool their client licenses. If each server has 25 licenses and one server crashes, how many licenses are available to the network ICA clients?

○ a. 25

○ b. 50

○ c. 75

○ d. None

Question 89

A MetaFrame server is a member of a Citrix server farm. Which Citrix utility can be used to remove the server from the server farm?

◯ a. Server Administration

◯ b. CCC utility

◯ c. PAM

◯ d. None of the above

Question 90

What must be available on each Citrix server in a load-balanced server farm?

◯ a. Published applications

◯ b. The same applications

◯ c. The ICA Browser Services utility

◯ d. Multihomed network cards

Question 91

Why are dedicated ICA browsers useful?

◯ a. They provide redundancy.

◯ b. They reduce network congestion.

◯ c. They manage ICA client mapping.

◯ d. They reduce the user load burden.

Question 92

With what Citrix tool do you configure a dedicated ICA master browser?

◯ a. Server Administration

◯ b. PAM

◯ c. Load Balancing Administration

◯ d. ICA Browser Administration

Question 93

What feature is associated with application launching?

O a. Applications are accessed within a Web page.

O b. When a Web page is closed, the ICA session is terminated.

O c. Clicking on a rectangular box in a Web page connects to a
Citrix server.

O d. None of the above.

Question 94

What two files are required on the Web server for a Citrix ICA Web client to
make a connection with a Citrix server? [Check all correct answers]

❑ a. ICA file

❑ b. java.exe

❑ c. HTML file

❑ d. ica.exe

Question 95

What features are associated with embedded applications? [Check all correct answers]

❑ a. Applications are accessed within a Web page.

❑ b. When the Web page with the ICA hyperlink is closed, the ICA
session is not terminated.

❑ c. Clicking on a rectangular box connects to a server.

❑ d. When a Web page is closed, the ICA session is terminated.

Question 96

Which client is automatically installed if you visit a Web page with an embedded application?

○ a. ActiveX control

○ b. Netscape plug-in

○ c. Java applet

○ d. wfica32.exe

○ e. All of the above

Question 97

Which Web client must be installed manually? [Check all correct answers]

❏ a ActiveX control

❏ b. Netscape plug-in

❏ c. Java applet

❏ d. wfica32.exe

❏ e. All of the above

Question 98

What are the two types of Java clients? [Check all correct answers]

❏ a ActiveX control

❏ b. Netscape plug-in

❏ c. Apple Mode

❏ d. Published Mode

❏ e. None of the above

Question 99

Which feature is associated with application launching?

○ a. Applications are accessed within a Web page.

○ b. When the Web page with the ICA hyperlink is closed, the ICA session is not terminated.

○ c. It is supported on a LAN network exclusively.

○ d. When a Web page is closed, the ICA session is terminated.

Question 100

What ICA client supports seamless windows?

○ a. Win16

○ b. Win32

○ c. WinCE

○ d. Web clients

○ e. DOS16

○ f. DOS32

○ g. Unix client

○ h. Macintosh client

○ i. Java client

Question 101

Client audio mapping allows users to hear server-based audio broadcasts and WAV files on their local workstation speakers. This capability is supported only for DOS and Windows clients, and all workstations must be equipped with a Sound Blaster-compatible sound card. Also, audio is not available when shadowing user sessions. Because audio can consume a great deal of network bandwidth, Citrix provides three different audio quality options. What are Citrix's three audio quality options? [Check all correct answers]

❏ a. High—1.3Mbps. This level delivers very high audio quality, but it also uses the most network bandwidth.

❏ b. Medium—64Kbps. This is the default setting. It compresses the data stream to 64Kbps and represents the best choice for most networks.

❏ c. Low—16Kbps. A compressed data stream of 16Kbps is the logical choice for dialup connections.

❏ d. High—2.3Mbps. This level delivers very high audio quality, but it also uses the most network bandwidth.

❏ e. Low—12Kbps. A compressed data stream of 12Kbps is the logical choice for dialup connections.

❏ f. Medium—84Kbps. This is the default setting. It compresses the data stream to 84Kbps and represents the best choice for most networks.

Question 102

The Occam Razor Corporation recently installed MetaFrame 1.8 (the original version without a hotfix or FR1 update) on its Sales and Marketing networks. You are its system administrator. The two networks are on separate subnets/local networks. The Sales network comprises 50 licensed users and includes 4 servers, 1 dedicated MetaFrame server as an ICA master browser, 2 additional MetaFrame servers, and 1 Microsoft Exchange server. The Microsoft Office suite is installed on one of the Citrix servers. The company's Marketing network has 40 licensed users and includes 4 servers, 1 dedicated MetaFrame server acting as an ICA master browser, 2 additional MetaFrame servers, and 1 custom ODBC database application.

Required Result
Make the Office applications installed in the Sales network available to the users on the Marketing subnet.

Optional Desired Results
Pool the ICA client licenses so that the Marketing department clients can use their licenses when connecting to the Sales department server (i.e., the server where the Office applications are hosted).

Allow all Windows and DOS ICA clients to access the Office applications via Program Neighborhood.

Proposed Solution
Establish a trust relationship whereby the Marketing department domain is trusted by the Sales department domain. Configure an ICA gateway on an ICA server in the Marketing network so that the Marketing employees can access the Sales department server applications.

Which results does the proposed solution produce?

○ a. The solution meets all required and optional desired results.

○ b. The solution meets the required result but meets only one optional desired result.

○ c. The solution meets only the required result.

○ d. The solution does not meet the required result.

Answer Key

1. c
2. d
3. a, b, c, d, e, f, g, h
4. a, c
5. a
6. a, b, c
7. b
8. a, b
9. b
10. d
11. d
12. b
13. b
14. e
15. d
16. d
17. d
18. d
19. d
20. b, c

21. c
22. c, d
23. d
24. b
25. c
26. d
27. d
28. b
29. b
30. a, c
31. b
32. b, c
33. b
34. b
35. b
36. d
37. b
38. d
39. c
40. c
41. d

42. c
43. b
44. c
45. b
46. c
47. c
48. d
49. b
50. a
51. a
52. c
53. a
54. a, b, c
55. a
56. c
57. b
58. e
59. a
60. b
61. d
62. a

63. a, b, c
64. d
65. a, d
66. c, d
67. b, c
68. a
69. d
70. d
71. a, d
72. c
73. c
74. d
75. c
76. a, b
77. d
78. a
79. a, c
80. c
81. a, b
82. b
83. a

84. f
85. d
86. e
87. c
88. b
89. d
90. b
91. b
92. a
93. d
94. a, c
95. a, c, d
96. a
97. b, c, d
98. e
99. b
100. b
101. a, b, c
102. d

Question 1

Answer c is correct because the Shadow Taskbar tool allows several ICA sessions to be shadowed simultaneously. There is no Shadow button or icon in the Citrix Connection Configuration utility or Program Neighborhood (PN). Therefore, answers a and d are incorrect. The Shadow button in Server Administration allows you to shadow only one user session at a time. Therefore, answer b is incorrect.

Question 2

Answer d is correct. Citrix Load Balancing improves availability by distributing user connections between the load balanced Citrix servers. SecureICA encrypts network traffic to provide data security. Therefore, answer a is incorrect. Resource Management Services (RMS) is used for centralized network management. Therefore, answer b is incorrect. Installation Management Services (IMS) is used for installing applications in Citrix server farms. Therefore, answer c is incorrect.

Question 3

Answers a, b, c, d, e, f, g, and h are correct. As always, it is preferable to use components that exceed the suggested minimum specifications. Before starting the install, determine the manufacturer and model number of the Network Interface Card (NIC) and of the Small Computer System Interface (SCSI) drives and controllers to verify that the components are compatible with Terminal Server Edition (TSE). For a complete list of components that are compatible with TSE, see the Microsoft Hardware Compatibility List (HCL) for Windows NT 4.

Question 4

Answers a and c are correct. Load Balancing enhances network scalability as Citrix servers can be easily added to accommodate more ICA clients (Citrix's Load Balancing automatically distributes the client connections to the least busy load balanced server). Redundancy of available resources is enhanced because a disconnected user can immediately log on to another server. A server crash disconnects the user, causing the data from the session to be lost. Therefore, answer b is incorrect. Load Balancing has no direct effect on available bandwidth. Therefore, answer d is incorrect.

Question 5

Answer a is correct because Data Source is an RMS component. Disk Administrator, Published Application Manager (PAM), and Client Resources Manager are not part of Resource Management Services (RMS). Therefore, answers b, c, and d are incorrect.

Question 6

Answers a, b, and c are correct. Resource Management Services (RMS) is made up of three components: data collection, analysis, and data source tools. The Data Collection Agent is installed on each monitored MetaFrame server and collects information on user access and application usage (note that Excel and text files are not compatible with RMS). The Data Collection Agent is the only component of RMS that must be licensed. The data source is any open database connectivity (ODBC)-compliant database. It can be a client/server database or a desktop database like Microsoft Access. Even though you can run the Data Source locally on a MetaFrame server, it is not recommended due to resource utilization. You should run this component on a remote database server. You can install the analysis tools on any Windows 9x or NT machine on the network. It is the component that gets the data from the Data Source and then presents it to the administrator. The analysis tools offer detailed monitoring of applications, users, and fees and can display system snapshots and current system status. Unlike with the Data Collection Agent, Citrix does not require you to license the data analysis tools. Answers d and e are incorrect because they are not components of RMS.

Question 7

Answer b is correct. Program Neighborhood is used to place application icons on client desktops. You use the Published Application Manager (PAM) to publish applications to a MetaFrame server. Therefore, answer a is incorrect. You use Citrix Server Administration to manage users and connections (among other functions). Therefore, answer c is incorrect. You use ICA Client Update Configuration to load new versions of the Independent Computing Architecture (ICA) clients into the ICA client database. Therefore, answer d is incorrect.

Question 8

Answers a and b are correct. Seamless desktop integration refers to a network environment where users can access network applications and printers in the same way they access their local resources. Answer c is incorrect because the TCP protocol must be configured to allow for Internet access. Answer d is incorrect because internal versus external email access is not a seamless integration issue.

Question 9

Answer b is correct. The maximum international encryption level is 40-bit. Answer a is incorrect because 28-bit encryption is less than the available 40-bit encryption. Answer c is incorrect because 56-bit encryption is not available with the international version of SecureICA. The North American version of SecureICA provides up to 128-bit session encryption to secure network traffic. Therefore, answer d is incorrect.

Question 10

Answer d is correct. Windows NT 3.51 is included with WinFrame. Answers a, b, and c are incorrect because the listed NOSs are not used with WinFrame.

Question 11

Answer d is correct. The IMS Synchronization Services do not exist. The Installation Management Services (IMS) Packager readies the application files for installation. Therefore, answer a is incorrect. IMS Application Publishing Enhancements loads the prepared files onto the servers. Therefore, answer b is incorrect. The IMS Installer executes the installation process. Therefore, answer c is incorrect.

Question 12

Answer b is correct. RMS works only with ODBC database products. Lightweight Directory Access Protocol (LDAP), remote monitoring (RMON), and Systems Network Architecture (SNA) are not database products. Therefore, answers a, c, and d are incorrect.

Question 13

Answer b is correct. Resource Management Services (RMS) is not compliant with Excel or text files. RMS is compatible with Access, SQL, and Exchange. Therefore, answers a, c, and d are incorrect.

Question 14

Answer e is correct. The terminals do not need hard drives because the data and applications are normally stored on the network server. Network terminals running Java have a CPU, memory, Network Interface Card (NIC), and video card. Therefore, answers a, b, c, and d are incorrect.

Question 15

Answer d is correct. The server-based models—Windows NT Terminal Server Edition (TSE), Citrix WinFrame, and MetaFrame—exchange only keystrokes, mouse movements, and screen refreshes between the servers and clients. With the Citrix products, this requires only 10K to 20K of local area network (LAN) or wide area network (WAN) bandwidth. The Traditional, Client/Server, and Network Computing Models, on the other hand, all generate substantial amounts of network traffic between the clients and servers. Therefore, answers a, b, and c are incorrect.

Question 16

Answer d is correct. Mainframe networks, like server-based Citrix or Terminal Server Edition (TSE) networks, handle all of the processing and data storage on the server rather than on the user terminals. But unlike server-based networks, mainframe networks do not offer network clients the familiar Windows applications and user interface. Answers a, b, and c are incorrect because the traditional, client/server and network computing models (unlike the mainframe paradigm) are not server-based models.

Question 17

Answer d is correct. Terminal Server Edition (TSE) needs at least 128MB and MetaFrame requires at least 32MB for the installation. Keep in mind that these are the absolute minimum requirements. Answers a, b, and c are incorrect because the hard disk minimums they cite are wrong.

Question 18

Answer d is correct. Anonymous users cannot log on to an NT domain controller. Answers a and c are incorrect because Explicit access requires a username and password. Answer b is incorrect because anonymous users must log on using a local guest account rather than an NT domain account.

Question 19

Answer d is correct. The Performance Monitor is used to monitor system resources on the network servers. You use Citrix Server Administration, the Citrix Connection Configuration (CCC) utility, and Program Neighborhood (PN) for administering MetaFrame-specific features. Therefore, answers a, b, and c are incorrect.

Question 20

Answers b and c are correct. After you enter the 21-character serial number during the MetaFrame installation, an 8-character machine code is generated. To activate the license, you must submit this combined character string to Citrix via phone, fax, or the Internet. Answers a and d are wrong as they cite incorrect procedures to use for licensing Citrix products.

Question 21

Answer c is correct. Although answers a, b, and d are legitimate server drive letters, the question asked for the default drive letter displayed when remapping the server drives.

Question 22

Answers c and d are correct. If the server drives are not remapped, the server uses the C:, D:, and so on drive letters. The client drives are labeled U:, V:, and so on. Answers a and b are incorrect because E: and F: are not assigned to the client drives if you do not remap the server drives.

Question 23

Answer d is correct. The user database is preserved. Answers a, b, and c are incorrect because all applications must be re-installed after the TSE installation.

Question 24

Answer b is correct. The hard drive partition should be 2GB or less. Answer a is incorrect because there is no minimum size for the partition. Answers c and d are incorrect because the Terminal Server installation will fail if the hard drive partition is larger than 2GB.

Question 25

Answer c is correct. Terminal Server always uses a fixed or static Internet Protocol (IP) address. Answers a, b, and d are incorrect because they allow the IP address to be dynamically assigned (rather than statically configured by an administrator).

Question 26

Answer d is correct. If an application is installed before any server drive remapping, the path to the application's working directory could be incorrect. (If the server drives are remapped from C:, D:, and so on to M:, N:, and so on and an application was previously installed to the server's C: drive, the application will not function.) Therefore, answers a, b, and c are incorrect because they suggest installing applications before or during the TSE or MetaFrame installations.

Question 27

Answer d is correct. MetaFrame is compatible with TAPI-compliant modems. Answer a is incorrect because MAPI is an email interface. Answers b and c are incorrect, although V.90 and 56Flex modem types can be used if they are TAPI compliant.

Question 28

Answer b is correct. Fifteen client licenses are included with the MetaFrame server license. Answers a, c, and d are therefore incorrect. However, more client licenses can be optionally purchased when you purchase MetaFrame.

Question 29

Answer b is correct. RAID 1, also referred to as mirroring, helps prevent the Disk Queue Length counter value in Performance Monitor from exceeding the desired value of 1.5 to 2 times the number of hard disk spindles. RAID 0 provides the best performance but no protection from data loss. Therefore, answer a is incorrect. RAID 5 protects against data loss but can give a high reading for the Disk Queue Length counter. Therefore, answer c is incorrect. (Note: In a real world network environment, data is often stored on separate file servers that can use RAID 1 or RAID 5 disk arrays. For the CCA exam, remember that a Disk Queue Length counter reading of 2.0 or higher indicates that the disk system of the TSE machine should be replaced.)

Question 30

Answers a and c are correct. Microsoft argues that because Terminal Server delivers a virtual NT desktop to clients, all non-NT desktop clients (like Windows 9x and DOS) must buy the Terminal Server Client Access Licenses (CALs) as well as the regular NT client licenses. Answers b and d are fictitious license options.

Question 31

Answer b is correct. The Per Seat option should be selected for all Terminal Server installations. This option allows clients to log on to multiple servers; with Per Server licensing, clients can log on to the licensed server only.

Question 32

Answers b and c are correct. Windows NT 4 and Solaris are both supported by MetaFrame 1.8. WinFrame includes NT 3.51. Therefore, answer a is incorrect. Linux is not yet supported (although there are persistent rumors that Citrix will support Linux in a future release of MetaFrame). Therefore, answer d is incorrect.

Question 33

Answer b is correct. If a license is not activated within the grace period, the software will stop working. (Thirty days is the correct answer for the CCA exam. In reality, Citrix normally allows 35 days before the software shuts down.) Answers a, b, and d are incorrect because they all cite the wrong grace period.

Question 34

Answer b is correct. When you set up a trust relationship between two NT domains, an account domain containing users and groups must be trusted by the resource domain whose files, printers, and other resources the users want to access. Answer a is incorrect because it describes a resource domain. Answer c is incorrect because it implies that the function of the account domain is to store NT licenses. Answer d is incorrect because the Performance Monitor tool is not "contained by" any NT domain.

Question 35

Answer b is correct. Microsoft defines a trusted domain as a domain containing the ("trusted") users and groups. Both of the domains will have their own Primary Domain Controller (PDC). Therefore, answer a is incorrect. The domain housing network resources (e.g., file and print servers) is known as the trusting domain. Therefore, answer c is incorrect. All NT domains have a domain controller. Therefore, answer d is incorrect.

Question 36

Answer d is correct. The trusting domain contains network resources. The trusting domain can be either local or remote. Therefore, answers a and b are incorrect. The domain containing the authorized users is called the trusted domain. Therefore, answer c is incorrect.

Question 37

Answer b is correct. After a two-way trust is established and an Independent Computing Architecture (ICA) gateway is set up at both locations, communication between the two server farms and the sharing of resources is enabled. The 32-bit Windows clients can then access the hosted applications using Published Application Manager (PAM) (the other ICA clients can use the Remote Application Manager—RAM—tool to access the published applications). The optional result of Load Balancing the published applications is achieved by installing the licenses on the Citrix servers. The second optional desired result of allowing administrators to shadow users in both locations is not possible because clients cannot be shadowed across domains.

Question 38

Answer d is correct. Users must log off then log back on to an NT network before any profile or policy changes can take effect. The user's security settings should not have to be changed. Therefore, answers a and b are incorrect. The question asks for the most likely source of the problem. If a change was made to the user's desktop that was beyond the capabilities of her workstation, this *could* be the source of the problem. However, the most likely source of the problem is contained in answer d. Therefore, answer c is incorrect.

Question 39

Answer c is correct. The user profile is activated before any of the options listed in answers a, b, and d. An application set is the set of published applications in a Citrix server farm. The application set programs can be made available to Independent Computing Architecture (ICA) clients after logon via the Program Neighborhood (PN) window, the Start menu, or from a desktop icon. Therefore, answer a is incorrect. There is no user activity log. Therefore, answer b is incorrect. The user policy is loaded after the user profile. Therefore, answer d is incorrect.

Question 40

Answer c is correct. The computer policy is enforced after the user profile and policy. Because the user profiles and policies are activated before the computer policy is applied, answers a and b are incorrect. There is no user log that is activated when an NT network user logs on. Therefore, answer d is incorrect.

Question 41

Answer d is correct. Anonymous user accounts are available with Citrix MetaFrame, but they cannot be located on an NT domain controller. Answers a, b, and c are incorrect because they all describe features that *are* included in an NT domain.

Question 42

Answer c is correct. The ICA PassThrough technology allows Macintosh ICA clients to use PN. None of the other options involve Independent Computing Architecture (ICA) PassThrough. Therefore, answers a, b, and d are incorrect.

Question 43

Answer b is correct. Low bandwidth connections should be set to MetaFrame's lowest quality setting of 16Kbps. Answers a, c, and d are incorrect because they list audio bandwidth settings that are not available for use with MetaFrame.

Question 44

Answer c is correct. When clients require high-quality audio and bandwidth is not an issue, map the client's audio to the High Quality setting of 1.3Mbps. Answers a, b, and d are incorrect because they cite bandwidth settings that are not available with MetaFrame.

Question 45

Answer b is correct. The described scenario dictates using MetaFrame's 64Kbps or Medium level of audio compression. Answers a, c, and d are incorrect because they list bandwidth settings that are not available in MetaFrame 1.8.

Question 46

Answer c is correct. SecureICA must be installed on both the MetaFrame server and on all ICA clients. Answers a, b, and d are incorrect because they do not mandate that SecureICA must be installed on both the Citrix server and on the ICA client.

Question 47

Answer c is correct. Although the New York and Toronto offices can use the 128-bit North American version of the SecureICA client, the Tokyo office cannot (the U.S. government has changed this, but it still holds true for the CCA certification exam). Tokyo users would be legally permitted to use only the international SecureICA client with 40-bit encryption. Thus, you cannot meet the required result of providing access for all clients using 128-bit SecureICA.

Question 48

Answer d is correct. Without SecureICA, MetaFrame connections provide Basic encryption. This is a fairly low encryption level but it is preferable to using no encryption (i.e., clear text). Answers a, b, and c are incorrect because they all list encryption levels that are not available with MetaFrame.

Question 49

Answer b is correct because MetaFrame can be installed from a network share. You use the Citrix Connection Configuration (CCC) utility to create and configure ICA connections. Therefore, answer a is incorrect. You use the Citrix Server Administration utility for to manage Citrix servers and user sessions (and more). Therefore, answer c is incorrect. The ICA Client Resources utility does not exist. Therefore, answer d is incorrect.

Question 50

Answer a is correct. The ICA Client Creator utility (accessed from the server desktop) can be used to create the client installation diskettes. The Win16/DOS Client Installation utility and Client Installation tool in the Server Administration utility do not exist. Therefore, answers b and c are incorrect. You cannot use MetaFrame installation diskettes to install ICA clients. Therefore, answer d is incorrect.

Question 51

Answer a is correct. A description of the connection is required when setting up a custom ICA connection. None of the other options is required for a custom Independent Computing Architecture (ICA) connection. Therefore, answers b, c, and d are incorrect.

Question 52

Answer c is correct. You must specify a network protocol when setting up a custom Independent Computing Architecture (ICA) connection. The user name, network bandwidth, and password are not required when you are configuring a custom connection. Therefore, answers a, b, and d are incorrect.

Question 53

Answer a is correct. Unix supports only the TCP protocol. Integrated Services Digital Network (ISDN) is not a network protocol. Therefore, answer b is incorrect. NetBIOS and Internetwork Packet Exchange/Sequence Packet Exchange (IPX/SPX) cannot be used for Unix clients. Therefore, answers c and d are incorrect.

Question 54

Answers a, b, and c are correct. DOS 16/32 clients support all major network protocols. Dynamic Link Library (DLL) is not a network protocol. Therefore, answer d is incorrect.

Question 55

Answer a is correct. Remote Desktop Protocol (RDP) supports only TCP/IP. RDP only supports TCP/IP, therefore, answers b and c are incorrect. Systems Network Architecture (SNA) is not a network protocol. Therefore, answer d is incorrect.

Question 56

Answer c is correct. DirectICA connections are high-speed serial connections that run directly to the multiVGA adapter on the server. This combination hardware/software technology is used for graphics-rich applications. Answers a, b, and c are incorrect because phone connections, modem pools, and Ethernet cabling cannot be used to establish the DirectICA serial connections.

Question 57

Answer b is correct. Each MetaFrame server has two idle sessions available for Independent Computing Architecture (ICA) connections.

Question 58

Answer e is correct. You use the Citrix Connection Configuration (CCC) utility to create and configure client-to-server connections. Therefore, answer a is incorrect. You use Load Balancing Administration to fine-tune a Citrix server's Load Balancing parameters. Therefore, answer b is incorrect. Program Neighborhood (PN) is a client-side tool that provides access to published applications. Therefore, answer c is incorrect. Router Configuration does not exist. Therefore, answer d is incorrect.

Question 59

Answer a is correct. The Citrix Server Administration utility is used to configure and manage ICA browsers. You use the Citrix Connection Configuration (CCC) utility to set up and configure Independent Computing Architecture (ICA) connections. Therefore, answer b is incorrect. You use the Published Application Manager (PAM) to publish and manage applications. Therefore, answer c is incorrect. Program Neighborhood (PN) is a client-side tool used to provide clients with access to published applications. Therefore, answer d is incorrect.

Question 60

Answer b is correct. The Server Administration tool is used to manage user sessions. You set permissions on ICA connections and set audio levels on user connections within the Citrix Connection Configuration (CCC) tool. Therefore, answers a and c are incorrect. Applications are published using the Published Application Manager (PAM). Therefore, answer d is incorrect.

Question 61

Answer d is correct. The Server Administration utility is used to monitor user sessions and to manage the listener ports. Shadowing is initially set up using the Citrix Connection Configuration (CCC) tool. Therefore, answer a is incorrect. License activation is performed using the Citrix Licensing tool. Therefore, answer b is incorrect. Application publishing is done using the Published Application Manager (PAM). Therefore, answer c is incorrect.

Question 62

Answer a is correct. The Server Administration utility is where you monitor domain information. You set up client clipboard mapping and set audio quality on an ICA connection using the Citrix Connection Configuration (CCC) tool. Therefore, answers b and c are incorrect. You configure user permissions in the Terminal Server's User Manager for Domains tool. Therefore, answer d is incorrect.

Question 63

Answers a, b, and c are correct. A Citrix administrator can shadow one or multiple users. She can also allow multiple users to shadow her session.

Question 64

Answer d is correct. Microsoft RDP clients cannot be shadowed using the Citrix shadowing tools. Win32 ICA, Win16 ICA, and DOS ICA can be shadowed in a MetaFrame network. Therefore, answers a, b, and c are incorrect.

Question 65

Answer d is correct. Administrators can shadow users hosted by MetaFrame and WinFrame servers. An administrator can shadow all users within her domain. Therefore, answer a is incorrect. An administrator cannot shadow across domains. Therefore, answers b and c are incorrect.

Question 66

Answers c and d are correct. You cannot use audio while shadowing and shadowing can be used only over an ICA session. You can use the Shadow button to shadow only a single user session. Therefore, answer a is incorrect. You cannot shadow Remote Desktop Protocol (RDP) clients using the MetaFrame tools. Therefore, answer b is incorrect.

Question 67

Answers b and c are correct. Only administrators or users who have been assigned Special Access permission can initiate or terminate shadowing sessions. Regular users cannot start or end shadowing sessions. Therefore, answer a is incorrect. Citrix shadowing permission cannot be granted using the Terminal Server utilities. Therefore, answer d is incorrect.

Question 68

Answer a is correct. For administrators to shadow a user session, their window resolution and color settings must be equal or greater than those of the user session they wish to shadow. You can use the Shadow button to shadow only one session at a time. Therefore, answer b is incorrect. Audio is not available while you are shadowing. Therefore, answer c is incorrect. You can do shadowing only from within an Independent Computing Architecture (ICA) session. Therefore, answer d is incorrect.

Question 69

Answer d is correct. The Minimum size bitmap cache is one of the required cache parameters. The auto bandwidth setting does not exist. Therefore, answer a is incorrect. Inherit user config is not applicable to the client cache. Therefore, answer b is incorrect. Maximum size bitmap cache is not a cache setting. Therefore, answer c is incorrect.

Question 70

Answer d is correct. Client clipboard mapping allows users to cut, copy, and paste data between server-based and local applications. You do not use clipboard mapping for copying data between clients, enabling the client clipboard, or for copying clipboard data to a printer. Therefore, answers a, b, and c are incorrect.

Question 71

Answers a and d are correct. To permit the sharing of resources, you must configure the correct trust relationships and establish ICA gateways on both networks. Independent Computing Architecture (ICA) PassThrough technology is used to allow non-Win32 clients to use Program Neighborhood (PN) to access applications. Therefore, answer b is incorrect. ICA licenses cannot be pooled across an ICA gateway. Therefore, answer c is incorrect.

Question 72

Answer c is correct. In a WinFrame or MetaFrame network, there is only one master browser for each network protocol.

Question 73

Answer c is correct. There is a master browser for each installed network protocol. There are three network protocols, not one or two. Therefore, answers a and b are incorrect. Citrix Load Balancing is a high availability feature, not a network protocol. Therefore, answer d is incorrect.

Question 74

Answer d is correct because MetaFrame requires one master browser for each installed protocol on each network. (In terms of Citrix browsers, each subnet is equivalent to a separate network.) This one master browser per protocol, per domain requirement also means that answers a, b, and c are incorrect.

Question 75

Answer c is correct. Rebooting a Citrix server will trigger a master browser election. Client licensing issues are not involved in master browser elections. Therefore, answer a is incorrect. Installing or restarting an ICA client has no effect on Independent Computing Architecture (ICA) browser elections. Therefore, answers b and d are incorrect.

Question 76

Answers a and b are correct. When an ICA client or browser fails to receive a response when querying the master browser, a master browser election ensues. Each subnet has its own master browser for each configured network protocol. Therefore, answer c is incorrect. Workstation problems do not cause master browser elections. Therefore, answer d is incorrect.

Question 77

Answer d is correct. In this scenario, a master browser election will occur and will shut down one of the master browsers based on the master browser election criteria. Answers a, b, and c are incorrect. They describe some of the election criteria used to determine which server will become the master browser rather than describing what happens when two master browsers are detected on the same subnet. (Note: For the CCA exam, remember that there is a master browser for each installed protocol on each subnet.)

Question 78

Answer a is correct. The most recent version number is the highest ranking master browser election criterion. The longest running browser is the third ranking criterion for configuring the correct trust relationship selection. Therefore, answer b is incorrect. The amount of server resources (i.e., the number and speed of the CPUs, amount of RAM, and hard disk space available) is not an election criterion. Therefore, answer c is incorrect. The most recently restarted browser is less likely to become the master browser than browsers that have been running longer. Therefore, answer d is incorrect.

Question 79

Answers a and c are correct. Independent Computing Architecture (ICA) master browsers maintain information on ICA servers, ICA server Load Balancing, and published applications. The master browser does not monitor clients or client bandwidth. Therefore, answers b and d are incorrect.

Question 80

Answer c is correct. After the 48-hour period, the pooled licenses will not be accessible until the Independent Computing Architecture (ICA) server is brought back to life. Because the licenses are not available indefinitely, answer d is incorrect. Answers a and b state that the licenses are not available until the server is brought back online. Since the pooled licenses are usable for 48 hours, answers a and b are incorrect.

Question 81

Answers a and b are correct. When you are configuring an Independent Computing Architecture (ICA) gateway, you must have a routable network protocol (such as Transmission Control Protocol/Internet Protocol [TCP/IP] and Internetwork Packet Exchange [IPX]) available. NetBIOS/NetBEUI is not a routable network protocol. Therefore, answer c is incorrect. 10bt is an Ethernet cabling standard rather than a network protocol. Therefore, answer d is incorrect.

Question 82

Answer b is correct. Licenses cannot be pooled across a subnet so each subnet can only use its own 25 client licenses. (This is true only for the CCA exam. The Feature Release 1 [FR1] MetaFrame update does enable license pooling across subnets.) Because each subnet can only use its own 25 licenses, answers a, c, and d are incorrect.

Question 83

Answer a is correct. The Citrix Load Balancing option routes ICA clients to the least busy servers during the logon process. Clients are not re-routed to different servers after logon. Therefore, answer b is incorrect. Remote Desktop Protocol (RDP) clients do not participate in Citrix Load Balancing. Therefore, answers c and d are incorrect.

Question 84

Answer f is correct. An Independent Computing Architecture (ICA) client sends a packet to the ICA master browser asking which applications are published. The ICA master browser responds with the list of published applications. Then, the

ICA master browser creates a numeric index from information provided from the ICA member browsers, which allows the master browser to calculate which Citrix server is least busy. Once an application is requested, the ICA master browser provides the client with the address of the Citrix server to connect with. The ICA client then makes a connection with the proper Citrix server. Therefore, the procedures cited in answers a through d are incorrect.

Question 85

Answer d is correct. A launched application runs independently of the Web page in a separate window. Closing the Web browser will not affect the application. Therefore, answer a is incorrect. The Back button would return Jim to the Web page with the Independent Computing Architecture (ICA) link, not to the application itself. Therefore, answer b is incorrect. The ICA session will remain available indefinitely, even if the user accesses other Web sites. Therefore, answer c is incorrect.

Question 86

Answer e is correct. The descriptions accurately summarize the features of each of these Citrix optional products. Load Balancing, Installation Management Services (IMS), SecureICA, and Resource Management Services (RMS) enhance MetaFrame manageability, scalability, and Web publishing capabilities.

Question 87

Answer c is correct because ICA gateways are configured using the Server Administration utility. Answers a, b, and d are incorrect because the PAM, CCC, and Load Balancing utilities cannot be used to configure ICA gateways.

Question 88

Answer b is correct. When a Citrix server goes down, its pooled licenses remain available to other Citrix servers on the same subnet for 48 hours. So the ICA clients would have the 25 licenses from the functional server and 25 more licenses from the crashed server (for a total of 50 licenses). Therefore, answers a, c, and d are incorrect.

Question 89

Answer d is correct. This is a tricky question because once a Citrix server becomes a member of a Citrix server farm, it cannot be reconfigured as a nonserver-farm member. Therefore, the utilities listed in answers a, b, and c cannot be used to remove the server from the server farm. (However, the PAM utility can be used to move a server from one server farm to another.)

Question 90

Answer b is correct. Balancing the load across a Citrix server farm requires that each server host the same, identically configured applications. In a load balanced farm, merely publishing applications is not sufficient. Therefore, answer a is incorrect. There is no Independent Computing Architecture (ICA) Browser Services utility. Therefore, answer c is incorrect. Multihomed network cards are not required on a load-balanced Citrix server. Therefore, answer d is incorrect.

Question 91

Answer b is correct. Using dedicated browsers reduces network overhead consumed by ICA browser elections. Independent Computing Architecture (ICA) browsers are not involved in network fault tolerance. Therefore, answer a is incorrect. ICA browsers do not manage client mapping. Therefore, answer c is incorrect. The browsers do not directly affect the user load burden. Therefore, answer d is incorrect.

Question 92

Answer a is correct. The Server Administration tool is used to configure and manage dedicated ICA master browsers. You use the Published Application Manager (PAM) to publish applications across Citrix server farms. Therefore, answer b is incorrect. You use Load Balancing Administration to set the load balancing parameters. Therefore, answer c is incorrect. The Independent Computing Architecture (ICA) Browser Administration tool does not exist. Therefore, answer d is incorrect.

Question 93

Answer d is correct. When a user clicks on a hyperlink that is associated with a launched application, it runs in a separate window. If the user wishes to close the Web browser window, the published application is not automatically closed, and it continues to run independent of the browser. Answers a, b, and c refer to embedded applications that run within the Web page. Unlike with a launched application, closing the Web browser window that contains an embedded application also closes the application. If a user chooses to load another Web page while using an embedded application, the connection is terminated. In addition, if the user scrolls the Web page, it also scrolls the application.

Question 94

Answers a and c are correct. Two types of files are required to establish an Independent Computing Architecture (ICA) session: ICA and HTML files. ICA files are plain-text files that can be created with the ALE Wizard in the Published Application Manager (PAM). They hold connection files containing a series of command tags needed to establish an ICA connection. HTML files are plain-text files that point to the ICA file. java.exe and ica.exe are fictitious files. Therefore, answers b and d are incorrect.

Question 95

Answers a, c, and d are correct. They refer to embedded applications that run within Web pages. Unlike with launched applications, closing the Web browser window that contains an embedded application also closes the application. In some cases, an embedded application appears as a rectangular box in a Web page that you can click on to connect to a Citrix server. If a user chooses to load another Web page while using an embedded application, the connection is terminated. Answer b describes launched applications, which run in separate windows. Therefore, it is incorrect.

Question 96

Answer a is correct. The ActiveX control can be automatically downloaded and installed on the client machine from a Web page on the Internet or intranet. When a Web page with an embedded application is accessed, the Windows ActiveX control Web client is automatically installed on the client machine. Netscape plug-ins, Java applets, and the wfica32.exe file must all be installed manually. Therefore, answers b, c, and d are incorrect.

Question 97

Answers b, c, and d are correct. Netscape plug-ins, Java applets, and wfica32.exe must all be installed manually. The ActiveX control is the only client that can be automatically downloaded and installed on the client machine from a Web page on the Internet or intranet. Therefore, answer a is incorrect.

Question 98

Answer e is correct. There are only two types of Java clients, Application Mode and Applet Mode. For the Java client to run in Application Mode, the Java Virtual Machine (JVM) 1.1 or higher must be installed on the client device. As with the full Independent Computing Architecture (ICA) client, the Java Application Mode client is installed on, and stays on, the client machine. When running in Applet Mode, the client and the application execute 100 percent on the server. The ActiveX control and the Netscape plug-in are not Java clients. Therefore, answers a and b are incorrect. Apple mode and Published mode are fictional clients. Therefore, answers c and d are incorrect.

Question 99

Answer b is correct. When a user clicks on a hyperlink that is associated with a launched application, it runs in a separate window. If the browser window is closed, the published application continues to run independent of the browser. Answers a and d are accurate for embedded applications that run within the Web page. Therefore, they are incorrect. Independent Computing Architecture (ICA) Web clients support local area network (LAN) and wide area network (WAN) connections. Therefore, answer c is incorrect.

Question 100

Answer b is correct. Only Win32 clients can take advantage of seamless windows. The clients cited in answers a, c, d, e, and f cannot use the seamless windows features of MetaFrame. Therefore, they are incorrect.

Question 101

Answers a, b, and c are correct. Citrix provides three different audio quality options, which can be selected based on the available bandwidth. The High (1.3Mbps) setting should be used only in networks with plentiful bandwidth to avoid local area network (LAN) or wide area network (WAN) congestion. The Medium (64Kbps) default setting provides good audio quality but consumes much less bandwidth than the High setting. The Low (16Kbps) setting is ideal for dialup connections. The audio bandwidth options listed in answers d, e, and f are not supported by MetaFrame so these answers are incorrect.

Question 102

Answer d is correct. The specified trust relationship is correct, but the proposed solution also calls for an Independent Computing Architecture (ICA) gateway to be configured on a server in the Marketing department. For an ICA gateway to work, it must be configured on both networks. The optional desired result of pooling ICA client licenses is not possible both because of the above-mentioned gateway issue and because licenses cannot be pooled across an ICA gateway. (For the CCA exam, remember that a gateway must be configured on both networks. However, with Feature Release 1 installed, only one network gateway must be configured and licenses *can* be pooled across a gateway.) The optional result of allowing Windows and DOS clients to use Program Neighborhood to access the Citrix servers is not possible because DOS clients cannot use Program Neighborhood to access applications (unless the ICA PassThrough technology is also installed).

Glossary

account domain
The NT domain where the users are located. It is also called the trusted domain. The network resource domain trusts the users in the account domain; the users are trusted by the resource domain.

Active Server Pages (ASP)
A standard for dynamically created Web pages that uses ActiveX scripting. As with CGI scripts, the scripts are executed on the Web server.

anonymous user account
Fifteen anonymous accounts are created when the MetaFrame base license is installed. These are local, non-authenticated accounts useful for providing Internet access. No explicit logon is required when you are using an anonymous account. You cannot install one on a domain controller (Primary Domain Controller [PDC] or Backup Domain Controller [BDC].

Application Launching and Embedding (ALE)
Used to Web enable applications, ALE allows Windows applications to be embedded into or launched from a Hypertext Markup Language (HTML) page. Embedded applications run within a browser. Launched applications open in a separate window and remain active even when the browser is closed.

application publishing
Citrix's technique of easily providing applications to large numbers of users. Published applications (or server desktops) are preconfigured to allow 16-bit and 32-bit Windows Independent Computing Architecture (ICA) clients to access them via icons in Program Neighborhood (PN), on the desktop, or from the client's Start menu. Non-Win32 clients can access published applications by setting up a custom ICA connection or by using ICA PassThrough technology.

Application Service Provider (ASP)

Hosts applications and offers data storage on its servers located at secure data centers. Users access applications over telephone lines or the Internet. ASP is a way for companies to outsource application hosting.

application set

The applications in a Citrix server farm that have been configured to be accessed using Program Neighborhood (PN). Each Citrix server farm has only one application set.

asynchronous

A form of communication whereby data is transmitted intermittently rather than in a steady stream. Modems use asynchronous connections.

Asynchronous Transfer Mode (ATM)

A WAN transmission technology that sends data in fixed-length cells rather than via Internet Protocol (IP) packets. ATM provides high-speed communication and is used for voice and video as well as data traffic.

Automatic Client Update

A Citrix tool used to update the network client database. After a new Independent Computing Architecture (ICA) client is installed in the server database, users can have their ICA clients updated to the latest version.

availability

A Citrix term that describes the percentage of time applications are available to the network clients. MetaFrame provides for a high level of application availability (but not fault tolerance).

Backup Domain Controller (BDC)

A computer that maintains a backup copy of the user security database—Security Access Manager (SAM). If the Primary Domain Controller (PDC) goes down, a BDC can take over and handle user authentications until the PDC is brought back online. *See also* "domain controller."

bandwidth

The capacity of network cabling, phone, or wireless connections to transmit data. Bandwidth is measured in MBs or Kbps (e.g., a 56K modem has a theoretical speed of 56Kbps).

base license

Required by each MetaFrame server. It can be thought of as a server license except that it also includes 15 client licenses.

bitmap caching

Allows often-used graphical objects (e.g., bitmaps) to be cached on a local hard drive, decreasing the amount of network bandwidth consumed. Bitmap caching is enabled on any connection that was originally set up for low-bandwidth connections.

caching

Used to reduce the traffic between a client and a server by storing repetitive information on a local hard drive.

Citrix connection

A virtual connection established between Independent Computing Architecture (ICA) or Remote Desktop Protocol (RDP) clients and Citrix servers. It works over all standard network protocols or

Telephony Application Programming Interface (TAPI) modems. Citrix servers use protocol-specific listener ports that monitor for client connection requests. Client requests are passed to one of two idle sessions that then establishes a client-to-server link.

Citrix Connection Configuration (CCC) utility

Used to add, change, or delete network and asynchronous Independent Computing Architecture (ICA) connections. CCC is also used to administer client device mapping, including drive, printer, COM port, clipboard, and audio mapping. CCC also manages security permissions for ICA connections.

Citrix Extranet 2

A new Citrix product used for securely providing applications to users across the Internet. It uses Virtual Private Network (VPN) technology and encryption to protect the data traffic.

Citrix Server Administration utility

Provides centralized management of users, user sessions, processes, and applications on multiple servers or server farms. It can be used to monitor session status or to connect/disconnect sessions. It can also be employed to log off or reset user sessions, to send messages to users, to shadow user sessions, or to terminate network processes. Another function of it is Independent Computing Architecture (ICA) browser and ICA gateway management.

client audio mapping

Allows DOS and Windows Independent Computing Architecture (ICA) clients to hear server-based WAV files or audio broadcasts on their sound card-equipped workstations. It provides three audio-quality options: High—1.3Mbps, Medium—64Kbps (the default value), and Low—16Kbps (for dialup or other low-bandwidth connections).

client clipboard mapping

Allows Independent Computing Architecture (ICA) clients to copy, cut, or paste data between server- and client-based applications. Windows Explorer can be used to copy, cut, and paste files and folders between the client and server applications.

client COM port mapping

Allows Windows or DOS Independent Computing Architecture (ICA) clients to redirect traffic going to the server's COM port to a local COM port. This enables applications running on the server to redirect COM port traffic to a client-side peripheral device.

client drive mapping

Client drives are mapped to drive letters on a MetaFrame server during logon. If server drives have not been remapped, they appear as C:, D:, and so on, whereas client drives are mapped as U:, V:, and so on.

client LPT mapping

Allows a client to print to a local LPT port from a server-based application or print spooler.

client printer configuration
MetaFrame clients can create and access Independent Computing Architecture (ICA) client printers. ICA clients can also create print queues if necessary (e.g., for DOS printers).

client printer mapping
Client printers are mapped during logon. This allows server-based applications to print to the local printers. As with the other types of MetaFrame device mapping, printer mapping allows users to access a network printer without any user configuration.

Client/Server Computing Model
Distributes the processing of applications among different network computers. The computers usually include a front-end server to pass client requests to back-end servers. The back-end servers are often database or mail servers.

client update configuration
Used to add the latest versions of the various Independent Computing Architecture (ICA) clients to the client update database. It is also used to configure the automatic client download process.

Custom ICA Connection folder
A folder in Program Neighborhood (PN) that allows you to configure a custom Independent Computing Architecture (ICA) connection to access a specific server or a published application within a server farm.

DirectICA
A combination software and hardware solution for users of graphics-intensive programs like AutoCAD or Photoshop. It provides a direct, high-speed serial connection to the server console.

domain
In Windows networks, a group of servers and client workstations with a common security database—Security Access Manager (SAM). Domain members can use a single logon to access all domain resources.

domain account
A user or group account on a Windows NT network. Without a valid domain account, users cannot log on to an NT network.

domain controller
A Windows NT Primary Domain Controller (PDC) or Backup Domain Controller (BDC) contains the user database—Security Access Manager (SAM)—used to validate user logons. A domain controller also provides a central location from which to administer domain users and resources.

domain management scope
A scope that provides backward compatibility for existing WinFrame 1.7 and MetaFrame 1 servers that host published applications. This scope also provides backward compatibility for Independent Computing Architecture (ICA) clients that do not support Program Neighborhood (PN). *See also* "server farm management scope."

doskdb

A Citrix command used to monitor and set the number of keyboard polls. If the polls exceed the configured value, the application is taken offline.

drive mapping

Used to set the server or client drive mappings. It allows clients to use the normal C: and D: letters for their local drives. Mappings can be configured either during the MetaFrame installation, or after the installation with the Disk Administrator utility.

embedded application

Unlike launched applications that run in separate windows, embedded applications run within the Web page. In addition, unlike with a launched application, closing the Web browser window that contains an embedded application closes the application. If a user chooses to load another Web page while using an embedded application, the user's connection to the Independent Computing Architecture (ICA) server and the embedded application is terminated.

Emergency Repair Disk

Normally created during the Terminal Server/MetaFrame installation, a diskette containing Windows boot, Registry, security, and system information files. You use it to recover from problems caused by any corruption or damage to the files. It should be updated after every software or hardware change.

Event Viewer

A Windows NT tool that permits administrators to examine a server's system, application and audit logs.

explicit logon

A Microsoft term meaning that a user must provide a username and password to log on to an NT server. The user logs onto a domain controller (Primary Domain Controller [PDC] or Backup Domain Controller [BDC]) which authenticates the explicit logon.

extranet

Essentially an intranet that is accessible to authorized outsiders. Business partners often use extranets to exchange data/information. An example is a manufacturer who allows authenticated suppliers to access inventory and purchasing information. Extranets are invariably protected from unauthorized access by a hardware or software firewall.

fat client

A workstation with its own floppy and hard drives that can perform all application processing locally. *See also* "thin client."

fault tolerance

The ability to fail-over to a backup hard drive or server in the event of a server crash. Network users can continue working with no loss of session data. MetaFrame and WinFrame offer high application availability, but not true fault tolerance.

Find New Application Set Wizard

A Program Neighborhood (PN) wizard that allows Win32 Independent Computing Architecture (ICA) clients to access applications on remote networks.

firewall

A router, computer, or other dedicated hardware or software solution that filters access to a network. All network traffic entering or leaving the corporate network must pass through the firewall. The firewall scrutinizes each message and blocks those that are not allowed.

Hardware Compatibility List (HCL)

Microsoft's list of hardware that is compatible with Windows NT and Terminal Server. MetaFrame is compatible with all hardware specified in the Microsoft HCL.

heterogeneous (mixed) computing environment

A network with a mix of different operating systems (e.g., Windows and Sun Solaris), different network protocols—e.g., Transmission Control Protocol/Internet Protocol (TCP/IP), Internetwork Packet Exchange/Sequence Packet Exchange (IPX/SPX), and NetBIOS—and/or different clients (e.g., Win16/32, DOS, Unix, Web, and Macintosh).

high encryption level

Refers to either the 128-bit, North American encryption level, or to the 40-bit international encryption level available using Citrix's optional SecureICA technology.

home directory

A location for storing a user's files. You configure a home directory using Windows NT's User Manager for Domains utility.

Hypertext Markup Language (HTML) file

A plain-text file that can be edited with virtually any text editor on any type of computer. HTML is the major authoring language of the World Wide Web. The links on a Web page can point to Independent Computing Architecture (ICA) files, which define the ICA connection parameters. Once the default HTML file is created using the Published Application Manager (PAM)'s Application Launching and Embedding (ALE) Wizard, a Webmaster can edit the page, move the links, and edit the text and graphics. The ICA files, along with the associated HTML files, must be located together on the Web server.

idle session

After receiving a client connection request from one of the server's listener ports, the idle session creates the client-to-server connection. Each Citrix server maintains two idle ports, and each port uses 1MB of memory.

Independent Computing Architecture (ICA)

A server-based protocol that works with the Windows Terminal Server or Sun Solaris multiuser operating systems. The ICA protocol separates the application's logic from its user interface, so only keystrokes, mouse clicks, and screen updates travel the local area network (LAN) or wide area network (WAN). Therefore, application performance does not depend on the network bandwidth, and 56K dialup connections operate at LAN-equivalent speeds.

Independent Computing Architecture (ICA) browser service

Used by Citrix clients to locate Citrix servers and published applications. All MetaFrame servers are Independent Computing Architecture (ICA) browsers. Each network and subnet has a master browser for each installed protocol. The master browser responds to client requests with information on published applications (including the location of the least-busy load-balanced Citrix server). Configuring a dedicated master browser can reduce network traffic by avoiding periodic master browser elections.

Independent Computing Architecture (ICA) client for 16- and 32-bit DOS

The 16-bit DOS Independent Computing Architecture (ICA) client is used for DOS 3.3 or newer clients. Thirty-two-bit DOS is used for DOS 4 or newer clients. Both DOS clients support the Transmission Control Protocol/Internet Protocol (TCP/IP), Internetwork Packet Exchange/Sequence Packet Exchange (IPX/SPX), and NetBIOS protocols as well as asynchronous dialup connections.

Independent Computing Architecture (ICA) client for Macintosh

Used for Macintosh clients running Macintosh OS 7.1 or later. Like the Java, Unix, and Web clients, the Macintosh client supports only Transmission Control Protocol/Internet Protocol (TCP/IP) server connections.

Independent Computing Architecture (ICA) client for Unix

Is available for almost all Unix varieties. It supports only the Transmission Control Protocol/Internet Protocol (TCP/IP) network protocol.

Independent Computing Architecture (ICA) client for Windows16/32

The Win16 client supports Windows 3.x, whereas the Win32 client works with Windows 9.x, NT, and 2000 workstations. Both clients support the Transmission Control Protocol/Internet Protocol (TCP/IP), Internetwork Packet Exchange/Sequence Packet Exchange (IPX/SPX), and NetBIOS protocols as well as asynchronous dialup connections. However, only the Win32 client can be used to take advantage of Program Neighborhood (PN) features.

Independent Computing Architecture (ICA) clients for the Web

There is an ICA Web client for Netscape Navigator and a separate client for Windows Internet Explorer. The Netscape plug-in must be manually installed, whereas the Internet Explorer client downloads automatically when the client connects to a Web page that contains an embedded application.

Independent Computing Architecture (ICA) connection

A virtual session, not a hardware link. It can be either a network—local area network (LAN), or wide area network (WAN)—or serial (asynchronous dialup or direct cable) connection.

Independent Computing Architecture (ICA) Connection Center

Win32 clients running applications in a seamless window can use the ICA Connection Center. This utility can be accessed from an icon in the System Tray. It allows the user to monitor active connections and currently active applications, close a window or log off of all active windows, or see whether open applications are local or server based.

Independent Computing Architecture (ICA) file

A plain-text file that contains a series of command tags needed to establish an ICA connection. ICA files are downloaded from the Web server to the client's Web browser so the ICA client can process them.

Independent Computing Architecture (ICA) gateway

Allows ICA clients and servers in one network to be configured to communicate with servers located in a different network.

Independent Computing Architecture (ICA) Java Web client

Used with clients that have a Java Virtual Machine (JVM) installed on their workstations (most Web browsers have a JVM installed). The Java client supports only Transmission Control Protocol/Internet Protocol (TCP/IP) server connections. The Java Web client can run in two different modes: Application Mode or Applet Mode. For the Java client to run in Application Mode, the JVM must be installed on the client device. As with the full ICA client, the Java Application Mode client is installed (and remains) on the client machine. However, to run in Applet Mode, both the client and the application must be located on the Citrix server.

Independent Computing Architecture (ICA) PassThrough technology

Enables non-Win32 clients to take advantage of Program Neighborhood (PN) features. To set up PassThrough, an administrator installs the ICA client on a MetaFrame server. When non-Win32 clients access the server, they can pass through the server's client to enable an ICA-over-ICA connection.

Installation Management Services (IMS)

Allows an administrator to install an application simultaneously onto multiple servers in a load-balanced server farm using Published Application Manager (PAM). IMS ensures that exactly the same version of an application is installed onto the load-balanced servers.

Integrated Services Digital Network (ISDN)

A switched, digital telephone service used for Internet access, remote local area network (LAN) access, and voice communication.

Internetwork Packet Exchange/ Sequenced Packet Exchange (IPX/SPX) protocol

Novell's network transport protocol. Like Transmission Control Protocol/ Internet Protocol (TCP/IP), IPX/ SPX is a routable protocol. *See also* "NetWare Link (NWLink)."

intranet

A private network (normally protected by a firewall) that is based on Transmission Control Protocol/ Internet Protocol (TCP/IP). Companies use intranets to provide communication among different departments and for transmitting sensitive information to employees.

Java

Sun's object-oriented programming language that is widely used for building applications. Small Java applications, called Java applets, are downloaded from a Web server and can be launched by any Java-compatible Web browser (e.g., Microsoft Internet Explorer or Netscape Navigator).

launched application

When a user clicks on a hyperlink that is associated with a launched application, the application runs in a separate window on the client's local desktop. If the user wishes to close the Web browser window, the published application is not automatically closed and continues to run independently of the browser.

license activation

All Citrix software—including MetaFrame, Resource Management Services (RMS), Installation Management Services (IMS), Load Balancing, and client license packs— must be activated or the software will shut down after the 30-day grace period. An activation code must be obtained from Citrix and entered into the Licensing utility to activate a license.

license pooling

By default, MetaFrame and WinFrame pool licenses across servers in the same network/subnet. An administrator can use the Licensing utility to remove some of the licenses on each server from the license pool. This prevents a busy server from using all of the available network client licenses.

listener port

On a MetaFrame server, each installed network protocol has a corresponding listener port that monitors network traffic for any clients asking to connect to the server. The protocol-specific listener port passes the connection request to one of the server's two idle sessions. The idle session then creates the client-to-server connection.

Load Balancing

An optional system service that dynamically and automatically routes Independent Computing Architecture (ICA) clients to the least-busy server. It allows you to load balance multiple WinFrame and MetaFrame servers into a single server farm. It's a very important component of Citrix's centralized, scalable, server-based computing architecture. A license must be purchased and activated on each Citrix server before Load Balancing can be used.

management scope
See "domain management scope" and "server farm management scope."

master browser
Houses a database that contains information about the network servers, their applications, license information, and each server's Load Balancing settings. Each Citrix network has one Independent Computing Architecture (ICA) master browser for each installed network protocol. A master browser uses the information in its database to route ICA client connection requests to the appropriate Citrix server.

Memory Load
One of the advanced Load Balancing parameters used to fine-tune a Citrix server's Load Balancing performance. It is defined as the ratio of total memory to available memory. The parameter is set in the Load Balancing Administration utility.

MetaFrame 1.1
A relatively new Citrix server product for Unix application deployment. Support is offered for Solaris 8, IBM AIX, or Hewlett-Packard's HP-UX Unix platforms. Like MetaFrame 1.8, it supports almost all types of client devices, network connections, and business applications.

Multipurpose Internet Mail Extensions (MIME) type
A specification for formatting non-ASCII (text) messages so they can be transported over the Internet. Each Web page on a Web server has a predefined content type that describes the type of data that is being sent to the Web browser. The Web browser uses the predefined content type to interpret the file and present it in the proper format—e.g., Hypertext Markup Language (HTML), GIF, JPG, and BMP—or as a Real Audio streaming video. These MIME types are all Internet standards.

multiVGA adapter
One of the hardware components of Citrix's DirectICA technology. It contains multiple VGA video adapters that enable a DirectICA terminal to receive a high-speed video feed from a MetaFrame server.

Multiwin
The component that allows multiple, concurrent users to run separate, protected application sessions on a Terminal Server Edition (TSE), MetaFrame, WinFrame, or Sun Solaris server. Microsoft licensed Multiwin from Citrix to provide the multiuser functionality of Windows Terminal Server.

NetBIOS/NetBEUI protocol
NetBIOS is the original network Application Programming Interface for DOS (and later for Windows). NetBIOS provides the network communication link for the NetBEUI protocol. NetBEUI is a simple, fast,

but nonroutable network transport protocol designed to support NetBIOS installations.

NetWare Link (NWLink)

A Windows NT protocol that supports Novell NetWare's Internetwork Packet Exchange/ Sequence Packet Exchange (IPX/ SPX) protocol.

Network Address Translation (NAT)

Maps internal, private Internet Protocol (IP) addresses to a single public, external IP address. This allows multiple computers to share a single IP address to access the Internet. The use of the internal IP addresses also enhances network security.

Network Computing Model

Works within a Java environment. The Java-based server stores all of the Java applications as well as the client data. The client downloads the requested Java-based application from the central server and then runs it on its local Java Virtual Machine (JVM). The data always stays on the server, but the applications can run wherever a JVM is running on a client workstation.

NFuse

Citrix's application portal solution that is used to make applications available to Independent Computing Architecture (ICA) clients via a Web browser. NFuse has virtually supplanted Citrix's Application Launching and Embedding (ALE) technology as the preferred method for Web enabling applications. NFuse

is a three-part product that has a Citrix server component, a Web server component, and an ICA client component that works with any standard Web browser. NFuse uses Secure Sockets Layer (SSL) encryption for security. *See also* "Application Launching and Embedding (ALE)."

Open Database Connectivity (ODBC)

An interface that allows applications to access ODBC-compliant databases such as Microsoft's SQL Server or Oracle's 8i.

Pagefile Usage

One of the advanced Load Balancing parameters used to fine-tune a Citrix server's Load Balancing performance. It is defined as the ratio of the current pagefile size to the allowed minimum free space in the pagefile. The parameter is computed as the percentage of time that the processor is busy and is set in the Load Balancing Administration utility.

Peer-to-Peer Network Model

In a peer-to-peer network, each PC can be used as a standalone system, not connected to the network. However, peers that are connected to a network can share file and print services. This differs from other network models, where dedicated network servers provide the file and print services to domain users.

Performance Monitor

A Windows NT utility for graphically tracking and logging many server (and network) components, including processors, memory, pagefiles, and hard disks.

persistent connection

A connection that is automatically renewed each time a user logs on to the network.

Point-to-Point Protocol (PPP)

A serial communication protocol used for dialup Internet connections. When used with Transmission Control Protocol/Internet Protocol (TCP/IP), PPP can automatically assign IP and DNS addresses to dialup clients.

power user

A heavy user of network resources who typically runs multiple applications and accesses multiple data files simultaneously.

Primary Domain Controller (PDC)

The domain server that maintains the security and user account database. The PDC periodically copies or updates its database to one or more Backup Domain Controllers (BDCs). *See also* "domain controller."

printer mapping

See "client printer mapping."

printer spooling

Sends all print jobs to a folder on the server's hard drive. The print jobs are stored in the specified folder before being sent to the printer.

Processor Usage

One of the advanced Load Balancing parameters used to fine-tune a Citrix server's Load Balancing performance. It is computed as the percentage of time that the processor is busy. The parameter is set in the Load Balancing Administration utility.

Program Neighborhood (PN)

Citrix's version of Windows NT's Network Neighborhood. It is a client-side utility that allows users and administrators to access and configure published applications, application sets, and server desktops. Win32 clients can use PN; other Independent Computing Architecture (ICA) clients must use the ICA PassThrough technology to be able to access published applications via PN.

published application

An application that has been configured on a MetaFrame server and that is available to authorized network users and groups via Program Neighborhood (PN), Remote Application Manager (RAM), NFuse, or a Web page. Published applications can be made available from the client's Start menu, or via icons placed on the user's desktop, or located within the PN window. Applications are published in either a Windows NT domain, or a Citrix server farm scope. If published to a server farm, Citrix's optional Load Balancing product can be deployed to load balance the applications across multiple WinFrame or MetaFrame servers.

Published Application Manager (PAM)

Used to both publish and manage applications, and to centrally manage multiple servers in a server farm. Applications and desktops that are published on a standalone MetaFrame server, or on multiple servers within a farm are automatically made available to Win32

Independent Computing Architecture (ICA) clients via Program Neighborhood (PN). PAM allows enterprise-wide management of individual or load-balanced applications. PAM is also the utility used to produce ICA and Hypertext Markup Language (HTML) files for Web enabling published applications.

ReadyConnect client

A Citrix feature used to make DOS and Win16 client installation diskettes. The diskettes are first configured on an Independent Computing Architecture (ICA) client workstation with the appropriate telephone numbers, Internet Protocol (IP) addresses, and Citrix server names. The configured diskettes can then be used to install identical versions of the clients on all DOS and Win16 workstations.

Redundant Array of Independent Disks (RAID)

A way of connecting two or more hard drives to a single controller card to realize faster performance and/or fault tolerance. RAID 0 offers improved performance, but not fault tolerance, through disk striping. RAID 1, also known as disk mirroring, offers fault tolerance by mirroring the contents of one drive to another. Unlike RAID 5, which offers disk striping with parity, RAID 1 offers no performance improvement.

Remote Access Service (RAS)

A Microsoft NT feature that allows network connections to be made over standard phone lines. RAS allows authenticated clients to open, upload, or download files from the network server. RAS ports cannot be accessed by Independent Computing Architecture (ICA) asynchronous clients.

Remote Application Manager (RAM)

Used to make connections to published applications and servers for Win16, DOS, Unix, or Macintosh Independent Computing Architecture (ICA) clients. RAM is an older Citrix tool that originated with WinFrame and requires users to manually find and configure the application connections. The connection parameters are Connection Type (network or dialup), Description (a unique application title), Network Protocol, Application Executable Name, Window Size And Color, and whether to enable sound.

Remote Desktop Protocol (RDP)

A multichannel protocol that carries mouse clicks and keystrokes from the client to the server, and screen refreshes from the server to the client. Though similar to Citrix's Independent Computing Architecture (ICA), RDP consumes more local area network (LAN), or wide area network (WAN) bandwidth, and does not support non-Windows clients.

resource domain

The NT domain containing the network resources that the users in the account domain access. It's also called the trusting domain. The resource trusts the users; the users are trusted.

Resource Management Services (RMS)

An optional Citrix product that provides in-depth application and system management for WinFrame, MetaFrame, and Windows Terminal Server. RMS works with an open database connectivity (ODBC)-compliant database to monitor user connections and accessed applications.

RSA RC5 encryption

Citrix licensed the RC5 encryption algorithm from RSA to provide secure communications for its optional SecureICA products.

scalability

Describes how a hardware or software system can adapt to increased demands. The scalability of a Terminal Server-based server farm depends on the user load, the type of applications running on the server, the server configuration, and the network bandwidth. When one or more servers in a Terminal Server Edition (TSE)/MetaFrame server farm is running out of resources, an administrator can simply add a server (or servers).

seamless integration

Allows MetaFrame clients to access network and local resources while working in a familiar desktop environment. Applications running on the server appear to run locally. Both server-based and local programs can be accessed by clicking on desktop icons or from the Start menu. Automatic mapping of drives, printers, clipboard, and audio is also part of Citrix's seamless desktop integration.

seamless window

A feature that allows Win32 Independent Computing Architecture (ICA) clients to run hosted applications via a MetaFrame server seamlessly on the client desktops. Even though the application is running on the MetaFrame server, it appears to be running locally on the user's workstation. A seamless window enables users to transparently multitask between local and hosted applications. Windows can be minimized, maximized, or resized just as in a standalone PC session.

SecureICA

An optional Citrix service that provides security by encrypting the client-to-server traffic. SecureICA uses RC5 encryption licensed from RSA, and is available in a 128-bit North American version, or a 40-bit international version.

Security Access Manager (SAM)

A Windows NT component that maintains the user account database. SAM authenticates usernames and passwords when users log on to a network domain. The SAM database is stored in the Windows Registry.

server application

An application running on a specific server that can be set up and run from a client workstation.

Server-Based Computing Model

Allows all processing to be done on the server, with only the keystrokes, mouse activity, and screen images passing between the server and the desktop. Applications are installed, managed, and executed 100 percent on the server. The Server-Based Computing Model uses a multiuser operating system like Windows Terminal Server for distributing the presentation of a user interface (UI) to a client device.

server console session

Occurs when you are working directly at the server console, or when accessing the server through a direct cable connection (i.e., a DirectICA link). By contrast, all local area network (LAN), or wide area network (WAN) connections are Independent Computing Architecture (ICA) connections that access the server across the network. All remote sessions are ICA sessions, not console sessions.

server farm

A Citrix term that designates a group of physically connected MetaFrame/WinFrame servers that share a common user database and can be jointly managed from a central location. Servers can be added to a server farm without making any changes to the client desktops.

server farm management scope

Published applications are viewed, managed, and created within either a server farm or an NT domain scope. Applications published in the server farm management scope are automatically added to application sets, which are then immediately available to Independent Computing Architecture (ICA) Win32 clients via Program Neighborhood (PN). *See also* "domain management scope."

shadowing

Allows administrators to remotely view single or multiple user sessions for support, troubleshooting, or training purposes. The default settings allow administrators to take over the user's keyboard and mouse while viewing the user session. Shadowing can be initiated from either the Shadow button in Server Administration, or from the Shadow taskbar, located on the Independent Computing Architecture (ICA) Administrator toolbar.

Shadow taskbar

Although the Server Administration's Shadow button allows you to shadow only one user session at a time, the Shadow taskbar allows you to shadow one or multiple users simultaneously. The Shadow taskbar is found on the server's desktop Independent Computing Architecture (ICA) Administrator toolbar. Shadowing can be enabled only within an ICA session. A MetaFrame/WinFrame console can neither shadow nor be shadowed.

Solaris

Sun's proprietary Unix operating system. In October 2000, Citrix announced that MetaFrame 1.1 is now available for use with Sun's Solaris, IBM's AIX, and Hewlett-Packard's HP-UX Unix operating systems. The Unix product includes several key MetaFrame 1.8 features, including application publishing, session shadowing, SpeedScreen, and seamless desktop integration.

SpeedScreen 2

Works by transmitting only the areas of the client screen that have changed since the last screen refresh. This can provide up to four times faster performance over low-bandwidth (i.e., dialup) connections. This server-based technology can lower band-width consumption by 60 percent. SpeedScreen 2 works by intelligently caching the unchanged parts of the screen images to the local hard drive.

subnet

A network segment separated from other network segments by a router. It's also referred to as a broadcast domain.

Swap Activity

One of the advanced Load Balancing parameters that can be adjusted in the Load Balancing Administration utility. This setting determines how frequently the pagefile is accessed.

swap file

A hidden hard disk file that stores data that will not fit into the computer's RAM.

system policy

Establishes a user's or group's access rights. A policy affects the user after successful authentication by restricting access to certain network resources. System policies can be applied to a single user, group, or a computer. An administrator can modify policies by using the System Policy Editor, a standard Windows NT Server tool. Individual policies

take precedence over group policies. Machine policies take precedence over all policies.

Telephony Application Programming Interface (TAPI)

Allows Windows-based PCs to connect to telephone services. Modems used in Citrix servers should be TAPI compliant. MetaFrame offers TAPI emulation support for DOS and Win16 Independent Computing Architecture (ICA) clients.

Terminal Server

When you are discussing MetaFrame, this refers to Windows NT 4 Terminal Server Edition (TSE) or Windows 2000 Terminal Services. MetaFrame loads on top of, and is an enhancement to, Microsoft's Terminal Server. Terminal Server, like WinFrame and MetaFrame, is a server-based, thin-client, multiuser product.

thin client

Can refer to a stripped-down user terminal or PC, or to Citrix's Independent Computing Architecture (ICA) client software. The Citrix ICA thin-client software leaves all processing chores to the Citrix server; it sends only keystrokes and mouse activity to the server, and receives only screen refreshes in return. With Citrix's server-based approach, all applications are installed, managed, executed, and supported on the server(s), rather than on the client workstations.

Thinwire

The most widely employed (and most important) of the Independent Computing Architecture (ICA) protocol's virtual channels. It's responsible for sending screen updates to the ICA clients.

Traditional Network Model

In this model, the network server stores data files or functions as a centrally located print server for the entire network. Client workstations can either download data files from a network server, or open a data file on the file server. When the client accesses a file located on the server, the server's file system locks the file and makes it read only. This mechanism protects the data from being changed while it is being accessed by more than one client at a time. Clients essentially use the network server like a remote hard drive or network printer. The Traditional Network Model is common in small and mid-sized business environments due to its relative simplicity and minimal maintenance requirements.

Transmission Control Protocol/Internet Protocol (TCP/IP)

This protocol suite is the standard for Unix networks and for the Internet. Because of the importance of the Internet, even older Windows and Novell networks are relying more and more on TCP/IP as their main network protocol (Windows NT uses TCP/IP as the default protocol).

trust relationship

A Windows NT method of joining two or more domains. Users in the trusted or account domain can access resources in the trusting or resource domain. A trust relationship eliminates the need for users to separately log on to the resource domain(s).

trusted domain

See "account domain."

trusting domain

See "resource domain."

Universal Naming Convention (UNC)

Provides a way to access shared network resources in almost all current IT environments (hence the Universal designation). The UNC path to the shared resource begins with two backslashes; e.g., \\myserver\littleblackbook\henrietta.txt. UNCs can also be used to identify and access shared peripheral devices such as printers.

Unix Integration Services

An optional Citrix product that allows X.11 terminals to connect to WinFrame or MetaFrame to run Windows applications. Unlike Unix Independent Computing Architecture (ICA) clients, X.11 clients using the Unix Integration Services cannot use some of the ICA features (e.g., Load Balancing). Conversely, the ICA Unix clients cannot use the Unix utilities (e.g., the Unix account administration services).

user interface (UI)

Can be either text based (DOS) or graphical (Windows). The UI is the user's working environment; i.e., a desktop, application interface, and the Independent Computing Architecture (ICA) client screen contents transmitted by a Citrix server. In a MetaFrame/WinFrame network, all processing is done on the servers, and only the user interface (UI) is sent to the client workstations.

User Load

Citrix's default Load Balancing configuration is calculated using the User Load parameter, located on the Basic tab of the Load Balancing Administration utility. The User Load Is 100% At setting determines the ratio of the current number of logged on users to the maximum number of users. The default maximum number of users is 10,000; it is recommended that this setting be reduced to the maximum number of users that will actually access the server.

user profile

Contains the user settings that load when a user logs on. Depending on the type of user, profiles may contain various desktop and Start menu preferences. Profiles can be stored locally on the user's machine, or in a network server folder that has been mapped on the Primary Domain Controller (PDC) with the User Manager for Domains administration tool. In Windows NT networks, system policies take precedence over the user profiles.

VideoFrame

An optional Citrix product that allows streamed audio and video to be sent to Program Neighborhood (PN) clients on MetaFrame networks. VideoFrame adjusts the streamed data to fit the available local area network (LAN), or wide area network (WAN) bandwidth.

Web client

In Citrix networks, the Independent Computing Architecture (ICA) client for Web computing. There are two main Citrix Web clients: Microsoft's ActiveX control and the Netscape Navigator plug-in. The ActiveX control loads automatically when the Web client connects to a Web page containing a Citrix embedded application. The Netscape plug-in must be manually installed. Citrix Web clients work only in Transmission Control Protocol/Internet Protocol (TCP/IP) networks.

wide area network (WAN)

A computer network spread over a relatively large geographic area. WANs usually consist of two or more local area networks (LANs). The computers in a WAN are connected by dedicated phone lines, or by the Internet. The Internet itself is the world's largest WAN.

WinFrame

Citrix's server-based product that includes the Windows NT 3.51 operating system. WinFrame and MetaFrame can co-exist in the same server farm. WinFrame clients can access MetaFrame server resources, and MetaFrame clients can access WinFrame server resources.

Winview

An early Citrix multiuser application
server product based on IBM's OS/2
operating system. Winview for
Networks was replaced by Citrix's
WinFrame product in the early
1990s.

X.11 terminal

A Unix-based workstation or device.
X.11 support is available with Citrix's
separate Unix Integration Services
product; there is no Citrix Independent Computing Architecture (ICA)
client that allows X.11 devices to
access MetaFrame 1.8 servers.

Index

Symbols

.wav files, 104
/ADDR command switch, 153
/APP command switch, 153
/CONTINUE command switch, 153
/COUNT:n command switch, 153
/DISC command switch, 153
/GATEWAY command switch, 153
/IPX command switch, 153
/IPXSERVER:x command switch, 153
/LICENCE command switch, 153
/LOAD command switch, 153
/NETBIOS command switch, 153
/NETBIOSSERVER:x command
    switch, 153
/PING command switch, 153
/RESET command switch, 153
/SERIAL command switch, 153
/SERVERFARM command switch, 153
/SIZE:n command switch, 153
/STATS command switch, 153
/TCP command switch, 153
/TCPSERVER:x command switch, 153
128-bit encryption, **106**, 180, **185–186**

A

Account domains. *See* Master domains.
Activation Wizard, 54
ActiveX control, **186**, **187**
Add ICA Connection icon, 97

Add ICA Connection Wizard, 97
Add/Remove Programs tool, 56–57
/ADDR command switch, 153
ALE, 170–173, **225**, **227**
    component overview, 173
    launching compared to embedding,
        171–172, **186**
    Web browser support of, **188**
Allow Background Download option, 136
ALTADDR command, 160, **161**
Analysis Tools, 16
Anonymous user accounts, 56, **75**, 27,
    200, **203**
/APP command switch, 153
Application demand, 45–46
Application Launching and Embedding.
    See ALE.
Application management, 125
Application publishing, 11, **221**, **222**
    Load Balancing and, 146
    with PAM utility, 126–127, **164**
    within server farms, 125
Application sets, 96
Applications
    embedded, 172, **187–188**
    hyperlinks to, 172, **186–187**
    launched, 171
    launching, 171
    Web page access of, **210**
ASP Model, 35–36, **37–38**
Asynchronous dial-up, 86
Asynchronous ICA connections, 88
Asynchronous Transfer Mode. *See* ATM.

Asynchronous user accounts, **208**
ATM, 86
Audio broadcasts, **105, 143**
    bandwidth, **208, 209, 228**
    mapping, 103–104
    session shadowing and, **215**

B

Backup Domain Controllers. *See* BDCs.
Bandwidth, 13, **105, 208**
    audio connections and, **208**
    audio mapping, 104
    ICA connection requirements, **23**
Base License, 48, 134, **141–142**
Basic encryption, 99
BDCs, 44, **81**, 114
Bi-directional gateways, 157
Billing reports, 16
Bitmap caching, 98–99
Browsers
    dedicated backup, 155–156
    dedicated master, 155–156
elections, 152, **165, 218**
By Default, Connect Only The Client's
    Main Printer checkbox, 130

C

Cache settings, **216**
CALs, 48, **204**
CCA exam, 10, 14, 44
CCC utility, 88–92, 114, 118, 129–132
    audio level settings, 92
    Client Settings dialog box, 90–91
    connection configuration with, 128
    Connection Permissions windows,
      91–92
    connection settings, 130–131
    Security/Permissions menu, 91
    session shadowing configuration, 132
Centralized management group, 115
Change Server Farm Wizard, 125
Citrix Activation Wizard, 135
Citrix Connection Configuration.
    See CCC utility.
Citrix Licensing utility, 54
Citrix Server Administration utility,
    157, **163, 213, 214**
Client Access Licenses. *See* CALs.
Client audio mapping, 103–104
Client cache settings, **216**
Client clipboard mapping, 104, **216**

Client COM port mapping, 103–104
Client Creator tool, 137
Client device mapping, 131–132
Client Download Mode options, 136
Client Printer Configuration utility, 137
Client printer mapping, 102–103
Client support, **21**
Client Update Configuration tool,
    136–138
Client/Server Computing Model, 30–32,
    39, 40
Clipboard mapping, 103, **216**
COM port mapping, 103–104
Complete Trust Model, 71
Connect Client Drives At Logon
    checkbox, 130
Connect Client Printers At Logon
    checkbox, 130
Connections, **207, 211**
    requests, **141**
    settings, 130–131
/CONTINUE command switch, 153
/COUNT:n command switch, 153
Custom ICA connections, 97, **211**

D

Data Analysis Tools, **197**
Data Collection Agent, 16, **197**
Data Source, 16, **196**
Dedicated backup browsers, 155–156
Dedicated ICA browsers, **224**
Dedicated master browsers, 155–156
Default To Main Client Printer
    checkbox, 130
Desktop integration, 14
Dial-Up Networking, 88
DirectICA environments
    connections, 88–89
    hardware recommendations, **212**
DirectICA solution, **110**
DirectICA stations, 89
Directory service, 66
Disable Client Audio Mapping
    option, 131
Disable Client Clipboard Mapping
    option, 131
Disable Client COM Port Mapping
    option, 131
Disable Client Drive Mapping
    option, 130
Disable Client LPT Port Mapping
    option, 131

Disable Windows Client Printer
  Mapping option, 130
/DISC command switch, 153
Domain master election, 151–152
Domain models, 68–72
Domain structure, 66–67
Domain trusts, **77, 78–79**
Drive mapping, 131–132, **201**
Drive remapping, 53, **61, 203**

E

Election packets, 152
Elections, 151–152
Embedded applications, 172, **86,**
  187–188, 225, 226
Emergency Repair Disk. *See* ERD.
Encryption, **106, 185–186**
    client-to-server connections, **210**
    export restrictions, 17–18
    International, 100, **198**
    North American, 100
    RC5 encryption, 177
ERD, 51
Explicit access, 56
Extranets, 172

F

Fat clients, 11,33
Firewalls, 158
Force Disconnection option, 136
Frame Relay, 86
Full client. *See* Windows ICA client.

G

/GATEWAY command switch, 153
Gateways, 157
Guest and Anonymous Users
  Groups, 127

H

High bandwidth audio mapping, 104, **228**
Hives, 67, **81**
HKEY_CURRENT_USER (HKCU)
  Registry hive, 73–74
Hot Fixes, 57
HTML files, 175, **189, 190–191, 225**
Hyperlinks
    to applications, 172, **186–187,**
      210, 225
    to ICA files, **190–191**

I

ICA
    Administrator toolbar, 118–120
    asynchronous connections, 88
    Browser Service, 150–152
    Browser tab, 153–154
    Client Creator utility, 94, 119,
      137, **211**
    Client Printer Configuration utility,
      119, 137
    Client Update Configuration
      tool, 119
    client software, 86
    Connection Center, 101
    connection types, 86–89
    DirectICA connections, 88–89
    File Encryption window, 177
    File Name window, 178
    File Size And Colors window, 176
    files, 175, **190–191,189,225**
    FileTCP/IP+HTTP ServerLocation
      window, 177
    gateways, 117, 156–158, **217,**
      220, 223
    network connection types, 87
    Java Web client installation, 184
    master browsers, **217, 219**
    packets, 89
    PassThrough, 98, **106, 109, 208**
    protocol, 12, **20,** 85
    sessions, **189**
    synchronous connections, **108**
    Web clients, 182–184, **186**
ICA browsers, 117
    dedicated backup, 155–156
    dedicated master, 155–156
    member browsers, 154–155
ICA clients, 11
    bitmap caching, 98–99
    connection requests, **162**
    installation, 93–94, **107,** 136, **211**
    seamless desktop integration, **197**
    seamless window, 101
ICA connections, **138, 139**
    custom, **211**
    security, 91
    creating, 157
    management, **213**
    connections, **186**
    hardware requirements for, 182
    installing, 184

Idle sessions, **213**
IMS, 15, **222–223**
IMS Packager, 15
IMS Synchronization Services, **198**
Independent Software Vendors. *See* ISVs.
Inherit User Config checkbox, 130
Installations
    ICA clients, 93–94, **107, 211**
    ICA Java Web client, 184
    ICA Windows Web clients, 184
    MetaFrame, 54–56, **200**
    MetaFrame uninstallation, 56–57
    NT 4 TSE, 49–52, **60**
    Terminal Server, **202**
    Terminal Services, **200**
    Win32 clients, 95
Integrated Services Digital Network.
    See ISDN.
International encryption level, 100, **198**
Internetwork Packet Exchange/Sequence
    Packet Exchange. *See* IPX/SPX.
Intranets, 172–173
/**IPX** command switch, 153
IPX, **21–22**, 84, **219**
IPX/SPX, 31, **212**
/**IPXSERVER:x** command switch, 153
ISDN, 86
ISVs, 35, **38**

J

Java
    applets, **186, 226**
    clients, **226**
    terminal, 32
    virtual machine, 32
jicaengj.jar file, 184
jicaengm.cab file, 184
jicaengn.jar file, 184

L

Launched applications, 171, **186, 189**
/**LICENSE** command switch, 153
Licenses, 48, 54, **220**
    activation codes, 135–136
    Base License, 48, 134, **141–142**
    codes, **201**
    grace period, **204**
    license pools, 134, 156
    Load Balancing, **161**
    network ICA clients, **223**
    Per Seat, 48

Per Server mode, 48
Per Server option, **204**
pools, **219**
server crashes and, **219**
Server Extension Licenses, 134
Licensing tool, 118
Listener ports, 128, **138, 139, 214**
/**LOAD** command switch, 153
Load Balancing, 13–15, **22**, 115–116,
    166–167, 195, 196, 220, 221,
    222–223, 224
    Advanced Load Balancing tab,
        149–150
    default settings, 148
    license, **161**
    overview, 146–147
    requirements for, 147
Load Balancing Administration utility,
    119, 122–124, 148–149
Logon process, 72–73
Low bandwidth audio mapping,
    104, **105, 228**

M

Macintosh ICA clients, **108**
Mainframe Networking Model, 26
Many-to-one shadowing, 131
Master browser elections, **165, 218**
Master domains, 68–69, **77, 80, 205**
Master ICA browser, 117
Medium bandwidth audio mapping,
    104, **228**
Member ICA browsers, 154–155
Memory Load parameter, 124, 150, **162**
MetaFrame Books Online tool, 119
MetaFrame installation, 54–56, **59**
    drive remapping, 53–54, **61**
    uninstalling, 56–57
MIME, 173–174, **188**
Modem support, **203**
Multichannel RDP protocol, **59**
Multiple Master Domain Model, 69–70
MultiVGA adapters, **212**
Multiwin component, 12, **20**

N

NAT, 159–160
NC client, 32
/**NETBIOS** command switch, 153
NetBIOS, **21–22**, 31, 84, **212**
/**NETBIOSSERVER:x** command
    switch, 153

Netscape plug-ins, **186**, **226**
Network administration, **61–62**
Network Computer client. *See* NC client.
Network Computing Model, 26, 32–33,
    37, **41**
Network connection types, 87
Network management, 12, **19**, **21**
Network shares, **107**
NFuse tool, 18
North American encryption level, 100
NOSs, **198**, **204**
NT 4 Terminal Server Edition, 11, **19**, 44
    accessibility, **60**
    base memory requirement, **59–60**
    default processor support, **61**
    hardware requirements, 47, **196**, **200**
    installation, 49–52, **60**
    requirements for, 46
    server scalability, 45
NT Client Access License, 48, **204**
ntuser.dat file, 73, **76**

O

ODBC database, **197**
One-to-many shadowing, 131
One-to-one shadowing, 131
Overall Adjustment parameter,
    124, 150, **162**

P

Pagefile Usage parameter, 124, 150, **162**
PAM, 114–115, 119, 125–128, **142**, **164**
    application publishing, 95, 126–127,
        146, **221**, **222**
    HTML file creation with, 176
    ICA file creation with, 176
PDCs, 44, **81**, 114
Peer-to-Peer Network Model, 26–28
Peers, 27
Per Seat licensing option, 48
Per Server licensing option, 48, **204**
Performance Monitor, 48, 58, **200**
/PING command switch, 153
PN, 12, 95–96, **105**, **106**, **197**, **229**
    Add ICA Connection icon, 97
    application sets, 96
    Custom ICA Connection
        feature, 96–97
    ICA PassThrough technology, 98
    icons in, 84
PN client. *See* Windows ICA client.
Power users, 45

Primary Domain Controllers. *See* PDCs.
Processor Usage parameter, 124, 150, **162**
Program Neighborhood. *See* PN.
Published Application Manager.
    See PAM.
Published applications, 95, **221**, **222**

Q

qserver command, 152–153

R

RAID, 48, **203**
RAM, 97–98, 147
RC5 encryption, 177
Remote Desktop Protocol. *See* RDP.
Resource Management Services.
    See RMS.
RDP, **59**, 62, 84, **212**
Redundant Array of Independent Disks.
    See RAID.
Remote access, 88
Remote Application Manager. *See* RAM.
/RESET command switch, 153
RMS, 15–17, **22**, **196**, **198**, **199**, **222–223**
Routable protocols, 156

S

SAM, 66, 67, **81**
Scalability, 45
Screen resolution, session shadowing
    and, **216**
Seamless desktop environment, 102, **197**
Seamless windows, 101–102, **227**
SecureICA, 17–18, 99–101, **109**, 177,
    180, **198**, **209**, **210**, **222–223**
Security Account Manager. *See* SAM.
/SERIAL command switch, 153
Serial numbers, 54, **201**
Server Administration utility, 115,
    119–122, **141**, 153, 157, **163**, **214**, **224**
    ICA Gateway tab, **223**
    session shadowing with, 132
Server console, session shadowing
    and, **215**
Server Extension Licenses, 134
Server farms, 13, 115–118, **140–141**, **142**,
    164, **206**, **221**, **224**
    application management, 125
    application publishing, 125
    Change Server Farm Wizard, 125
    configurations of, 116

Server-Based Computing Model, 11, 26, 33–34, **38**, **39**, **199**

/**SERVERFARM** command switch, 153

Service Packs, 57

Session shadowing, 13, 92–93, 119, 132–134, **143**, **195**, **214**, **215**
    audio broadcasts and, **215**
    limitations of, 132
    screen resolution and, **216**
    server console and, **215**
    Shadow taskbar, 133–134
    single user sessions, 133

Sessions, 124, 150, **162**, **214**

setup.class file, 184

Shadow icon, **195**

Shadow Taskbar, 119, 133–134, **143**

Shadowing, 13, 92–93, 119, 132–134, **143**, **195**, **214**, **215**
    screen resolution and, **216**

Simple HTML files, 175

Single Domain Model, 69, **79**

Single user session shadowing, 133

/**SIZE:n** command switch, 153

SpeedScreen 2, 84

/**STATS** command switch, 153

"Stripe set" configuration, 48

Sun Solaris, 11, **19**

Swap Activity parameter, 124, 150, **162**

System monitoring, 22

System policies, 73–74, **75**

System Policy Editor, **76**

T

TAPI modem support, **203**

/**TCP** command switch, 153

TCP port 1494, 159

TCP/IP, **21–22**, 31, 84, **108**, 172, 212, 219

/**TCPSERVER:x** command switch, 153

Terminal Server, **62**, 84, **202**
    optimizing, 57–58
    RDP client for, **212**

Terminal Server Connection Configuration utility, 129

Terminal Server Edition. *See* TSE.

Terminal Services, licensing, 48

Thin clients, 11, **23**, 33, **41**

Thin pipes, 13

Tolly Research, 84

Traditional Network Model, 26, 29–30, **40**

Transmission Control Protocol/Internet Protocol. *See* TCP/IP.

Trust relationships, 71, **205**, **229**

Trusted domains, 68, 69, **77**, **80**

Trusting domains, **77**, **205**

Trusts, 67–68

TSE, 11, **19**, 44
    accessibility, **60**
    base memory requirement, **59–60**
    default processor support, **61**
    hardware requirements, 47, **196**, **200**
    installation, 49–52, **60**
    requirements for, 46
    server scalability, 45

Two-tier network model. *See* Traditional Network Model.

Typical users, 45

U

UDP port 1604, 151, 158, **163**

User accounts, **75**
    alterations to, **207**
    anonymous, 56, 127, **200**, **203**
    asynchronous, **208**

User authentication, 72, **78**

User Datagram Protocol ports. *See* UDP ports.

User Load Is 100 % At parameter, 123, 148

User Manager for Domains utility, 74, **76**, 91, 115, **192**

User network demands, 45

User profiles, 73–74, **75**, **207**

V

Verbose HTML files, 175

Version Checking options, 136

VideoFrame, 120

Virtual group. *See* Centralized management group.

Virtual machine. *See* VM.

VM, 32

W

Web pages, application access from, 172, **186–187**, **210**, **225**

Web servers, 174

wfica32.exe, 183, **186**, **226**

Win32 client, 95, **105**, **214**

Windows ICA client, 183

Windows NT 4 Terminal Server Edition,
    11, **19**, 44
        accessibility, **60**
        base memory requirement, **59–60**
        hardware requirements, 47
        installation, 49–52, **60**
        requirements for, 46
        server scalability, 45
WinFrame, 10, 14
Write An HTML File window, 179